Prai‹

Whispers from the Valley of the Yak

———— ⚬♋⚬ ————

"In *Whispers from the Valley of the Yak*, Jacquelyn Tuxill breaks away from a confining childhood with parents committed to their medical work.... Her vivid descriptions of panoramas in Alaska and China mirror the wild beauty she ultimately finds within herself. This memoir will take readers on a journey they won't want to end."

— LOUELLA BRYANT, author
of *Sheltering Angel*

"A story of familial struggles and reconciliation with the grandeur of revelation amid the high mountains near Jackie's Chengdu birthplace ... fine travel writing."

— JOHN ELDER, author of *Reading the Mountains
of Home* and teacher of English and
Environmental Studies, Middlebury College

"In her autobiography, Jacquelyn Tuxill shares her deep-seated passion for wild mountain landscapes, gained first as a campaigner in the national effort to protect Alaska lands. Returning to China where she was born, she discovers the soaring mountains, raging rivers, and deep gorges of the Tibetan Plateau's eastern rim. Tuxill vows both places will remain in her heart forever. A great storyteller, she uses flowing, beautiful language to shape the inspiring chapters of her life."

— CHARLES CLUSEN, chair, Alaska Coalition
1977-1981; chair, Protect the Adirondacks

"*Whispers from the Valley of the Yak* is a story about landscapes. From her birthplace in China to her connection with Denali, North America's tallest peak, Tuxill navigates her early years as a mom in the shadow of her rocky relationship with her own mother. Ultimately Tuxill explores how she came to terms with the unexpected landscape of her own heart. A wonderfully rendered story."
— KAYLENE JOHNSON-SULLIVAN, author
of *Our Perfect Wild*

"Jacquelyn Tuxill's deeply moving, profound memoir embraces family, place, redemption, and beauty. While plumbing the depth of family struggle, she explores how the essential contributions of unique places and powerful memories offer opportunities for rebirth and discovery. In *Whispers from the Valley of the Yak*, Tuxill welcomes readers into her journey as she celebrates her family and rejoices in our shared humanity."
— JEFFREY P. ROBERTS, author
of *Salted and Cured*

"Jacquelyn Lenox Tuxill's adventurous, curious spirit shines forth in this memoir of self-discovery. With honesty and empathy, she details the inner journey that allowed her to forgive her flawed yet remarkable parents and rediscover the land of her birth, China, through their eyes. . . . Tuxill guides us from the wilds of Alaska to the mountains of Tibet and into her own treasure trove of memory, delivering a bold tale of journeys within and without."
— SUSAN RITZ, author
of *A Dream to Die For*

Whispers
from
the Valley
of the Yak

Whispers from the Valley of the Yak

A Memoir of
Coming Full Circle

Jacquelyn Lenox Tuxill

SHE WRITES PRESS

Published 2023
Printed in the United States of America
Print ISBN: 978-1-64742-549-4
E-ISBN: 978-1-64742-550-0
Library of Congress Control Number: 2023905705

For information, address:
She Writes Press
1569 Solano Ave #546
Berkeley, CA 94707

Interior Design by Tabitha Lahr
Map by Mike Morgenfeld

She Writes Press is a division of SparkPoint Studio, LLC.

To Marilyn,
who was always there for me.

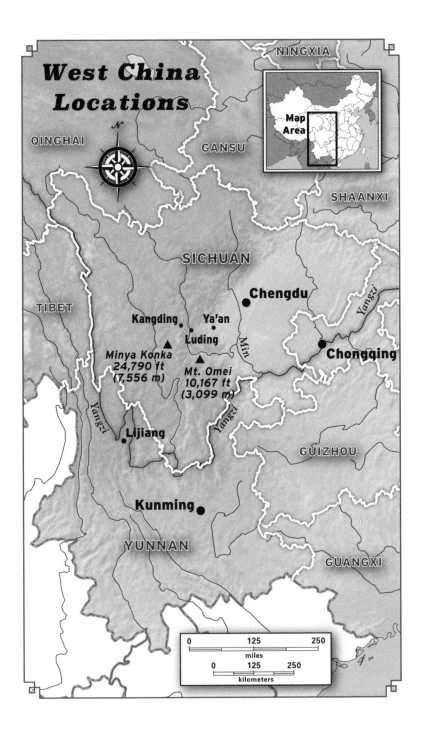

West China Locations

NINGXIA

Map Area

QINGHAI

GANSU

SHAANXI

SICHUAN

TIBET

Chengdu

Kangding • Ya'an

▲ • Luding

Minya Konka
24,790 ft
(7,556 m)

▲ Mt. Omei
10,167 ft
(3,099 m)

Min

Yangzi

Chongqing

Yangzi

Yangzi

Lijiang •

GUIZHOU

Kunming •

YUNNAN

GUANGXI

| 0 | 125 | 250 |
miles

| 0 | 125 | 250 |
kilometers

My parents speak to me from the valley of the yak.
They whisper on the wind,
telling me come on, come on.
This is the way.

— Yulongxi Valley, 2016

Contents

◈ *Part III: Finding Myself*

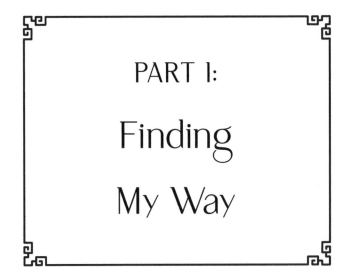

PART I:

Finding

My Way

 Chapter 1

The airplane touched down on the tarmac, bringing me back to my birthplace: Chengdu, China. I tried to ignore my stomach jitters, caused by feelings still lurking from childhood of wanting nothing to do with this country. Even at thirty-eight I seldom revealed where I was born. Yet here I was in the spring of 1980, accompanying my parents on a tour of the People's Republic of China. They'd been eager to visit Sichuan Province and Chengdu ever since the country reopened to western tourism. This tour was the first they had found that included the western provinces. But my parents weren't tourists. They were doctors, medical missionaries who had lived here for fourteen years. For them, this was a kind of homecoming.

Our plane taxied to a stop in front of a drab concrete terminal. I stood and took a deep breath, gathered my travel bag and camera, and followed my parents up the aisle toward the door. Waiting our turn to descend the stairs, Mom gave me a tight smile, fidgeting with her still naturally blond hair. Dad leaned toward me, gleeful, his blue eyes crinkling.

"Are you ready for this, Jackie?"

"As ready as I'll ever be, I guess."

At the doorway, I glimpsed flat agricultural fields stretching into a distant haze and stepped down into the steamy subtropical air of a sunny spring day. Reaching the tarmac, I moved briskly to keep up with my eager parents as they strode toward the terminal door.

Four Chinese people waited just inside, all dressed in dark gray Mao-style jackets and pants. Only their heights defined a difference—the two women diminutive, the men both a head taller. All four were scanning the incoming travelers, mostly westerners. I watched their expressions transform from somber concentration to elation when they recognized my parents.

Mom, proceeding apace and not expecting an airport welcome, started to rush by.

"Mom!" I said and put my hand on her shoulder.

Then she recognized them. The women bowed shyly as my mother reached toward them. They clutched hands, all three smiling and crying at the same time. Dad, shorter than the two men, beamed and shook their hands enthusiastically. A lively conversation in Chinese broke out, punctuated by hand gestures and laughs. Dad stopped talking briefly to introduce me in English. The four were Mom's medical-school classmates and Dad's former medical students at West China Union University. I shook hands with them, and they resumed their conversations as passengers from our flight continued to trickle by.

I stood outside their circle, transfixed by the women's tender, poignant reunion. My mother's constant mask of stress had fallen away, leaving only joy. I could not recall her ever showing love so openly to me and my siblings, or even to Dad. My eyes pooled as I backed away and leaned against the beige wall. Large, side-by-side pictures of Chairman Mao and Premier Zhou Enlai gazed at me from across the hall. My chest tightened as if in a vise, and time slowed down. I saw only what was before me: my mother chattering away with her friends, delight emanating from her every look and gesture.

I was stunned to my core. Who was this woman? Certainly not the mother I'd grown up with.

Minutes later we bade a temporary farewell to my parents' friends. We would see them the next day at a gathering of their Chinese medical colleagues when we would leave our tour for the day. Still reeling from what I'd witnessed, I wondered what other revelations awaited me.

Rejoining the tour group, we boarded a bus that took us to our hotel in the city. The only thing on our itinerary that evening was a briefing on Chengdu history and dinner—my first chance to try the famously fiery Sichuan cuisine.

This trip came at an unsettled time for me. My marriage had developed fissures, although my relationships with my children, a son twelve and a daughter ten, were close and rewarding. After seventeen years tending to others' needs, I was at long last thinking about what I wanted to do in life.

My decision to accompany my parents had surprised me. Growing up in a small West Virginia town following World War II, I hadn't wanted anyone to know about our connection to China as it drew attention to how different we were from others in town. At the same time, I knew they were concerned about the growing upheaval in China. They scoured newspapers and magazines for updates as the Nationalist and Communist armies battled for control. I heard the worry in their voices as they wondered how their Chinese friends were faring. Dad did not resign his medical missionary appointment until 1948, when there was no hope of returning. The next year, Mao Zedong established the People's Republic of China, and the country closed to the world. My parents heard nothing more from their Chinese friends.

Years later as my childhood memories receded, I became curious about my birthplace. When visiting my parents, I looked through their old photo albums and asked questions. I had grown up with my father's vivid storytelling of snow-covered mountains, warlords, and Tibetan valleys with yak and now imagined seeing firsthand the landscapes that had inspired his stories. As China reopened in the 1970s, my parents began looking for a tour that included Chengdu. Upon learning Coca-Cola would soon sell packaged soda in China, I knew western influence would change the country. I wanted to see it before that happened. So when Dad and Mom mentioned this tour, I signed on too.

That first night in my Chengdu hotel room, I replayed the airport scene over and over as I readied for bed. The roommate assigned to me for the tour had canceled at the last minute, and I was grateful that night not to make small talk. Witnessing my mother with her classmates had reordered my world. While much of my childhood remained fuzzy, I remembered Mom as often distant. At times she erupted in volcanic rages. Dad was even-tempered, but when she aimed her anger at him, he eventually countered her verbal jabs, although never with her level of acrimony. Now I'd glimpsed a different person. What had caused Mom to close off to her family?

Repetitive sounds drifting through the open window broke my thoughts. I crossed the room to investigate. The dim streetlight illuminated a woman in a dark blue Mao jacket and trousers sweeping the sidewalk three stories below. The streets of China always teemed with people, but fewer were out at this hour, and they detoured around the street sweeper as she worked. A bamboo pushcart nearby was filled with brooms of several sizes, each handmade of twigs lashed to a bamboo pole. One surprise of the trip so far was how little mechanization I'd seen in China, shown most starkly by the bicycles choking the streets and the lack of cars.

As the night was warm and muggy, I left the unscreened window open, despite noting the mosquito netting hanging above my bed. The faint breeze coming in felt good. I settled in bed, turned off the lamp, and arranged the netting in anticipation of nighttime visitors. Sleep was slow to come. I lay awake, the image of Mom greeting her classmates in my head. She had made these friends when she was twenty-four, living in a country so different from what she knew. I couldn't imagine what that must have been like for her. My parents had spent their first two years in Chengdu in language study. Then Dad began teaching in the medical school—in Chinese—and Mom, having had one year of medical studies in the United States, entered the school as a student. Her experiences bridged language and culture, cementing friendships that withstood thirty-five years of separation.

As I lay hoping for sleep, a memory surfaced of a visit to my parents after I had married. Mom was at work, and Dad had brewed tea for us. Settling beside me on the living room couch, he had handed me a yellowed newspaper photo with a caption about Philadelphia's annual spring flower show. An attractive young woman in a flapper-style dress kneeled on the grass. With a hint of a smile, she reached toward a lavish display of potted flowers.

I had put my teacup down to look more closely. "That's Mom—she's gorgeous! Where did this come from?"

"I found it last week in an old file and thought you'd enjoy seeing it." He chuckled. "That photo played a big part in our getting together."

They'd met in Philadelphia in autumn of 1929. Dad had his MD from the University of Pennsylvania and was in his last year of training for internal medicine. He had just been appointed by the American Baptist Foreign Mission Board to teach in Chengdu. Mom was in her first year at Women's Medical College of Pennsylvania.[1] Having been refused admission by a school close to her South Carolina home, she had ventured north of the Mason-Dixon Line for the first time.

"Tell me more about the photo and what happened."

"If I was going halfway around the world from my family, I wanted companionship—a wife. Someone who could laugh and talk seriously too," he said. "By then I had only six months to find the right woman and convince her to marry me."

"Tall order," I said, taking a sip of tea. "Especially when you're going to China."

He laughed. "Ah, but then I'd already met her." He turned toward me, his eyes shining. "I met Clinky at a student forum at the Chestnut Street Baptist Church early in the school year. We all introduced ourselves. I was impressed she was studying medicine. She was vivacious and easy to talk to." He gave a sly grin. "She laughed at my jokes, too—obviously a very intelligent woman."

"Ha!" I gave him a playful poke with my elbow. "Did you ask her out?"

He shook his head ruefully. "I had duty every night till ten thirty and was so tired I'd go home and fall into bed. In truth, she was a bit intimidating—seemingly perfect. I talked with her several more times at church."

"So the photo changed things?"

"It was a reminder." He picked up the photo. "This *Philadelphia Inquirer* photo was the nudge I needed. I hadn't seen her for several months, but I tracked her down."

"Well, I'm glad you did, or I wouldn't be here." I had leaned my head briefly on his shoulder. I knew what came next but let him tell the story. He was enjoying his memories.

"I wrote a note asking if she could pull away from her studies and go to a talk about medical missions on the Labrador coast." He'd beamed. "I've never forgotten what she said in return. 'Oh! Gee! I'd love to! I have an exam that day, so I'll be ready to go out!'"

Still awake in my hotel room in Chengdu, I rolled onto my side, trying to imagine my parents in their twenties. A whirlwind courtship had followed, so their first date must have been memorable. Two months later he'd asked Mom if she would pack her trunk and go to China with him—his exact words, according to her.

Although more women sought work in those years, my mother was bucking the norm of wives tending to home life and husbands being the sole breadwinners. Her determination to become a doctor was fierce, and she was lucky to have met Dad, a progressive thinker who had supported her ambitions.

At some point, I drifted off to sleep in the humid Chengdu night. I awoke bleary-eyed the next morning when my alarm rang. The tiny spots of blood on my sheet spoke of the middle-of-the-night battle with mosquitoes that had found their way under the netting. Getting up, I retrieved the thermos of piping-hot water that appeared every morning outside my door. Making a welcome cup of tea, I thought about the gathering my parents' friends had planned for the day. Mom had written to a Chinese colleague several months before our tour to say we were coming. She'd sent the letter to the medical school, hoping it would be delivered. Just days before we left, a brief letter arrived saying a celebration was planned.

As I drank my tea and thought about their friends, I recalled visiting my parents in 1968 when China's Cultural Revolution was wreaking havoc. The Red Guards had rampaged across the countryside, destroying temples and cultural objects, accusing elders and academics of clinging to traditional values and western thought. During my visit, we had watched Walter Cronkite one night on their black-and-white television. A video from China came on showing people being paraded through the street in dunce caps, wearing placards with Chinese characters proclaiming their "crimes." Most people were older, so some may have been former academics.

Mom had become distraught during the video and had turned to Dad, her brow furrowed. "Johnny, they don't say where this was taken. I'm afraid to watch for fear of seeing Zhang Meilan or Guo Wenliang."[2]

He had reached to squeeze her hand. "Don't lose hope. We have to believe they're okay."

Mom's mention of their friends by name had personalized the news video for me. They'd had no word from China since Mao had assumed power, but their friends were never far from her thoughts, as I had learned later in that same visit. Mom and I were having lunch the next day when she got up to get more coffee. While she was in the kitchen, I had looked up at the painted scroll hanging on the wall depicting China's last empress dowager. Growing up, we kids had nicknamed her "the freckled lady" because of the slight mildew bloom across her cheeks.

When Mom returned, she had shared the story of her friendship with her classmate, Dr. Zhang. "When we were getting ready to leave China for good in 1944, she and I pledged to keep our memories of each other alive." She gazed out the window and was quiet for a moment. "Every month we look at the full moon and remember the other halfway around the world watching the same moon. For more than two decades now. . . ." Her voice trailed off as sadness veiled her face.

"That's a beautiful story, Mom." I was touched—and surprised. She rarely shared something so personal. "I'm glad you had such a close friendship."

Looking down, she had clutched her hands together and said, almost in a whisper, "I just hope she's okay."

In my hotel room, as I dressed to meet my parents for breakfast, I realized Dr. Zhang had not been among the friends who had welcomed us the previous day. Would she be at today's gathering? Another question surfaced immediately. Would knowing more about my parents' time in China help me understand this puzzle that was my mother?

This thought would launch me on a journey that brought me to a better understanding of both my parents and a closer relationship with them. Only decades later did I realize the more fundamental breakthrough: China was the key to discovering my authentic self. I would return to China several more times. I would form my own friendships there, including one with Dr. Zhang's daughter, and explore landscapes that tugged at my soul with their beauty. I would bring my adult children and my niece to China, enabling them to experience firsthand their grandparents' legacy and link the generations in a profound way. These discoveries and more were all set in motion by that poignant reunion in the Chengdu airport.

 Chapter 2

I knew from an early age I didn't fit in.

When I entered Miss Mason's second grade at Philippi Elementary School in September 1948, I faced my third set of new classmates in twelve months. Everyone stared as Miss Mason introduced me, and the thought of making friends yet again terrified me. I didn't speak with the local West Virginia accent, just one of the things that made me shy and self-conscious.

My life until then had been so unlike my classmates' lives. I was acutely aware of these differences, even if they were not. Few of them had been outside the state, maybe even the county, whereas I had lived the first three years of my young life on the other side of the planet. My family had escaped war-torn China and lived for six months as refugees in Mumbai, India.[1] The mercy ship MS *Gripsholm* rescued us along with several hundred other missionary families and brought us through the Suez Canal and "home" to the United States.

With my family making multiple moves in the three years after reaching these shores, my concept of home was shaky. We lived for a year in Rochester, New York, in housing provided by Colgate Rochester Divinity School for missionaries on furlough, while my parents investigated places to settle. Philippi, in north-central West Virginia, offered a promising combination: a small town, a Baptist-affiliated college, and a regional medical clinic with job openings for both my parents. We moved in 1946, and Dad joined the clinic's practice. But Mom's foreign degree blocked her from obtaining a state medical license, even though West China Union University was chartered through the State of New York and offered an accredited program of western medicine. Foreign doctors had flooded the United States after World War II, and a foreign diploma was no longer sufficient to practice medicine in most states.

Mom applied to several medical schools and explained her dilemma, asking for admission into the fourth-year class. Women's Medical College in Philadelphia, where she first began her studies, accepted her. In August 1947, my mother, my two siblings and I, and our live-in housekeeper moved to Philadelphia for Mom's school year. We saw little of Dad during that time. As the newest clinic doctor, he was often on call for emergencies. He arranged a few days off around Christmas, though, and came by train to visit. Mom graduated in June, earning her second medical diploma. We returned to West Virginia, and she joined the clinic, seeing pediatric patients.

Philippi nestled among rolling hills with the Tygart Valley River and the adjacent railroad threading through town. An imposing pink sandstone county courthouse anchored the central square amid several blocks of stores, offices, and restaurants. At the west end of Main Street, a white two-lane covered bridge bearing the words FIRST LAND BATTLE OF THE CIVIL WAR spanned the river, while a two-story brick building housing both elementary and high schools anchored the east end. An underground coal mine was tucked in a hollow several miles from town, and a fair number of my schoolmates came from families whose men worked in the mine.

I began second grade in Philippi as a six-year-old, a full year younger than my classmates, having been promoted from kindergarten to first grade halfway through my Philadelphia school year. Although my age factored into my shyness, my greatest embarrassment was my family's connection to China.

With "Red China" frequently in the news, my parents often gave talks about their fourteen years in Chengdu, wanting to put a human face on the Chinese and boost understanding of this ancient culture. China's closure to the outside world had revived decades-old stereotypes of Chinese people and reinforced the postwar fear of communism. My parents remained fluent in Chinese, often speaking it at home and occasionally in public. Explaining a few words in a speech was one thing, but when they switched to Chinese in a store to discuss a purchase, I was mortified.

Over time I developed friendships. Jeannie became my first friend, maybe because she also had a different family situation. For reasons unbeknownst to me, she lived with her grandmother. Her grandma was warm and kind and reminded me of the children's book character Mrs. Piggle-Wiggle, who always smelled like cookies. By the end of third grade, my circle of friends also included Janet and Judy. We called ourselves "the four J's." I was sad when Jeannie and her grandma moved away after third grade, but a new girl, Juanita, soon joined our class, and we adopted her into our J club.

Even in fourth grade I rarely spoke out in class and never talked about China. Then one day the subject surfaced in social studies class when Mrs. Jones made an announcement.

"For the next few weeks, children, we'll study the world's major countries." As she talked, she listed countries alphabetically on the blackboard. "I'll divide you into groups by country. Each group will put together a report and make a salt-dough map to show the geography and location of major cities."

My stomach lurched when she wrote the word "China." I

wanted the floor to open up and swallow me. What happened next was worse than I'd expected. She had already decided the country assignments and began calling out names.

After finishing with Australia, Mrs. Jones said, "Now, with China we're lucky to have someone who knows a bit about this subject. Jackie, since you were born in China, I've put you in that group. You'll be in charge of the report."

My cheeks flushed as several classmates turned to look at me. One boy pulled his eyes into slits. I was so humiliated I didn't hear who else was in the group. Now all my classmates knew my deepest secret. My parents probably approved of this assignment, but for me it was an exercise in embarrassment. I don't remember much more except lining up in front to give our group report and then sitting down with relief at my desk, out of the spotlight.

During fourth grade my family moved to a house two blocks from school. Every day I walked to classes with Janet, who became my best friend throughout our school years. Sometimes she invited me into her house in the afternoon. Her mother always offered me an after-school snack and asked about my day. My family no longer had live-in housekeepers, but an older woman from church came to be with us at lunchtime and after school. She was nice enough, but it wasn't like having a mom at home.

At times the neighborhood kids gathered in our backyard for a pickup softball game, but I seldom invited anyone in to play, even when my parents were there. Inside, my home looked more Chinese to me than normal American, further emphasizing how different we were. In the living room, for example, four large vertical scrolls with giant calligraphic characters hung over the sofa. A huge brass bowl etched with dragons sat on a hand-carved wooden side table, each leg an elephant trunk curving up to a head complete with ivory tusks and three-dimensional leaflike ears. A brightly painted red-and-green Tibetan mask loomed gargoyle-like over a door, its eyes fierce, a sword held crosswise in its teeth. And much more. To me, normal was Janet's home. That's where we usually played or sometimes on the big swing on my front porch.

My mother was often critical and controlling. Appearances were important to her. She would back me up to a doorjamb for perfect posture—"Tuck your hips under, Jackie; you don't want a swayback"—and fuss with my stick-straight hair, giving me home perms or pulling it into painfully tight barrettes or braids.

When I was ten and my sister Marilyn twelve, we convinced our parents the two of us and our brother Don could manage on our own after school. At an earlier age I'd wished my mother were at home like other mothers, but by then I was relieved to do as I pleased.

I never shared our family secret of Mom's periodic rages. I only knew these episodes to happen at home, and they contributed to my feeling uneasy in my own skin, unable to ever get anything right. Emotional distance, intellectual conversation only, and no talk about feelings—these were the constants in my family. The tongue-lashings were unpredictable. I never knew what would set Mom off, and her anger was often out of proportion to whatever triggered the blowup. When she directed her ire at me, I figured it was my fault, that I'd done something wrong. Even with tirades aimed at others, my stomach filled with dread and I wished to be invisible.

We all avoided setting Mom off, yet without thinking, I did that one Saturday when I was fourteen. My parents had tickets for the football game at West Virginia University, an hour's drive away. The weather was nasty—blustery, cold, spitting snow—and I didn't want to go. I found Mom in her cramped bedroom closet, searching through hangers of blouses. Despite sensing her irritation, I blurted my question.

"Do I have to go to the old football game, Mom?"

She looked at me and frowned, her eyes narrowing. "Yes. We're all going."

"But I really don't want to."

"That doesn't matter," she said, her voice cold. "All five of us are going, so go get dressed right now. We have to leave soon." She returned to her searching.

"Shit!" The word just slipped out.

She spun around, her eyes tight with fury. "What did you say?" Her hand shot out and grabbed my arm, hard. "I don't want to hear that word again, young lady."

"Shit, shit, shit," I said, unable to help myself.

She squeezed my arm harder. "You'll do as I say," she hissed, her voice dripping with derision. "No one wants to hear such foul language. You won't amount to anything if you keep this behavior up." Her eyes darkened. "Go get ready—now!"

As I left her bedroom, I mumbled, "I hate you!"

I didn't think she would hear me, but there was nothing wrong with her hearing.

Her bitter voice trailed after me. "What a miserable pill you are."

The thought of sparking Mom's temper usually tamped down any inclination I had to talk back. When she got mad, her words cut through my heart, and each time the hole became a bit bigger. I learned that expressing anger in return or reasoning with her made the situation worse. I learned that sharing vulnerable feelings, even in a normal conversation, could backfire, as she might turn my vulnerabilities back on me in a rage and humiliate me. I learned to navigate my precarious home environment by being a "good" girl and not drawing attention to myself. This became my approach with all authority figures, including Dad and my teachers.

I don't remember ever talking with anyone in my family about Mom's temper until long after I was on my own. Nor do

I recall Dad intervening. All four of us—Dad and we kids— dealt with Mom's anger independently, alone. Unconsciously, I buried my feelings and the associated hurt and shame. To avoid Mom's ire, I became ever watchful of what went on around me and did what I thought would bring me approval.

Despite all the angst, there was laughter in our home. My father engaged in all kinds of banter, from jokes to puns to physical humor, which lightened the atmosphere. He took such delight in silliness that everyone around him would laugh too. Not even Mom could remain angry when he entered a room and barked like the terrier they had in China or oinked like a pig or acted out some funny story. More than once at a social event, I saw him "bend" a good silver teaspoon almost double, the children's eyes growing wider, the hostess looking on uneasily and then laughing in relief as he removed his hands from the intact spoon.

Within the privacy of our home, my discomfort with China diminished some. Both my parents had fond memories of living there, so anything related to China brought out the best in them. We all loved Chinese food and often had rice and stir-fried vegetables. Occasionally my parents prepared sumptuous six-course feasts for company. For two days they would stay up late, slicing meats and chopping ginger, garlic, and vegetables. One dish I've never found on a restaurant menu: angular chunks of carrot and beef simmered with *jiang-yu* (soy sauce), ginger, fermented black soybeans, star anise, and crunchy *mu-er* ("tree ears" or lichens). We used the Chinese porcelain dishes and set a traditional table with a small plate, small bowl, and chopsticks at each place. My siblings and I gleefully flouted western custom. We drank soup straight from the bowl or used chopsticks to shovel rice and vegetables from the bowl into our mouths. We laughed when we burped, the ultimate Chinese compliment to the cook.

Every year I looked forward to our annual road trip, always two weeks in August. Our first car was a used 1940s Desoto that had terrible visibility from the back seat. Dad placed an orange crate on end behind the driver's seat, and that's where I sat until I grew tall enough to see out the window without it. My father treated these trips as adventures. He was relaxed and weathered Mom's criticisms with good humor. Every other year, we drove to South Carolina to visit Mom's family. In alternate years we traveled to places like Niagara Falls or Maine, or we visited Dad's brothers and sister in Pennsylvania, Ohio, and Michigan.

Even as a youngster, I recognized the contrast between my parents' families. I never knew my paternal grandparents. My grandfather, an American Baptist minister, died while Dad was in college, and my grandmother passed away not long before we left China. Whenever Dad and his siblings got together, they joked and told stories on each other, laughing boisterously. There seemed to be plenty of stories about Dad, the youngest. He and Uncle Merrill, less than eighteen months apart, had been best friends growing up. More than once I heard Uncle Merrill tell a story about Dad as a toddler.

"John, do you remember when you were two and a half and you crawled under the pews during Father's church service?"

I never knew if Dad remembered this or just the telling, but he'd start to grin.

"No one noticed you," my uncle continued, "so Father must've been preaching a pretty good sermon. Mother didn't miss you until you started pinching the ladies' ankles and saying, 'Fleabite, fleabite.' That disrupted the service while Mother retrieved you." Then my uncle broke into his distinctive laugh, "Ahuh, ahuh, ahuh."

I looked forward to the immersion in good-natured bantering that happened on visits with Dad's siblings. I wished our family were more like that.

Mom's childhood had little in common with Dad's. Her parents lived in the Deep South their entire lives. My grandmother had grown up on a farm in northeast Georgia, just across the border from my grandfather's family in South Carolina. One summer we drove to the rundown farm near Granddaddy's family home where Mom had lived as a child, before the family moved to Greenville when she began high school.

"Daddy was very clever," Mom said. "He crossbred cattle and devised systems for us to have running water and electricity long before others had them." Then her veneer of pride vanished and her voice turned flat. "He ran our household with an iron hand. Children were to be seen and not heard."

I sensed little lightness or joy in the few times she spoke of her childhood, and my own experiences from our summer visits reinforced this impression.

Granddaddy and Hapink (a nickname bestowed by a cousin) lived in a small brick house with two bright red crape myrtle bushes gracing the front walk. Hapink's round, pretty face was framed by dark hair that she colored until late in life. The mouthwatering meals she fixed were different from ours at home: grits with redeye gravy made from Granddaddy's own salt-cured ham, fried chicken, green beans cooked all day with a ham bone, and delicious hand-cranked peach ice cream. Hapink was a poet. Her poems, sometimes printed in the newspaper, were filled with references to family, flowers, and the beauty of nature, often with religious overtones. Mom helped her publish a small book of poetry in 1958.

Granddaddy was a medium-sized balding man with wispy red hair and a cruel glint in his eyes. He had a sour demeanor and was often berating someone—usually Hapink and at times another of my relatives, but never my family.

One morning, coming into the kitchen for breakfast, I slid into the booth seat and instantly sensed tension. Several adults besides my grandparents were there. Hapink put a plate of fried eggs and grits in front of me. Inhaling the tantalizing aroma of buttered eggs, I realized I had walked into one of Granddaddy's rants.

"Bertie, I've never heard such ridiculous drivel," he said to Hapink, shaking his head. "You're always taking up for the underdog. That's just downright stupid."

My grandmother pursed her lips and looked down but didn't respond. No one said anything, though someone coughed or cleared a throat. The spiteful words triggered memories of similar instances at home with Mom, and the familiar flush of shame crept up my face. I bolted down my now-tasteless eggs and escaped.

Granddaddy had a ritual he performed whenever there were several grandchildren around. With a fiendish expression in his ice-blue eyes, he'd look at each child in turn, then yell, "Granddaddy wants chicken meat!" Then he'd sit back with a smirk and watch the children scream and scatter. I don't know about the others, but I screamed out of terror, not fun. I never knew what he intended, but I had images in my head of him grabbing me and gnawing on my neck or pinching me unmercifully. I wasn't going to wait to find out.

One of Hapink's poems was titled "The Words We Utter." It contains these lines: "watch well the things you say, my dear one, / repress the cruel words that give such pain." She never raised her voice to Granddaddy as far as I know. I never heard any family member confront him on his behavior or criticize him out of earshot.

On more than one visit I overheard Mom say to a sister or brother, "Jackie is so like our family. Marilyn and Don both take after Johnny."

This comment stayed with me. I know now she meant physical attributes, but at the time I absorbed more: resemblance, personality, behavior. But I knew I didn't want to be like her family, especially Granddaddy.

Not until much later did I recognize the counterbalance my father provided to the negative influences of my childhood. Besides his optimism and humor, Dad was a master storyteller. Some of my most enjoyable childhood memories involved him describing the adventures he and Mom had in China in the 1930s before we were born. I listened with rapt attention, never tiring of hearing the same stories over and over.

In one, Dad set out from Chengdu to walk to Mount Omei (now Emeishan), a sacred mountain three days away by foot. He and Mom had planned a month at the missionaries' summer retreat—a compound of cabins built on an Omei foothill on land rented from a Buddhist temple. Mom had gone ahead with friends and was already there. On his way, Dad became trapped between two battling warlords. He tried route after route to get through the military lines, to no avail. For ten days no one knew where he was. Friends sent messages back and forth: "Where is Lenox?" Finally making his way back to Chengdu, he sent a message to Mom saying he was safe and would stay put there.

Another time, as he accompanied a sick missionary down-river, soldiers began shooting at them, intending to confiscate the boat. The captain maneuvered to the bank where Dad, speaking Chinese, negotiated with the warlord himself to let them continue. Upon learning my father was a doctor, the warlord insisted Dad examine his ailing concubine before allowing him to proceed.

My favorite story was of their six-week trek into Tibet in 1932, traveling part of the ancient tea road and trade route to Lhasa. They had ten porters to carry their supplies: tent, cots, clothes, books, canned food, and medicines. They stayed in village inns or set up camp in the countryside. Best of all, they made a side trip by horseback to see the snow-clad Minya Konka, the highest mountain on the eastern rim of the Tibetan Plateau, which they had glimpsed from the summit of Mount

Omei. Making their way into a high, remote valley one ridge removed from the Minya Konka, they encountered a summer encampment of local Tibetans who had brought their yak to graze on the tender young grasses. They camped one night near the Tibetans' large black tents made of woven yak hair. Whenever Dad told this story, I knew from the faraway look in his eyes that he was transported back in time to that valley with the yak.

Although my father was unable to shield us from my mother's anger, he lightened the tension in our home with humor. He also modeled optimism and kindness. These traits, along with his stories of adventure, provided a lifeline that allowed me to escape, if only briefly, the sadness pervading my childhood.

 Chapter 3

I was a blank slate when I graduated from high school. I always knew what would follow—with my parents, college was a given—but I gave little thought to the future beyond college. Not until quite recently did I understand why.

In a writing workshop several years ago, the instructor asked us to write for fifteen minutes about what we had dreamed of becoming when we were children. Everyone else began to write and, after fifteen minutes, shared how they wanted to be a firefighter, a teacher, a doctor, and more. Stunned that I had nothing to write about, I sat motionless, absorbing the knowledge that thinking about the future hadn't occurred to me as a child.

Dreaming and imagining the future would have required turning inward, where pain and humiliation lay stored. I focused outward, always monitoring what was happening around me so I could please my parents and avoid my mother's temper and harsh words.

As a result, upon finishing high school I was timid, indecisive, and immature. I had no idea what I wanted to do in life. Most of my high school classes had been uninspired and boring, and I'd made good grades with little studying. Not one teacher provided a role model that attracted me to their profession or to their field of study. With no career guidance at my high school and my parents not wanting to unduly influence us, I was on my own.

I took the easy route, following my sister Marilyn to the same liberal arts college in Ohio with little more than a cursory glance at other schools. I also followed her into a biology major, a chemistry minor, and, after she graduated, the job she'd had as a student lab assistant in the biology department. Although we were not close then, she blazed a path that seemed like safe terrain. I thought little about what I would do with a biology degree. Yet I absorbed from my parents the desire to work in some capacity that served a larger purpose beyond myself.

In college I discovered a pleasure in learning. In addition to courses in my declared subject areas, I took history and psychology courses. Most of my biology classes related to the human body, but in the fall semester of senior year I veered into a field ecology course on winter tree identification. We made weekly field trips off campus into November. Even in the bare-branch stage, I delighted in identifying a tree by its bark, the shape of a winter bud, or the thickness and character of a leafless twig. A peaceful feeling always washed over me upon entering the Ohio woods, especially as the trees assumed their autumn colors.

On our class field trip the October week of peak foliage, with the trees cloaked in vibrant hues of gold, reddish-orange, and crimson, I realized why these forays into the forest struck such a deep chord. My father had taken us kids for Sunday walks in the West Virginia woods in the fall, his favorite time of year. He pointed out the colorful trees and named the birds we saw. Before turning for home, we picked up the prettiest fallen leaves to take home to Mom.

I met my future husband, Tom, at college. Although we were classmates, our paths crossed little until junior year when his premed major meant we had similar schedules. In classes we were friendly competitors for grades and conversation came easily, a new experience for me. When he teased me in the labs, the dimples that appeared when he smiled made my heart melt. I knew he was on the football team, and that spring when we began dating, I learned he also threw the shot and discus for the track team. In addition to being athletic, he was self-confident and had known for years he wanted to be a doctor—qualities I found attractive in part because I lacked them.

Tom and I married in June 1963, a week after graduation and a few months after my twenty-first birthday. I hadn't gone to college seeking a husband like some women of my generation; I was in love for the first time, and marriage seemed a natural next step. In hindsight, I should not have married so young. But no one counseled me to wait, not even my mother, who had married at twenty-two. Not that I would have listened! Marriage allowed me to avoid what I was ill-prepared to do— to make my own decisions and act on them. By marrying, I transferred dependency from my parents to my husband.

We moved to Rochester, New York, where Tom entered medical school. He had a large extended family living east of Rochester in the Finger Lakes region. My first big gathering was Thanksgiving dinner, held at the home of one of Tom's uncles. When we entered the house, the first person to greet us was an aunt.

Seeing me with Tom, she said, "Jackie, how nice to meet you at last. I've heard so much about you, dear." And she embraced me in a big bear hug.

I was startled, being used to the awkward clinches of my family that substituted for hugs. After my first thought—*oh my god, they're huggers*—other relatives surrounded me and drew me farther into the house, also offering affectionate hugs. From the beginning I felt loved and accepted in a family very different from my own. I soon relaxed and began to enjoy the warm tribal camaraderie of my in-laws.

In Rochester I worked as the supervisor of a medical research lab investigating gastric enzymes—not a subject I chose but the position available when I applied near the end of college. My job was to oversee the research process and keep the lab running smoothly. The pay was pathetic, even for the times. As a medical student, Tom's wages for three months' work during the summer was equivalent to my annual salary.

As a university employee, I could take classes at little cost. In Tom's first year of medical school, I took a graduate-level physiology course and later met with a biology professor to discuss a master's program. We lived on a shoestring, and I explained my need to take classes part-time. The professor said the department had just decided to accept full-time students only, regardless of qualifications. Who knows what would have happened if I'd questioned his response. I put graduate school aside for the time being. I didn't share my thoughts about future graduate study with Tom, and he, preoccupied with his own classes, didn't encourage me further.

These medical school years coincided with the growing turbulence of the mid-1960s. Like everyone, I was shocked by President Kennedy's assassination and watched the funeral tableau on our small black-and-white television. The following summer President Johnson signed the Civil Rights Act, and within weeks riots and looting erupted across the city from our apartment. The riots were quelled by National Guard soldiers, but the unrest provided a glimpse into the turmoil engulfing the country.

Despite these events and the growing Vietnam War protests, we lived mostly in a bubble, going to the medical center every weekday—Tom to classes, I to the lab. Our weekend social life consisted of an occasional movie or get-togethers with a small circle of married friends, the husbands in Tom's class and the wives all working to put them through school. At times I had doubts about where my life was going, but I stuck with the coping habits that had helped me through childhood: to live day by day and not think about the future.

We saw our parents mostly on holidays or school breaks. On one visit to my folks, I came across the photos taken during our family road trips as I was growing up. Sitting cross-legged on the floor, I looked through the pictures. In the first one, Mom sat at a picnic table as my brother and I horsed around in the background. As a kid I'd intuitively connected Mom's anger with unhappiness, yet the naked sadness on her face astonished me. She stared into the distance, oblivious to the camera, lost in her own thoughts. I put that photo down and lifted the next to see a different setting but the same scene: a somber Mom paying no attention to what was going on around her, interacting with no one. As I went through the photos one by one, only the ages of the children and the outdoor setting changed. Dad must have taken the photos because he appeared in none. Mom was at best pensive, more often downcast or despondent.

Growing up, I had wondered if she wanted to be a mother. Sitting with the photos that day, another question came to mind. Was her marriage the cause of her unhappiness? I kept these thoughts to myself too. In my relationship with Tom, as with my birth family, we avoided uncomfortable, personal subjects.

As Tom's last year of medical school approached, a decision loomed: where to apply for his year of internship. That summer we drove to the West Coast, camping along the way in national parks and national forests. This was my first time in the Rocky Mountains and the Cascades. I was gobsmacked by the sweeping views, extensive forests, and crisp air. One day in Glacier National Park, we hiked to a mountain pass and back, a total of thirteen miles. We hadn't intended to hike so far, but I kept wanting to see what was beyond the next curve in the trail or the view from the next rise. Not accustomed to such strenuous exercise, I was sore for the next week, but the exhilaration of being in the wilderness stayed with me.

As we made our way through the Pacific Northwest and down the coast to California, I found myself thinking about Tom's internship and raised the subject one day in the car.

"You know, your internship is only for one year. We could live in an entirely new place."

"Uh-huh." He glanced at me, then turned his attention back to driving.

"This is such gorgeous country. What would you say to living out west somewhere, trying it for a year?"

"Sure, we can think about it," he said, although he didn't sound excited about the idea.

We never discussed the topic further as Tom soon decided to join the navy in exchange for the government paying for his last year of school. Despite my disappointment, I didn't argue because it would ease our tight financial situation.

With Tom's graduation in 1967, I took a tiny step toward becoming my own person. Four years of medical research was enough for me. I still had a desire for work that contributed to society but didn't yet know what that might look like. Reflecting on a career had to take a back seat anyway because I was pregnant. We were both thrilled with this imminent change in our family. Tom was assigned to Bethesda Naval Hospital for his internship, and we spent the next year in the Washington, DC, area.

Our son, John, named after my father, was born in November. The first time I held him I fell deeply in love with this tiny human being, responding to him intuitively—a new reaction for me. With my new baby, I allowed my heart to lead without further questioning or shielding my feelings. I was experiencing unconditional love for the first time, although unaware of the concept then.

With Tom's long hours, the childcare fell solely to me. Tom would come home and pick Johnny up to play with him.

I would soon find him lying on the couch or the floor with this wee baby on his chest, father and son both asleep—a scene so sweet it never failed to warm my heart.

After his internship Tom opted for six months of flight surgeon's training. We moved to Pensacola, Florida, where Johnny learned to walk on the white sand beaches. Duty assignments came in early 1969 near the end of the training, when the Vietnam War was raging. The newly minted flight surgeons had to choose between operational duty—assignment to a specific squadron of navy pilots and the certainty of going to Vietnam—or a nonoperational assignment to a specific base for the duration of military duty. Tom chose the latter, which put him into a lottery. He called me immediately after the drawing.

"I got Olathe, Kansas." When I burst into tears, he asked, "Jackie, what's wrong? With my parents now in Wichita, we won't be far from them."

"What's the navy doing in Kansas?" I asked, my heart sinking. I had seen the list of openings but must have skipped over Kansas. With our western camping trip still in mind, I'd been hoping for one of the West Coast openings or even the base in Iceland.

"It's a Naval Reserve base," he replied. "Hey, if you really don't want Kansas, I have an hour to trade assignments. I'll see what I can do."

"Thanks, Tom. I'd really appreciate that."

I hoped someone in the class wanted to live in Kansas. The next hour was pure torture, and I was hovering by the phone when it rang.

"Jackie, only one person wanted to trade. This guy grew up in Kansas City and preferred Olathe to Kodiak, Alaska. So that's where we're going. I hope you're okay with living on an island in the Gulf of Alaska."

I let out a huge breath of utter relief.

It is no exaggeration to say Tom's trade transformed my life. I had never heard of Kodiak, an island southwest of Anchorage, one hundred miles long and famous for king crab and the giant Kodiak brown bear. We traded vehicles with the Marine couple who lived in the apartment next to ours—our station wagon for their Volkswagen camper—and in April 1969 we headed north from Pensacola. After spending a week with friends in Rochester, Tom dropped me off at my folks'. My father, always up for an adventure, climbed into the camper with Tom for the drive across the country and north through Canada to Alaska. They parted in Anchorage, Dad flying home and Tom taking a ferry to Kodiak.

I followed with Johnny by air in mid-May, arriving during the spring rains. For two solid weeks clouds hung low, and rain fell steadily. I wondered what I was in for. When the clouds lifted, I beheld a lush landscape: mountains cloaked in a sumptuous new green and the slate-gray ocean rolling in waves onto black volcanic-sand beaches. The kitchen of our base duplex faced the aptly named Barometer Mountain. One glance out the window gave a reading on the cloud ceiling and current weather. I embraced the Kodiak mantra: "When the sun shines, drop everything and go outside, for the rains will return."

The town of Kodiak and the base just south are located on the northeast end of the island, with Native Aleut villages scattered on the coast farther south and on the western side. The island then had forty-five miles of roads that linked the town and the base, extending a bit north of town and more extensively south of the base, with side roads to scenic or fishing spots. The roads were gravel except for pavement between the town and the base.

We headed south at every opportunity. The road snaked around the bays leading to beaches where we found driftwood, tiny pink shells, and occasionally the coveted beachcombing prize: three-inch-diameter floats of teal-colored glass, once attached to Japanese fishing nets. At times we spied bald eagles in the few trees scattered along the roadside—a sight unusual then in the rest of the United States due to DDT use. During salmon spawning, the eagles feasted on the fish clogging the rivers. Coho salmon returned to spawn soon after I arrived. We often drove to a fishing beach and brought home our limit.

Adapting quickly to life in Alaska and loving it, I discarded my umbrella, a useless encumbrance with rain blowing sideways in the ever-present wind. I bought a red, all-weather jacket, a red-and-black-checked wool shirt, sturdy hiking boots, and insulated boots for winter. I learned where to pick luscious, reddish-orange salmonberries and find the succulent white angel wing mushrooms that grew on decaying wood. Tom liked to hunt, so we ate moose and venison often. On his days off, we'd go fishing or hiking with Johnny in a backpack. Stephanie was born in 1970. Once she took over the pack, Johnny developed into a hardy little hiker. I loved pointing out the birds and flowers to him, much like my father had done for me. Even at three, he absorbed these nature lessons avidly.

My parents came for a visit when Steph was three months old. We rented a truck camper in Anchorage for a week's travel on the mainland. My parents took to camper travel right away. Mom seemed less prickly than I remembered, her hair-trigger temper perhaps muted by the mountain beauty. Because no one wanted to miss anything, we crowded four across the truck's bench seat—Tom driving and my parents and I taking turns holding the sleeping baby. Johnny claimed the bunk window over the cab.

This was my first time exploring the Alaskan mainland, and I was astounded by the magnificent scenery. Even our earlier trip through the Pacific Northwest hadn't prepared me for the wilderness we saw from the camper. I had never seen anything like the scale of the landscape and the seemingly endless mountains with their "zebra" striping, a result of snow melting on exposed ridges but remaining in protected areas. We drove the Glenn Highway to the Matanuska Glacier and then connected with the road going south to Valdez.

I was curious about Valdez, a fishing village situated on scenic Prince William Sound and the epicenter of the massive 1964 earthquake. This village had been proposed as the southern terminus of a pipeline to bring the recently discovered North Slope oil to a port for loading onto tankers. I was glad to see Valdez in its pristine setting before oil development changed it.

We took the state ferry across the sound, sailing close enough to the Columbia Glacier to see minor calving from the glacier into the water. I was used to Dad's joy of the outdoors, but Mom's whole demeanor changed as the week passed—she seemed more at ease, game for anything. The ferry docked at Whittier on the western shore of the sound. We drove the camper onto a car train that took us through a tunnel, delivering us to the highway along scenic Turnagain Arm south of Anchorage. The next day we said goodbye to my parents, dropping them off at the airport, where they joined a tour going to remote Native Alaskan coastal towns. We returned the camper, picked up our Volkswagen bus, and headed for the Kodiak ferry.

By the time Tom's navy commitment was up at the end of 1971, Alaska had claimed my soul. Living on Kodiak had awakened me from the fog of my childhood. The extraordinary beauty of our forty-ninth state, the healing power of nature, and the unconditional love coursing through me with the birth of my children had combined to crack my heart open. Some long-held fear or defense mechanism gave way a little, and the shackles binding my emotions loosened. With a certainty rare for me, I recognized an inner resonance that told me Alaska was where I belonged.

 Chapter 4

As our departure from Kodiak drew near, Tom was accepted at the University of Rochester for three years' training in ophthalmology. While on Kodiak, he had participated several times on a US Public Health Service team providing medical services to remote Alaska Native villages. On these trips he'd struck up a friendship with Sam, an eye doctor from Anchorage, and they'd discovered a mutual love of hunting. After several hunting trips together, Sam invited Tom to join his practice upon completing his training.

Putting down roots had always seemed so far into the future that Tom and I hadn't talked seriously about where to settle. Despite the decision being several years off, with Sam's offer we had something concrete to consider. Although Tom kept his options open, the thought we might end up in Anchorage made it easier for me to leave Kodiak when our time there ended.

In Rochester we bought our first home in a quiet neighborhood near the university where most families were associated in some capacity with medicine. There were children Johnny and Steph's ages and friends for me in a similar phase of life. Although Rochester was familiar, I was aware now of the flat topography and missed the outdoor life we'd had on Kodiak.

Tom and Sam stayed in touch, and I held on to the hope that we would return to Alaska.

During this time, I often heard Peggy Lee's Grammy-winning recording "Is That All There Is?" on the radio. People interpret the song's meaning in varying ways, from disappointment and disillusionment to survival and optimism. My take was disillusionment, but what drew me to the song was the title, which mirrored my thoughts as I approached the second decade of my marriage. I don't remember which came first, hearing the song or the bouts of insomnia that began midway through our three years in Rochester. My life then consisted of caring for my two small children and managing the household—a typical 1950s image of a woman's life. When the insomnia began, one question kept surfacing as I lay awake, Tom sleeping soundly beside me: Is this all there is to life? At first, I didn't know what to make of it. I told myself I should be happy. I had two wonderful children, and my husband was a good man who had chosen a profession that would provide a comfortable life for us. And the end of Tom's training was in sight.

So why the discontentment with my life?

I began compiling a list. First were the things I missed about Alaska—the stunning mountain beauty and outdoor adventures. The closest mountains to Rochester, the Adirondacks, were too distant with Tom's busy schedule. Next were the habits Tom and I had developed early in our marriage. Despite my full-time job during his medical school, I'd taken on all the cooking and housework since his classes and studying had seemed more important. I had grown up with my parents sharing cooking duties, but neither did much housework—they paid someone for that. Tom had grown up in a traditional household, and he rarely offered to help. Having children reinforced the roles we had unconsciously assumed. I didn't mind the cooking, but shouldering all the housework frustrated me. I'd had no model growing up for talking about feelings, and Mom's temper had conditioned me to not speak up. So I had swallowed my frustration.

During those midnight hours I realized happiness wasn't guaranteed by falling in love and getting married. I didn't yet understand that a successful marriage needs continuous nurturing, good communication, a willingness for give-and-take, and a mutual ability to share emotions. These skills, although practiced to some extent by my father, had been mostly lacking in my family or too subtle for a child to comprehend.

One might assume having a mother laser-focused on her career would have influenced me, but I had absorbed conflicting messages growing up. With Mom's apparent unhappiness and her tendency toward anger and shaming, I'd never considered emulating her. The perky stay-at-home moms in the television programs of my youth had all looked happy, but now I found that role unsatisfying.

In the decade I had helped put Tom through medical school and cared for two small children, society had undergone a sea change. I'd spent the better part of those years in the bubble of medical school and the isolation of island military life, aware of the social changes but several degrees removed. Entering the second decade of marriage, I felt adrift, without guidance, still trying to please others because that was how I had survived childhood. But I was more aware now and understood I didn't have to conform to a traditional view of a wife and mother.

I needed to decide what I wanted from life and create a plan for getting there. My inclination to pursue graduate school after college had been thwarted but was still a possibility, along with volunteering or finding a job I liked. However, even with women demanding greater social freedoms and career opportunities, no career path had yet spoken to me. So I drifted from day to day, discontented.

What I lacked at thirty-one was a sense of agency, an understanding that my happiness was in my own hands. I was comfortable with parenting, and unlike my experience growing up, I expressed my love freely and often with my children. Still trying to please everyone, though, I coped with life much as I had as a child: if I'm a good mother and a good wife and keep a perfect house, then everyone will be happy and love me. At long last, I realized taking care of everyone else while ignoring my own needs and desires was a recipe for unhappiness.

As the children grew and the work related to their care lessened, I filled my time with creative endeavors. I tried macramé and knitting, sewed clothes for Steph and me, made curtains and even a slipcover for the sofa. I planted an elaborate organic vegetable garden and baked bread, pies, and cookies. Feeling distant from my science years and ill-equipped to carry on an adult conversation, I joined a book club and volunteered for a local nonprofit group. But the hollow inside remained.

Still, I said nothing about my discontent to Tom or to anyone, nor did I share my ambitions, unformed as they were. As with so many aspects stemming from childhood, I didn't know people shared such personal thoughts. I wasn't alone in this. Neither Tom nor I talked about our fears or hopes for life or our marriage. We never argued, and we both backed away from expressing anger. I feared being like my mother. As a result, neither of us learned to air our grievances or work through our differences. Even if I had been accustomed to analyzing my feelings, I would have had difficulty at the time putting my thoughts into words. There was only the vague discontent surfacing during my midnight insomnia: *is this all there is to life?*

To my delight, as the end of Tom's training neared, he and Sam agreed to give partnership a go. Tom and I flew to Anchorage in autumn of 1974 so they could finalize details for sharing the practice. We also bought a house and planned to return when Tom's training ended in December.

To save money, we decided to drive ourselves and our belongings via the Alaska Highway, despite it being wintertime. I looked forward to the adventure, considering it an epic road trip. We bought a used rental truck and began to pack. Tom's father volunteered to come with us and drive the truck, which we gratefully accepted, as we were also taking our Ford station wagon. We prepared our little caravan for a winter road trip, installing CB radios in both vehicles and a plug-in block heater in the truck. The traffic associated with oil development had increased, and gas stations, lodging, and outdoor electrical outlets for overnighting vehicles were numerous. Rather than put a block heater in the station wagon, we would leave the car running all night if temperatures plummeted. Our final purchase was the latest edition of *The Milepost*, which listed facilities along the Alaska Highway mile by mile.

After goodbyes to friends and family in upstate New York, we spent Christmas with my parents in Pittsburgh, where they had recently moved. After I went to college, Mom had left Philippi to take further training in pediatrics and pediatric cardiology at Children's Hospital, part of the University of Pittsburgh Medical Center. She had been recruited as the second physician in the new pediatric cardiology division of Children's Hospital. Soon after, Dad had moved from West Virginia to join her, eventually teaching a lab course in the medical school's dermatology department and working in student health part-time diagnosing skin conditions.

On our last day in Pittsburgh, Dad came to me with an "adolescent" Christmas cactus he had grown. The plant was lush and still blooming.

"For your new home," he said with a grin. "Do you have room in your box of plants?"

I'd brought a box into their apartment with a baby spider plant, an African violet, and a jade plant the same size as the Christmas cactus.

"Thank you, Dad." I took the plant from him and fitted it into the box. "I'll think of you and your emerald-green thumb every time I look at it."

He beamed as I hugged him.

After saying our goodbyes, we departed in the station wagon, the box of plants between Tom and me up front and the kids in back where we'd put the seats down to give them room to play. We rendezvoused with my father-in-law, who had driven the truck from upstate New York, and picked up our route angling northwest through North Dakota and the border. With crisp, clear weather, we traveled uneventfully across the Canadian plains. I reveled at signs of ever-more-northerly latitudes: the low angle of the winter sun, shorter days, more spruce trees, and ravens. One evening as Tom drove into the night, I awoke from dozing to see sparkling stars and the dancing greens of northern lights in the vast nighttime sky. A peacefulness washed over me. I was going home.

We arrived late afternoon in Dawson Creek, British Columbia, milepost zero of the Alaska Highway. We had sixteen hundred miles of driving still ahead of us, the first twelve hundred miles a gravel road. My journal says the temperature was zero degrees Fahrenheit. The next morning it was minus twenty-five and snowing lightly. Starting out, we encountered heavy truck traffic. Each time we passed an oncoming truck, a small blizzard of whirling snow followed, obscuring the snow-packed road for a few seconds.

Not long after lunch the CB radio crackled to life.

"Just wanted you to know my speedometer's stopped working," my father-in-law said. "The voltage regulator is acting weird too."

"Let's stop at the next town or service station to see what's going on," Tom said.

This was our first discovery of how extreme cold can monkey with a vehicle's electrical system. Long after sunset, we called a halt for the day when the wagon's interior lights began blinking on and off continuously. The next morning brought clear weather and plummeting temperatures. The wagon's side and back windows frosted over, making the kids' space into a cozy cave. They played well together, devising elaborate stories and activities for their stuffed animals and Steph's doll. We drove through a winter wonderland of heavily frosted trees and ice fog hovering over the rivers. When we stopped that night it was forty below zero.

"The wagon idles tonight," Tom said.

Each evening I'd carried the box of plants, well covered, into our lodging and back out the next morning once the car had warmed up. That night I threw a second layer over the box before bringing it in. My father-in-law plugged the truck in for the night. After getting extra blankets at the front desk, we went to bed.

Tom checked the car first thing in the morning and found it fine, still with a half tank of gas. But the truck was stone cold. A trucker had arrived late, plugged his big rig into the same outlet as our truck, and blown the circuit. We learned at breakfast the temperature was minus forty-eight and forecast to drop even further. After we waited several hours, someone arrived from the nearest town with a blowtorch to thaw the truck. We left the motel at noon with the temperature at fifty-one below. Despite the cold and wind chill, I marveled at the pristine beauty around us. I'd been hoping for several days to spot at least a moose for the kids but saw no wildlife during those frigid days.

"I guess the critters are smarter than we are," I said. "They've hunkered down."

Sunset came at three thirty, and again we had to deal with a bizarre electrical system. The wagon's interior lights blinked on and off, and then the headlights went out, leaving us with only running lights. Soon they began blinking too.

"We must look like a flashing Christmas tree," I said to the kids, prompting giggles.

Tom radioed his father to stop so we could confer. We decided to follow right behind the truck to benefit from its taillights and take our chances on the next motel. We maneuvered the curves and hills slowly and after eight miles saw the lights of Johnson's Crossing Lodge. I was prepared to spend the night no matter the accommodations and was pleasantly surprised to find a nice homey place—not fancy but clean and at half the cost of previous lodgings. That night I wrote in my journal: "Temperature a nippy -61°. Pile those blankets on!"

The next morning I was concerned that, despite my best efforts, the plants appeared bedraggled with leaf edges wilted and browning. At breakfast we sat beside a big south-facing window with shelves and shelves of healthy, happy plants. With more frigid cold forecast, I accepted the inevitable.

"I think I'd best leave the plants here," I said, gesturing to the shelves beside me. "Clearly these folks like plants."

"Good idea," Tom said. "By the way, I've talked with Dad. From here on, we're traveling only in daylight to avoid the problems with the lights."

After breakfast I spoke to the woman at the front desk and explained our situation, asking if I could leave my plants.

"Of course," she said. "We'll take good care of them."

I thanked her, feeling sure the plants would thrive. Nevertheless, leaving the Christmas cactus was like leaving a little piece of my father behind.

After several short days of driving only in daylight, we reached Haines Junction, where the temperature was a balmy thirty-five below. We learned a snowstorm four days before had closed parts of the highway, a sobering thought given what we'd just experienced.

Throughout the long trip, I had thought often about returning to the state that had felt like home to me, wondering what it would hold for us. The closer we came to the Alaska border, the more certain I was we had made the right decision. Driving ever more north through the snowy wilderness landscape, the beauty of the mountains all around, I felt a soul-deep stirring inside, like a reawakening from a long sleep.

We crossed into Alaska with 360 miles to go. The good weather held, warming gradually. Reaching Anchorage, we agreed the frigid trip had been quite the adventure, and we were grateful the winter gods had been kind to our naive caravan.

As we settled into our new home, my excitement at being back in Alaska overrode the doubt that had crept into my thoughts in Rochester. Although I was living in another large city, all I had to do was look out my living room window at the snow-covered Chugach Mountains or take in the extended alpenglow of this northerly latitude or watch the puffed-up hoary redpolls at our bird feeder, and my soul was at rest. I looked forward to what life in Anchorage would bring.

 Chapter 5

The first weeks in Anchorage I awoke each morning eager for the day. The extraordinary winter beauty took my breath away, especially the sunsets when the sinking sun bathed the snowy slopes in dazzling hues of mauve and gold. Crisp air and the lack of humidity made it comfortable to be outdoors in single digits above and below zero. Looking north from our cul-de-sac, under certain conditions we could glimpse Denali in the distance, the highest mountain in North America—a wondrous surprise as it had been hidden in clouds when we decided to buy the house.

I enrolled Steph in a preschool three mornings a week, and Johnny entered first grade at the nearby school. For a month he walked to school with neighbor kids as the day was dawning and returned home with sunset colors. Tom could enjoy this beauty only on weekends until the lengthening February days enabled him to drive to and from work with the sunrise and sunset.

One morning soon after the children were settled in their schools, I decided to explore the city center. In the frigid January cold, the snow crunched under my tires as I drove down the main street under the banner proclaiming "Anchorage, All-American City." I parked the car and started walking. The downtown was a mix of buildings from different time periods. I spotted the 1940s frontier outpost in the log cabins, bars, pawn shops, and peep shows, while the two- and three-story buildings marked the 1960s downtown. The newer, taller office buildings and hotels had likely come with the oil development that began during our Kodiak years.

Near the central downtown I came upon a small log cabin with the sign "Alaska Center for the Environment." I'd been following the growing environmental movement ever since the June 1969 *Time* cover photo depicted Ohio's Cuyahoga River ablaze from oil-soaked debris. I had worried about the effects of DDT on bald eagles and other birds and had noticed smog hanging over the larger cities on airline flights between the northeast states and Alaska. Although I hadn't studied ecology in college, my biology degree helped me understand the importance of a healthy environment.

On impulse I opened the cabin door and found myself in an open space that took up half the interior. At the central desk a lanky woman with a pleasant expression looked up and asked how she could help.

"I've just moved here," I said. "I was walking around and saw your sign. Can you tell me more about your organization?"

She smiled. "Welcome to Anchorage! The Center formed about five years ago to provide a citizen voice on environmental issues."

"Do you have volunteer opportunities? My younger child is in preschool, and I have several mornings free."

"Most of us here are volunteers. We can always use another pair of hands."

She showed me around and talked about the Center's priorities. When I left twenty minutes later, I had agreed to volunteer two of the mornings Steph was in preschool. Looking forward to getting involved, I couldn't stop smiling on the drive home.

That evening at dinner Tom raised his eyebrows when I mentioned my decision to volunteer. His questioning look made me feel defensive.

"It's only two mornings during Steph's preschool. You know I'm interested in environmental issues. I want something to do in my free time."

"Well, if that's what you want," he said, getting up from the table.

As I stood to clear the dishes, I almost expected him to pat me on the head.

I couldn't foresee then that volunteering with the Alaska Center would open the door to thirty-five years of conservation work. I started out clipping newspaper articles that discussed environmental issues or mentioned the organization. While the work wasn't challenging, I learned what was going on in my adopted state. Contributing even in this small way made me feel useful.

Anchorage, then with two hundred thousand residents, was booming from the prospect of oil production. Milly, another volunteer, told me Anchorage had been a sleepy town of just a few thousand hardy people less than four decades earlier. Her family had regularly seen wolves along the traplines they ran in what was now the downtown. The early growth during World War II and the Cold War years had been military in nature, but the later expansion came from resource development. I learned the city was considering a new master plan. I attended some public-information meetings and expressed my opinion to the editor of the *Anchorage Daily News*.

When I went to the Center the following week, Peter, the only salaried person on staff, came to me with a newspaper clipping of my letter.

"Jackie, you write well," he said.

"Thanks, Peter." I felt my face flush.

"We'll have to find something more substantial for you than clipping articles. Why don't you choose a topic that interests you and start monitoring it? You'll find lots of information in our resource library."

"I'd love to do that."

"Read up on the issue and then let me know if something surfaces that needs action or a position statement from us."

"I will. Thanks again."

When Tom arrived home that evening, I was still riding a wave of excitement. When I said Peter had given me an assignment with more responsibility after reading my letter, he seemed perturbed rather than pleased for me.

"Does this mean more time?" he asked, frowning.

"I don't know, not necessarily. But it's more interesting than filing articles." His tone bothered me, but I let it go.

I decided to follow coastal zone management and the plan the state was drafting. No one could have accused me of being unambitious. Alaska has more coastline than all the other states combined and was experiencing many pressures, including fish and wildlife concerns, pollution, and oil development. Over the next months I learned enough to compose a position statement on the draft plan for Peter and the Center's board of directors to consider.

On weekends our family went exploring. That first winter we took our new cross-country skis to Russian Jack Springs Park, a forested area not far from our house. There we found eskers—sinuous ridges of sand and gravel thirty or forty feet high, formed in glacial times when streams dropped their rock loads under the glacier. We found the trails up and down the eskers perfect for us beginning skiers—steep enough for a short downhill run but not too high to climb back up on our skis. We often saw signs of moose—tracks as well as "Yukon pecans," the local term for their droppings—and occasionally the moose themselves. At stream crossings we stopped to watch American dippers, chunky little gray birds that dash into cold rushing waters even in winter to catch water bugs hiding among the rocks.

In late spring on one of my volunteer days, Peter came to me again. The Tuesday daily coordinator was stepping down, and he asked if I would consider taking her place. The Center operated in a unique way. Five volunteers managed the organization's daily business, each responsible for a specific day of the week. They dealt with phone calls, supervised other volunteers, and handled any questions or concerns people brought in the front door.

Pleased he'd asked me, I accepted with the caveat of finding after-school arrangements for my kids. The rest of the morning, thinking about what I was taking on, I alternated between feeling upbeat and having jitters. But I had to trust myself. I could do this.

Johnny and Steph each had a friend in the cul-de-sac, and their stay-at-home moms agreed to watch them after school on Tuesdays. It never occurred to me to wonder if my children resented the afternoon each week when I wasn't there after school, as I had resented my mother not being home when I was their age. I gave them my full attention when I arrived home, asking about their day and what they'd done with their friends. I soon was able to handle the daily coordinator tasks with no difficulty. In early autumn Peter asked me to join the Center's board of directors, my first-ever experience with this level of responsibility and something totally unexpected. I took the invitation as a sign the organization appreciated my contribution and felt good about that. I accepted, although that inner part of me that felt unworthy—which I now recognize as rooted in the belittling words my mother used when angry—caused me to feel some trepidation. Tom didn't say much, which I took to mean he accepted this as what I did in my spare time.

As a family, we made good use of the longer summer days—four hours of darkness at the summer solstice—and spent our weekends exploring farther afield. We rode bicycles on the trail into the city and hiked in the Chugach Mountains where wilderness awaited just beyond the city boundary. We drove south from Anchorage to the Kenai Peninsula to fish for salmon and drove north for more exploring. I hadn't been an athlete growing up, but now, hiking regularly on challenging trails, I could feel myself getting stronger.

Even little things added to my sense of being in the right place. I planted a small garden that first summer and gloried in weeding at eleven at night, bathed in the lengthening sunset colors. Alaskan gardens are productive with the extended daylight, although my veggies didn't approach the record-setting produce from the Matanuska Valley just to the north, which produces twenty-pound zucchini and cabbages exceeding a hundred pounds.

With my volunteering, our outdoor adventures, and the sheer joy of living in Alaska, life had turned around for me. I'd found the something more I'd craved in Rochester. In less than a year, my volunteer work had gone from being a worthwhile spare-time endeavor to something I was passionate about, despite a lingering lack of self-confidence. The kids were thriving, doing well in school academically and socially. Sharing the outdoor experiences as a family and seeing my children embrace hiking and the wild beauty around us made my spirits soar. Alaska was a terrific place to raise them. Tom and I hadn't talked about our new life, but he seemed to enjoy it as much as I.

In the fall he developed excruciating knee pain, a flare-up of an old sports injury. Following surgery he had more pain and a longer recovery than anticipated. Although he returned to work in January, he seemed subdued and not his usual self. One evening after the kids were in bed and I was cleaning up in the kitchen, he appeared in the doorway to the dining room.

"Jackie, we need to talk."

Knowing something was wrong by his tone of voice, I stowed my sponge and turned to see a strained look on his face. "What's the matter?"

He rubbed the back of his neck, not yet looking directly at me. "I've decided to leave the practice."

"What? You're leaving the practice?" Had I misheard him? "It's only been a year."

He sat down at the dining table with a big sigh and finally looked at me. "It isn't working out with Sam. I can't stay here." He ran his hand through his thinning hair. "I've been offered a fellowship in Rochester to learn about laser treatment of cataracts and retinal problems."

My brain stopped processing after hearing "I can't stay here." Dismay settled over me like a cloak. I sat down opposite him. Unable to speak, I waited for him to explain, my eyes glued to his face although he was no longer making eye contact.

He played with a saltshaker for what seemed like ages, then looked up again. "I can't live in Alaska anymore."

My hands went clammy. Time stood still. "You can't live here anymore?" My brain didn't seem to work beyond repeating what he'd just said. "You can't live here?"

Then, my heart pounding in my ears, I found my voice. "Why haven't you said something before now?"

He laced his hands together on the table, the knuckles white. With a quiet sadness he said, "I miss seeing my family. I don't like living thousands of miles away." His eyes shone with unshed tears. "I thought I could do it, but this is different from Kodiak. It's permanent."

I was torn between empathy for him and a mounting sense of unfairness. This couldn't be happening now, just when things were looking up for me.

"It sounds like you've made your decision. . . ."

He nodded.

". . . without talking it over with me first." I stood and

walked a few paces away. "Or even saying a word."

I turned around to see a sheepish look on his face. What the hell?

"How could you make such a momentous decision without talking it over with me first? And we have to uproot the kids?" Once I started, I couldn't seem to stop. "They both have good friends here. Steph and Tracy are best buddies, and she's just starting to build her memories of Alaska and understanding why it's such a great place to have been born."

I was roiling inside, but years of stuffing my feelings, anger especially, blocked me from venting or saying more about what *I* was feeling inside.

"I agreed to move back to Alaska," he said, his tone pleading, "because you wanted so much to return."

"But you never expressed any reservations about returning! Our time on Kodiak, your hunting trips into the Brooks Range, your trips to Native villages—I thought you enjoyed all that."

"I did, then. But now I can't live here."

I felt completely upended but heard the finality in his voice. I was furious yet unable to yell or fume or explode. My mother still sat on my shoulder silencing me. When I was a child, her belittling words had hurt and shamed me, but talking back had only made things worse. Of all the emotions, anger was the one I could not allow myself to express.

"The fellowship is for three months, beginning in June. We have to decide where to live after that." His voice lightened as if a load were off his chest.

Right, I said to myself. *You've delivered your speech. My hell is just beginning.*

He continued, "I've given this some thought. I'd be happy living either in the Finger Lakes or the capital area of New Hampshire. Think about it and let me know your decision."

With no apology and seemingly no remorse at the unfairness of his unilateral decision—or the limited choice he'd bestowed on me almost as an afterthought—he stood and left the room, patting my shoulder as he passed. I felt like slugging him.

I sat there for another half hour, still having difficulty accepting what was happening. I knew our marriage had problems, but I had not seen this coming. Two thoughts kept going through my mind: *What am I going to do? How can I leave Alaska?*

If we'd had better communication skills, perhaps we could have discussed a wider range of options. But we had never practiced those skills. I felt up against a brick wall, not knowing how to argue or negotiate. My new life, which had seemed so promising, was crashing around me. I had so little experience expressing my feelings I was unable to share how environmental work was filling a fundamental inner need to contribute to something beyond being a wife and mother. He knew I loved living in Alaska, but I'm not sure he understood what it meant to have a soul-deep connection to a place or to nature. I couldn't find the words to explain that either. I was starting to recognize my feelings, to discover who I was and what I wanted in life. But with this chasm opening, I was unable to share even the excitement of this personal growth.

In the days that followed, I kept my heart at bay while I considered the two options Tom had given me. Our best friends from medical school had moved to Concord, the capital of New Hampshire, and we'd visited them before moving to Anchorage. Finally, I decided if I had to leave Alaska, my preference was to live in New Hampshire rather than upstate New York.

Tom gave Sam notice he would leave the practice at the end of May. Over the next few weeks, the more I thought about moving, the more internally distraught I became. I was numb and couldn't carry on a conversation with Tom—and didn't want to—beyond the most mundane subjects. I had difficulty imagining getting on an airplane to leave. The break would simply be too abrupt. Then my next step came to me. I would assert myself on the one thing I had some control over.

"I'm not spending the summer in Rochester when I can spend it in Alaska," I told him. "I'm staying here with the kids. And I'm not flying out of here either. You come back after your fellowship and we can drive east, back down the Alaska Highway."

He conceded, and we planned how the summer would unfold. I would pack our things and handle selling the house and hiring a moving company. We would trade our station wagon for a camper. Tom would return to Anchorage in late August, and the four of us would drive across the country together. For me this provided a more gradual leave-taking. We could have some adventures along the way and sell the camper in New Hampshire.

When I was finally capable of telling my friends and my Center coworkers, they were all stunned. My unhappiness must have leaked from every pore in my body.

One woman, trying for humor, blurted, "Well, Jackie, you'll just have to get a divorce so you can stay."

I don't know what lame response I made, but I felt as if a brick had landed full force in the pit of my stomach. I hadn't considered divorce, but after her comment I couldn't get it out of my head.

Throughout the spring the thought of leaving Alaska lay heavy on my mind. In many ways it was akin to working through grief when a loved one dies. In April the Center board held a potluck with spouses, and Tom went with me. He made no attempt to converse with anyone. I was in no mood to cater to him and spent most of my time chatting with friends. At one point I glanced at him sitting in a chair across the room, brooding and watching me with a fury on his face I had never seen before. I didn't care. I let him stew until I was ready to leave.

I had finally found something outside of the home I could do well—work that fulfilled me both personally and professionally.

Tom seemed to feel increasingly threatened by that, which upset me. I was not neglecting my family. Environmental work energized me and made me happy. It offered a future when I'd been finding only dead ends. But it wasn't centered on family, and that may have been the problem. Tom's model for a wife and mother was his own stay-at-home mom. She was a warm, generous person, and I loved her dearly. Despite having spent a good portion of her formative years in foster care—or maybe because of it—family was everything to her. Her passion was nurturing the ties of the extended family she had married into. Although I admired her, I had to be myself and follow my passion—just as my mother had done, I realized with a start.

As spring wore on, I weighed the idea of divorce but discarded it. Although not confident our marriage would survive, I wasn't ready to split our family. The old fear of being independent and making my own choices resurfaced. I knew Tom was a good father, and he loved his children. If I stayed in Anchorage and he moved east, one of us would become a distant parent. I could not imagine that for myself, nor did I want it for him or our children.

As best I could, I put aside my devastation at having to leave Alaska and focused on the tasks I'd agreed to for the move.

 Chapter 6

One cloudy April afternoon as I was leaving our cul-de-sac to get groceries, the unexpected view of Denali caused me to idle the car for a full minute before continuing to the store.[1] The high clouds in Anchorage extended partway north, but the full sun beyond the clouds highlighted the peak with a stunning golden brilliance. The clarity of the air made the mountain, a hundred miles to the north, seem closer than the few other times I'd seen it from this vantage point. The image stayed with me and became symbolic over the next months of all I was losing in moving to New Hampshire—but also everything I was determined to remember.

The previous summer I had camped in the national park surrounding Denali with my family. (The official park name then was Mount McKinley National Park; it was changed to Denali National Park in 1980.) What made this park truly special for me was the opportunity to gain a sense of the Alaskan wilderness without needing to backpack or fly into a remote area. The park's shuttle buses stopped whenever opportunities arose to view wildlife—grizzly bears, moose, Dall sheep, caribou, even wolves—and stopped at trailheads along the park road to let hikers on and off.

During my last summer in Alaska, I had several occasions to spend time at Denali National Park. Tom had not yet left for his summer course in Rochester when I attended a May meeting at the park hotel. Alaska and national environmental groups had convened to lay the groundwork for a new land protection effort in the state. The effort was rooted in the land claims of Native Alaskans going back decades, even before statehood. Growing pressure to determine a pipeline route to carry Prudhoe Bay oil south to Valdez had finally forced the US Congress to act. The new land claims law, signed in 1971, conveyed legal ownership to Native Alaskans of forty-four million acres and green-lighted the decision on a pipeline route. The law also provided for establishing eighty million acres of new national parks and wildlife refuges in the state—the reason for this first meeting of what they called the Alaska Coalition. I was thrilled at the idea of protecting large pristine areas around the state from mining and oil and gas development. At the same time, my heart was heavy. What a time to be moving three thousand miles away!

The meeting took place before the park had opened for the season. After lunch the first day I took a walk along the park road with June, another Center board member. Although Denali lay out of sight here, the view was scenic with the rolling tundra and smaller mountains.

"It's great to be here before visitors arrive," I said.

"Yes," she said, then lowered her voice. "Look!" She pointed to a ptarmigan still mottled with winter's white sitting on the road a short distance ahead. "That ptarmigan thinks he's invisible. We're only seeing him because there've been no tourists for months."

We slowed our pace, closing to within twelve feet before the bird exploded into flight.

As we resumed walking, I said, "I want so much to help in this effort, but just as it's starting up, I'm leaving."

June smiled sympathetically. "This will be a fifty-state press, you know. Perhaps you can work on it in New Hampshire."

"I hope so. It would help me deal with my Alaska withdrawal symptoms."

She chuckled. We walked in silence for a few minutes before turning back to the hotel. Looking around at the beauty of the tundra, I soaked up the landscape details. I knew life would be different in New Hampshire.

That afternoon the environmental groups each outlined how they would contribute to the collaboration. When the National Audubon Society pledged to have someone in every state gathering support for these "national interest lands," my spirits lifted for the first time in months.

"Maybe that's my chance," I whispered to June, sitting beside me.

She smiled and nodded.

I was too new to the issue and intimidated by the directors from the national groups to speak to anyone from National Audubon. But several days later at the Center office I thumbed through a national directory of environmental groups and found the Audubon Society of New Hampshire listed in Concord. *Okay, that's it*, I thought. *Once we arrive, I'll visit the chapter office and volunteer to be their Alaska person.*

Before Tom left for Rochester, we bought a small camper with inside access between the cab and the living area. The cozy living space had everything we needed: a small yet serviceable galley, decent storage, a toilet/shower combo, and adequate sleeping space for the four of us. My favorite feature was the dining nook and picture window across the back.

In July amid my packing, my parents came for several weeks. For the first few days they took turns playing with the kids and helping me pack. After adding the boxes to a growing stack in the living room, the five of us piled into the camper for a planned rendezvous with my sister and her family in Canada's Yukon Territory. Marilyn had moved west for graduate school, married Tim, a Seattle native, and now lived in Vancouver, BC. Their daughter, Jennie, was a year younger than Steph, and the girls had become fast friends on past visits.

I had become comfortable maneuvering the camper and did all the driving. Following the Alaska Highway into Canada, I retraced in reverse some of the frigid trip we'd made moving to Anchorage a short eighteen months before. We met up with Marilyn and spent a week camping together, her family tenting, as we explored the gold rush country. Traveling along the rivers, we saw the signs of hydraulic gold dredging from the 1800s in the rock piles still snaking along river channels and visited several gold rush towns now thriving from tourism.

Saying goodbye to Marilyn and her family at the end of the week, we began the drive back to Alaska. That afternoon I stopped for a break in a mountain pass where a chill wind blew across the treeless tundra. As I began assembling snacks in the galley, Dad drew silly pictures with Johnny and Steph in the dining nook.

Mom pulled on a jacket. "I think I'll take a walk and get some fresh air. I won't be long."

She stepped down from the camper and walked a short distance. I glanced out the back window several times and saw her stooping to pick up things from the ground.

"Snacks are ready," I called out the door five minutes later. "No rush, though."

She soon returned. "Look what I found!" She slid into the seat opposite the kids and spread her treasures on the table.

I brought her a mug of tea and sat down beside her. Everything in her collection was miniature: several gnarly sticks looking like alpine driftwood, two rocks dotted with minute yellow-and-black lichens, a twig with two tiny cones, and a shard of bleached bone.

"What's this, Mommy?" Johnny asked, picking up the piece of bone.

"My guess is it's from the leg bone of a small mammal. What do you think?"

"You mean like a lemming or a ground squirrel?" At eight and a half he was a budding biologist.

"Yep, could be." I exchanged delighted glances with my father.

"I love the tiny lichens on the rocks," I said, then pointed to the twig with the miniature cones. "This may be scrub alder. It's pretty common."

"I didn't see trees of any size, but maybe the wind carried it." Mom picked up her tea mug. "It probably blows constantly, huh?"

"I expect so, but scrub alder isn't particularly big," I said, getting up to put things away.

Mom turned to Dad. "Don't you think this place resembles the high valleys in Tibet?"

He grinned. "The elevation is lower but otherwise, yes. Broad pass, no trees, alpine vegetation." Then, his eyes teasing, he said, "But it's missing one thing—no yaks."

I smiled at the reference to my favorite of Dad's China stories. Mom left the table, her treasures nestled in a clean paper napkin, and put the bundle gently into a bag of her things. For the rest of her life she kept these mementos on her dresser in a small glass box.

We drove north to Denali National Park before returning to Anchorage. My parents talked often about the Minya Konka, the mountain they'd visited in Tibet in 1932, and I wanted to show them my favorite mountain. The day was clear when we hopped on the park's shuttle bus at Teklanika campground, where we were staying. The driver stopped briefly for pictures at Stony Dome, a pullout halfway along the park road with the first full view of the mountain, thirty miles distant. Then we continued to Eielson Visitor Center, where we had another gorgeous view of Denali. My parents were suitably impressed.

When we were back on the park bus returning to the campground, I asked, "So, how does Denali compare to the Minya Konka?"

"Where to start?" Dad shook his head slightly, a big grin on his face. "Denali is impressive—the sheer mass of it looming over its neighbors."

"In vertical rise Denali is taller than Mount Everest," I said. "Its base begins at a much lower elevation."

"And that's the thing," Dad said. "It's hard to compare them, mountain to mountain. The Minya Konka is higher—the tallest on the eastern rim of the Tibetan Plateau. It has a distinctive pyramidal shape. But those are just physical details." He paused as if collecting his thoughts. "I don't get a sense of Denali's aura. Maybe that's it."

He turned to my mother. "What do you think, Clinky?"

"Both are awe-inspiring," she said, "but I can't separate the Minya Konka from its Tibetan context." She looked at my father. "Like the valley we rode into from the pass, where the Tibetans had their summer encampment, and we thought those two bull yaks were going to fight. And the tiny village where we stayed overnight at the headman's house before riding up the ridge and setting up camp right across from the Minya Konka—"

"Yes!" Dad interrupted. "That's it! The Tibetans consider the Minya Konka sacred, and the day we finally saw it with no clouds, only one deep narrow valley separating us, its white snout rising abruptly into the air so far above us...." He looked at me and made the clucking sound with his tongue and teeth that he reserved for something special. "That moment was sacred for me too. That's the aura of the Minya Konka. Denali surely has its own aura, too, but I can't tell from this distance."

I was speechless for a few seconds. "Wow! I know the Minya Konka is impressive from your photos. But I've never heard you talk about it that way."

"You never asked the question before." He smiled, his face beaming. "I said at the time I didn't expect to see anything in my lifetime to compare. Right, Clinky?" He looked at her and reached over to take her hand.

"You did indeed," she said.

"I've never thought of mountains having an aura," I said. "I love being surrounded by them, but it's been a physical experience, a visual appreciation. You're talking about something more intimate, more spiritual." I looked at my parents, feeling the grin spreading on my face. "You've given me something to think about."

We stayed two nights at Teklanika campground, named after the river running alongside it. The Teklanika River is braided, its channels meandering and intertwining across a riverbed two hundred yards wide in places, its milky waters a telltale clue of their glacial origin. The gravel bars consist of smooth, water-washed rocks of many hues—shades of gray, tan, green, reddish-orange, and mauve—some speckled, some striped, some glinting with mica.

On our second evening after the kids were asleep, I picked up Steph's hooded sweatshirt from the camper floor, surprised at its heaviness. She had filled her pockets with rocks.

"She's as taken with these as I am," I said, emptying the contents of her pockets onto the table in front of my parents.

"I see why," Dad said, picking up a stone. "This one's a beauty."

"Do you remember the book you gave to Johnny when he was little?" I asked. "The book with no words, just wonderful rock drawings?"

"Yes," they said in unison, then smiled at each other.

"These Teklanika stones always remind me of that book," I

said, my voice catching suddenly. Tears prickled my eyes. "How can I leave Alaska? It's where I belong."

Dad came over and hugged me. "I wish you didn't have to, Jackie. But life has twists and turns we can't always predict. I'm confident you'll find ways to make up for the loss you feel now."

I gave him a weak smile. "Well, I don't have any choice, do I?"

My parents returned to Pittsburgh in late July. Afterward, I thought about our time in the camper and how it had gone. Although I still thought of myself as timid and dependent, being responsible for driving my family around in our bulky camper had taken courage. And there was Mom's surprisingly good humor. Marilyn once told me she and Tim had taken our parents tent camping before Jennie was born, sleeping on the ground with only foam pads as cushioning. She said Mom had enjoyed herself and seemed less tense. I'd been surprised then, but that's exactly how Mom was this time and on the camper trip when they visited us on Kodiak. I knew she liked being around her grandchildren. I thought back to the time I'd looked through the family photos from our road trips and wondered if my parents had marriage troubles. They'd gotten along well on this trip, but perhaps work stress had caused that melancholia. Would I ever figure Mom out?

The summer respite from the constant strain of my relationship with Tom had been a relief. When he returned toward the end of August, there was a coolness between us. I wasn't eager to tap into the anger I knew was still inside. We fell into old patterns and didn't talk about whether or how our time apart had changed our outlooks. My focus was on wringing all the pleasure possible out of my farewell to Alaska.

In early September we restocked the camper, said goodbye to friends and colleagues, and headed north to Denali one last time. The fall colors were nearing peak. The few birches had turned a bright gold, the scrub alder a yellowish-brown. The rich autumn hues came from the ground cover, the brilliant red leaves of crowberry, bearberry, and blueberry. Clouds obscured the view when we arrived at Wonder Lake, the campground closest to the mountain. Glancing out the camper window a bit later, I noticed the white tip of the mountain peeking through an opening in the clouds, seeming improbably close and high in the sky.

"Hey, the mountain's coming out!" I called.

We all stopped whatever we were doing and converged on the picnic table, where we sat oohing and aahing as the clouds melted away. The unbroken view across twenty-seven miles of tundra to Denali's massive snowy profile was spectacular. I wondered briefly what it might be like to be close enough to feel its aura. As I concentrated on burning the image into memory, it seemed as if The Great One were saying farewell to me. My chest ached as a wave of sadness, always just below the surface those days, swept over me.

The next day, with glorious weather, we took the shuttle bus and hopped off at Igloo Mountain. Pushing carefully through the alder thicket, we soon heard grunts and rustling nearby and glimpsed a huge bull moose, his massive scoop-like antlers dangling shreds of bloody velvet. Rutting season was no time to disturb him. We quietly backed up, made a wide detour, and continued up the mountain. An hour or so later we came to a rocky outcrop overlooking the valley and stopped for lunch. I savored the wilderness view as I ate my peanut butter sandwich, storing the sensual memories—what I saw, heard, smelled, touched. We could see the moose still below us, and Johnny spotted a grizzly meandering through the alder not far from the moose.

Then in the distance I heard a wild primal howl.

"Did you hear that?" I asked. "A wolf!"

This was the one animal I hadn't seen on my visits to Denali. The sound resonated through me with tendrils of awe tinged with a seemingly primordial fear. I felt it to my bones. As the howl trailed off, the echoes continued for a few seconds before dying out. The spell lasted a bit longer as I wished for the wolf to howl again.

After finishing lunch Tom spied ten Dall sheep a little above us and suggested we try to get closer for photos. I started out, the kids behind me, Tom bringing up the rear. The path was essentially a wildlife trail at that point. Fifteen minutes later I rounded a bend to see a talus slope before me. I paused at the edge to study the beckoning path, an indentation made by the feet of sheep and other animals traversing the small angular rocks. *If Dall sheep can walk across this rockslide, I should be able to,* I thought, and I impulsively stepped onto the talus.

Halfway across, the rocks under my feet began to slip ever so slowly downhill. *Shit, what was I thinking?* Too late, I remembered talus slopes have not necessarily reached equilibrium. Fear settled in the pit of my stomach. My mind began ticking through options as time seemed to slow down. The slope fell away to my left. I couldn't see the bottom of the talus where the largest boulders would lie. If I continued sliding over the edge and hit those boulders, I would be dead. I had a sour taste in my mouth but couldn't seem to swallow to get rid of it. Silently commanding myself to get a grip, I took a deep breath.

Carefully, in slow motion, I turned to my right to face into the slope, gingerly repositioning my feet and placing my hands as lightly as possible on either side of me. I leaned bit by bit closer to the talus. Not until I was almost spread-eagled, the tip of my nose a hair's breadth from the slide, the sharp rock edges pricking my palms, did I feel the movement cease. I took a slow, deep breath and willed myself calm.

Turning my head ever so slowly to my right, I saw Tom and the kids standing silent at the slide's edge, bodies frozen, eyes wide, fear stamped on their faces. Relief flooded me. Thank god no one had followed me.

Tom called, "Stay there. I'll come over."

He began edging across a little above me at a snail's pace, trying not to disturb the slide further. But when he got near, he too began to slip. Instinctively I reached out and rested my hand gently on his arm. The rocks stopped moving. Again in slow motion, each stabilizing the other if we started to slip, we inched back to solid ground. Gratitude overwhelmed me as I embraced Tom and whispered my thanks.

Then I hugged my children and stooped to be at their eye level. "Always remember to keep your head about you in the wilderness," I cautioned, my voice a bit shaky. "Don't do something stupid like I just did."

All desire to pursue sheep now gone, we started down the mountain to catch the bus back to Wonder Lake. I was so glad to be safe it was lost on me that Tom and I had made it to safety by working together. In a crisis we had supported each other as a team, but in everyday life we seemed at cross-purposes. My heart had softened, though, and I was feeling kindlier toward him.

On our last morning in the park we woke to a dusting of snow. Packing up in the cold, we headed toward the park entrance. Along the way I spotted four caribou trotting effort-lessly over the tundra. With antlers in velvet, nut-brown winter coats, and creamy neck ruffs, they were magnificent against the backdrop of snow-touched autumnal ground cover. They moved with a lightness as if they had springs in their feet. I could easily visualize them migrating the hundreds of miles between their summer and winter habitats.

Leaving Denali, we began our long trek south in the camper along the Alaska Highway through Canada and then east across the plains. I lived in the moment of our adventure, glad I'd insisted we drive instead of flying across the country. Reaching upstate New York at September's end, we stopped to see Tom's relatives and picked up the red Volkswagen Rabbit he'd purchased in June.

The next day, the last of our journey, Tom and Johnny climbed into the camper while I drove the Rabbit with Steph. Crossing the Connecticut River into New Hampshire, I was alone with my thoughts as Steph slept. New Hampshire's landscape was pleasing—scenic vistas, forested mountains, quaint villages. But it seemed compact and tame. The immense scale and wildness of Alaska—the endless mountains, broad valleys, braided glacial rivers, and iconic wildlife—defined the state's profound impact on my soul. Tears streamed down my face as I silently gave way to my grief. I didn't know what was in store for the future or for my marriage, but I wept for what I had lost.

If I'd understood then the circumstances surrounding my parents' departure from China, I would have seen the parallel to Dad's leaving a situation that had been so rewarding for him. There was even a similarity in the landscapes we each had to leave—the mountains and rugged terrain that promised adventure. I wish I could have talked with him about these similarities, but this insight came later, after his death. I did, however, have his wisdom to guide me. My father, giving up what he had loved in China, looked for the benefits and opportunities offered by change and new experiences. He didn't dwell on what he'd left behind but incorporated what he had valued from past experiences in creating a new path.

In my own way, I kept Alaska in my heart and moved forward into my new life. Denali would remain a touchstone for me, emblematic of the role Alaska had played in my personal and professional growth.

 Chapter 7

Arriving in New Hampshire, Tom and I rented a house outside Concord and settled the children in school, Johnny in third grade and Steph in first. Tom opened a solo practice in ophthalmology, taking over the first floor of a house converted to offices in downtown Concord. He hired staff, but in the early days I also helped part-time to save money. He and I seemed on a new footing, our personal issues having receded as we drove east.

True to my pledge, I visited the Audubon Society's headquarters soon after arriving. As I entered the small red former farmhouse on the outskirts of Concord, the woman at the nearest desk looked up and smiled.

"Is the executive director in?" I asked. "I have an environmental issue I'd like to discuss."

"Tudor? Yes, he is."

She showed me to a small room lined with bookshelves where a gray-haired, patrician-looking gentleman sat behind a desk covered with messy piles of paper. He rose as I introduced myself, motioning me to sit in the chair opposite his.

Sharing that I'd recently moved from Anchorage, I said, "I'd like to discuss National Audubon's Alaska initiative."

"I don't know of this initiative," he said with a note of puzzlement. "But New Hampshire Audubon is an independent state organization, not a chapter of National Audubon."

"Oh, I didn't realize that." My heart sank.

"Yes, there are a handful of us upstarts in the northeast. We go back nearly as far as National Audubon." His eyes gleamed and his shaggy gray mustache couldn't hide his grin of pride. "They began in 1905, we in 1914."

Not having planned for this turn of events, I said the first thing that popped to mind. "In Anchorage I volunteered with an environmental group and helped follow issues like coastal zone management. Would you have volunteer opportunities for someone like me?"

"Oh my, yes," he said, rising from his desk. "Come with me. I'll introduce you to Jane. She's our lead board member on conservation topics."

I followed him into the spacious wood-paneled library. A small white-haired woman with soft gray eyes stood as Tudor and I approached the table where she was working. He mentioned my interest in volunteering and left us to talk.

We sat, and I described what I had done with the Alaska Center for the Environment, focusing on tracking pertinent issues, and expressed an interest in doing something similar. Jane explained the group's mission—protection of wildlife and wildlife habitat along with environmental quality—and the scope of their programs. She was friendly and seemingly mild mannered, though I soon found she was not to be underestimated. A half hour later I said goodbye, having agreed to help track environmental issues two days a week during school hours. I was especially pleased I could get into the nitty-gritty of issues right away.

Driving home, I wondered briefly how Tom would react given my experience in Anchorage. Then my frustration about the Alaska issue sparked. *Damn*, I thought. In moving to New

Hampshire, I'd made a bargain with myself to stay involved with the Alaska Coalition. I would have to find a way to do that.

When I mentioned my arrangement with Audubon to Tom that evening, he just shook his head and walked away. *Oh boy, here we go again,* I thought. *Why is he like this? I'm not neglecting the kids or him. Well, this is how I want to spend my spare time, so he'll have to get used to it.*

Before long I met Will, another Audubon board member and a contemporary of Jane and Tudor's. Will was a forester, tall and a bit gaunt, whose irreverent sense of humor and tendency toward puns reminded me of Dad. He was astute on local and national issues, and he knew of the Alaska Coalition. He was also gifted at political strategy, and his ideas often provided the nugget for action projects. We became instant friends.

Over the next months, Jane and Will mentored me, sharing their knowledge of the state's environmental scene. Since Concord was the state capitol, much of my work with Jane involved following legislative bills and drafting comments for public hearings before the New Hampshire Legislature. In addition to state legislation, we also tracked national issues related to wildlife and environmental quality, such as pesticides and endangered species. My contributions to Audubon soon became more substantive than what I had done in Anchorage. I knew Jane and others appreciated my contributions, which made me feel good.

In the spring as I settled into a routine with Audubon, a letter arrived from the Alaska Coalition inviting me to a national colloquium on the Alaska lands issue in Washington, DC. I showed the invitation to Tom.

"I'm going to go to this. I want to find out what they're planning." I saw the tension around his eyes. Trying to keep my voice pleasant, I added, "I'll see if Nancy will agree to take the kids after school. You could pick them up on your way home from work." Nancy and her husband were our best friends from medical school.

"Where's all this going? First Audubon and now Alaska, too?" he asked irritably.

"I don't know. But Alaska is important to me. I want to help with this." I was learning to speak up for myself.

Nancy agreed to watch Johnny and Steph after school for the three days I would be gone. I signed up, booked a flight, and went to Washington with high hopes.

The colloquium was an intensive minicourse. The Coalition aimed to galvanize a network of citizens across the country who would press their congressional representatives to support new national parks and wildlife refuges in Alaska. Most of the history and background I already knew from the Denali meeting. We also learned about various competing bills before Congress, what the Coalition's position was, and why certain bills fell short. At the colloquium I talked with several Anchorage colleagues who now worked in DC, reconnecting with the excitement I'd felt in discovering environmental work. Over the two days I sensed a growing communal energy and camaraderie and knew being part of this effort was right for me.

At one point we broke into groups by region, and Coalition presenters described how public programs would be key to building grassroots support. The Coalition had copies of a National Park Service movie and other resources, including a large map of the proposed national parks and wildlife refuges for us to use for programs. As the only colloquium attendee from New Hampshire, I became by default the Coalition's main contact for the state. I returned home eager to get to work but prepared to face a less-than-enthusiastic husband.

My first step was to ask Tudor if New Hampshire Audubon would cosponsor the Alaska programs I gave, which would lend me credibility. He agreed, and I gained support from other state groups as well. My first presentation was to a friendly audience at New Hampshire Audubon's annual meeting, held with field trips on a July weekend. I was the dinner speaker. I invited Tom, but he declined, although John and Steph came with me. I wrote down what I wanted to say about the Alaska lands issue and read it word for word. It must have been dreadful.

Public speaking did not come naturally to me. As far back as my college speech class, the idea of speaking before even a small group of friends struck fear in my heart. It was fourth grade all over again. My mouth became dry and my face flushed. My tongue felt thick, my knees knocked, and I sweated profusely. But my passion for Alaska and the lack of anyone to share the task pushed me forward.

After the first few programs, I put my talking points on three-by-five-inch cards and made sure to have water on hand. Gradually I became more comfortable and shortened my prompts. I posted the large map with the proposed parks, refuges, and wilderness areas. After describing the opportunity we had to protect these lands, I showed the movie, outlined ways people could help, and urged them to sign up for my periodic newsletters.

Then one night I left the cards at home.

Oh god, they have to be here, I thought, rummaging through my bag of materials. *The program is starting in twenty minutes! I've already put up the map, but where are those damn cards?* I pulled from my bag the sign-up sheet, the books about Alaska, and the handouts and set them on the display table as my dismay grew. No cards bound with a rubber band lay in the bottom of the bag, and I'd already searched my purse.

Shit . . . they must be at home.

A moment of sheer panic slammed me in the gut. I talked myself down silently. *Calm yourself, Jackie. Take a deep breath, and another. You know the subject better than anyone who will be here.* I looked up then to see the first people arriving. Pasting a smile on my face, I went to greet them. And the presentation proceeded smoothly. I made sure to take the cards to my next program, but after that it didn't matter. Going cold turkey had shown me I didn't need the prompts. My fear symptoms took longer to disappear, but eventually they did, one by one. Six months after the colloquium, I was giving programs every few weeks, relaxed enough that my love for Alaska showed throughout my presentation.

I never had anyone come to my talks who was opposed to this initiative. Most folks were eager to learn more. Many people feel an almost mystical connection with our forty-ninth state, inspired by the beauty and the idea of wilderness, even if they've never been there. The folks who attended ran the gamut of ages and were usually outdoorsy. I made some lasting friends through these programs, like Carl with the bone-crushing handshake, an always-enthusiastic Presbyterian minister and someone I could count on to speak out on Alaska and other environmental issues.

My task, as the Alaska Coalition's contact, was to ensure the votes of my state's congressional delegation—two senators, two congressmen—in favor of the strongest bill. At the spring colloquium, we were given pointers on how to lobby. I had visited the offices of the two congressmen while in DC and met with staff aides, my first such meetings ever. Although my voice wobbled a bit and my hands trembled, all had gone well. I realized having lived in Alaska lent credibility to what I said, which helped over time to set a reasonable tone with the legislators. But my work was cut out for me: my own representative opposed the idea of new national parks, and the other supported a weaker, competing bill sponsored by a colleague of his. My two senators from the beginning were generally receptive, although I didn't take their support for granted. At a later point one of them became the lead sponsor of the Coalition-backed bill.

Over the next eighteen months I made at least six trips to Washington to attend Coalition meetings or to lobby at key times. My mailing list grew to nearly 250 people who also pressed our delegation, reinforcing my message. On one DC trip I was one of a few dozen people to come from around the country to testify before a House subcommittee in support of legislation. Although intimidated at first, after several sentences I was surprised to feel a power in speaking about something I cared about deeply.

Tom was never happy about my times away, nor did he express support for me and what I was doing. Except for that aspect, my life was full and rewarding. In addition to looking after the kids and our home life and working on the Alaska initiative, I volunteered regularly at New Hampshire Audubon. As the Alaska presentations helped me find my public voice, I also began delivering some Audubon statements in state legislative hearings, taking turns with Jane.

In the first months of 1978 I accepted the offer to join Audubon's board of trustees. At my first meeting I struck up a conversation with John, another trustee, who was a professor of natural resource policy at the University of New Hampshire. I'd been thinking again about graduate school, wanting a better knowledge base for my environmental work. I arranged a time to talk with him on campus about the master's program in his department. When we met and talked in greater depth, I found the program interesting and exactly the subject matter I was seeking. John encouraged me to apply. Even the hour's drive to the campus didn't dampen my enthusiasm.

That evening after the kids had left the dinner table, I described my meeting to Tom and how the program dovetailed with my needs.

"I'm going to apply. The materials say they're looking for students who have life experience." I chuckled. "Guess I have that, huh?"

He was quiet for a moment, fiddling with his hands before finally looking up. "Well, I guess that's okay as long as you fulfill your wifely and motherly duties."

I was dumbstruck. Wifely and motherly duties? Where had he been? This was 1978, well into the wave of feminism. My father had supported Mom in her career aspirations fifty years earlier. Couldn't he at least be happy for me?

I found my voice and heard the chill as I said, "I wasn't asking for your permission."

He got up abruptly and left the room. I sat back in my chair, foreboding growing in the pit of my stomach. His response instantly took me back to Anchorage when I had been struggling with his decision to leave. Had nothing changed? Had I put my life on hold for two years? Then I realized we had recreated the same life we had in Anchorage, except Tom was now happier in his work. I was glad for him, but I felt in the same damn place, not measuring up to what someone thought I should be, which reminded me of childhood with Mom.

But I wasn't in the same place. I knew environmental work was my calling. Tom's proclamation only strengthened my resolve to go to graduate school. If my marriage failed, the extra education would better position me to get a job. I wasn't turning back. The only option I saw was to continue doing it all: be a good mother, keep a decent house, and continue in my career. I needed to prove to him—and myself—I could do it. I was accepted into the master's program starting in the fall term. My class schedule worked well with my Audubon responsibilities, and I made an effort to get home so the kids wouldn't be alone.

During the hours I spent in the car driving to Audubon or the university or to give a program on Alaska, I often thought about the deteriorating state of my marriage. Tom and I rarely fought or argued. At some point we had just stopped talking. I was angry he never supported anything I did, even though

I'd helped him at various points in his career. Not once had he attended one of my programs on Alaska. John and Steph had come with me to several more Audubon annual meetings as well as a whale watch and a bird-banding weekend. Although I invited Tom to these activities, he never joined us.

At the time I told myself it was okay if we did separate things. We just had different interests. Yet beyond inviting him to my outdoor excursions and getting together with family, neither of us sought activities we could do together, and we drifted further apart. Alone in the car, I remembered the comment of my Alaska colleague—"Jackie, you'll just have to get a divorce"—and increasingly found nothing to counter that thought.

I'd always had considerable energy, able to juggle a lot. But now the juggling grew more difficult. After the first semester of graduate school, I cut back from twelve credits to eight and then six. My grades were fine, but my energy flagged and with it my ability to handle a full schedule of courses along with everything else. I could barely drag myself out of bed in time to see the kids off to school. I was depressed but didn't realize it. Driving to campus, I thought about my three separate lives: my environmental work with Audubon and the Alaska Coalition, graduate school with my university friends, and my home life with Tom, the kids, and the friends we now rarely socialized with.

Although Tom wanted us to entertain more, I was tired of doing all the work. I offered once to do the cooking if he would do the inviting, but he never took me up on the offer. The few times we had our closest friends over were emotionally exhausting. One of the men invariably baited me, belittling my environmental views. I always refuted his remarks, but Tom remained silent. In the car by myself I would rant about this. Why the hell didn't he say something?

Even as it became evident my marriage was unraveling, I knew I couldn't turn away from environmental work and go back to being a stay-at-home mom. I believed I wasn't asking for a lot, but the crackling tension told me Tom was unable to move past his unhappiness with me.

Many nights after John and Steph were asleep, I attempted a conversation about the state of our marriage, but my efforts ended up being monologues.

"Tom, we need to talk. We need to face the fact we have problems."

Silence.

"Our marriage is in trouble. I'm not happy. Can we go to a marriage counselor?"

More silence.

Sometimes I said things just to provoke a response.

"Please talk to me. Say something—anything! At least then it would show you care."

I was finally voicing my unhappiness, trying in every conceivable way to say we had issues we needed to address. No matter the tack, I couldn't engage him. He remained silent with the same look of fury on his face I'd first seen at the Alaska Center's potluck back in Anchorage.

Any intimacy in our life had vanished long before, and my late hours didn't help. Although my excuse for staying up when he went to bed was the need to study or work on a paper, I brooded and accomplished little. Often I had a late-night drink or two. My parents were teetotalers, so I hadn't grown up with alcohol in the house, but Tom and I kept a well-stocked liquor cabinet. For both of us—Tom upstairs in bed, me stewing downstairs with my glass—the resentment and disappointment simmered, threatening to explode our separate lives.

Into the midst of this tumultuous home life came a distraction. My parents had reopened a connection to China. One aspect of warming relations between the United States and

China in the 1970s had been the arrival of Chinese scholars at major US universities. In 1972 the University of Pittsburgh hosted a contingent of visiting graduate scholars who came for several years of study. My parents were thrilled and began holding periodic gatherings of a dozen or so scholars in their apartment. With my parents still fluent in the language and their home decor at least quasi-Chinese, the visiting scholars must have felt comfortable and relaxed. My parents in turn were delighted to converse in Chinese and learn firsthand how the Chinese people were faring.

On several of my trips to Pittsburgh, my parents hosted a tea, and I talked with scholars who had become their good friends. One time I looked through an album of my parents' photos from China with a woman who was fascinated to see pictures from the 1930s and '40s. She said all such photos involving westerners had had to be burned during the Cultural Revolution. I enjoyed these conversations and began to pay closer attention to what was going on in China. I knew my parents were looking at trips offered by travel companies, but they hadn't yet found a tour that included Sichuan and Chengdu.

At the time, when nothing felt good about my marriage, I welcomed these distractions. My touchstones then for some sense of self-worth were my children and my work. I tried to keep my routines and spirits up around Johnny and Steph, not realizing they were well aware of the ever-present tension at home.

 Chapter 8

I visited my parents in the summer of 1979, just after they had signed up for a trip to China that included Chengdu, scheduled for the following April. In an earlier phone call, Dad had mentioned finding this trip and asked if I wanted to come along. I said I didn't have time, but after the call I found myself thinking about it. A break from the stresses of my marriage would feel good, and perhaps the time away might help Tom and me gain new perspective.

As we sat talking after my arrival, I said, "I've been rethinking what I said about the trip to China. I'm now leaning toward joining you."

Dad flashed a grin of delight. He jumped up and headed to his study. "A preliminary itinerary just came," he called over his shoulder. "Let me get it."

He returned with the tour schedule and their world atlas. He sat on one side of me on the couch and placed the atlas on the coffee table in front of us, while Mom sat on my other side.

"Chengdu comes at the midpoint," he said, opening the atlas to China and starting to trace the tour. "From Hong Kong, we make a big circle. First the southern cities of Guangzhou and Nanning, then west to Kunming and Chengdu, north and east to Xi'an, Luoyang, and Beijing, and then back to Hong Kong via Guangzhou."

The itinerary indicated traveling by train between some cities and flying between others. Dad pointed to western China. "We're scheduled to fly between Kunming and Chengdu, but Mom and I want to take the train. There was no train in 1944 when we left." His face beamed as he described the wild rivers, steep gorges, and soaring mountains between the two cities.

His infectious enthusiasm clinched it for me. "The train sounds wonderful," I said. "Count me in!"

I wondered about spending twenty-six days with my parents, the most time in their company since summers in college. Increasingly curious about my birth country, though, I wanted to see it firsthand. Who better to help me understand what I was seeing? I signed up for the trip and mailed my deposit. Dad applied for visas for the three of us and asked permission to take the train, explaining they knew the two cities and spoke Chinese fluently. Our request was denied. Tourists were required then to stay with their groups when traveling between cities.

Arriving in Hong Kong the following April, I was in a fog for two days due to the long flight and twelve-hour time difference. For me, the tour began when our group of twenty-five boarded the train for Guangzhou. We left the Hong Kong skyscrapers behind, and somewhere in open country with no fields or villages we crossed into the People's Republic of China.[1] Soon we passed a few rice paddies, then more. People in the fields wore the wide conical straw hats typical of Asian farmers. I glimpsed a man herding a flock of ducks, the birds flowing in a synchronous white cloud through the paddies and over the dikes. We passed villages with clusters of small houses the color of the reddish-brown soil. Rice paddies, periodic groves of bamboo, and larger scattered trees added touches of intense spring green to the landscape.

Living in Alaska had opened my eyes to the subtleties of landscapes. I had known China mostly through my parents' black-and-white photos. Now the colors and quintessential scenes from the train brought those photos and Dad's stories to life. Over the next few days my heart softened as the last remnants of childhood indifference vanished, and I opened to the country of my birth.

At our hotel in Guangzhou (Canton), my room overlooked the Pearl River. The many boats plying the waters—barges, steamships, junks of all sizes—were mesmerizing. The junks provided a peek into people's lives, the larger ones serving as homes, the smaller ones ferrying people, vegetables, and other goods to shore. My parents' window introduced me to a different beauty: a sea of undulating gray tile roofs broken intermittently by upturned eaves decorated with real or mythical animals.

With several hours of free time, my parents and I left the hotel to investigate the narrow cobblestone street lined with small shops. Periodically alleyways branched off to a warren of small houses—the roofs I'd seen from my parents' window. I noticed the shops had no doors; rather the entire storefront opened onto the street. Dad explained the owners lived in the back. At night they closed the shop by stacking boards horizontally, edge to edge, into grooves on either side of the front opening.

After two nights we moved on to Nanning. I awoke before dawn the next morning to a muffled *pad-pad-pad* sound drifting through my second-story hotel window. Curiosity drew me to the window. The air, already warm and humid, hinted at a sticky day. Sandal-clad men ran through the street, pulling two-wheeled wooden carts in the fashion of rickshaw drivers. They were all headed in the same direction, their carts laden with produce—watermelons, carrots, peppers, eggplants, greens of all types, and more. Soon bicycles appeared, most going in the same direction as well, the riders weaving through the farmers' carts. Many bicycles towed carts, while others had platforms cantilevered behind the rider with unbelievably large loads lashed on: bamboo chairs and baskets, small tables, big cardboard boxes, and who knows what else. There were no cars; only officials had automobiles in 1980. The musical *b-r-r-i-n-g, b-r-r-i-n-g* of bicycle bells dominated the street sounds like violins in an orchestra.

My mind wandering, I thought about experiencing the country of my birth for the first time as an adult. I now had a better context for understanding my parents' experience here. I was surprised to feel drawn to this country, something I wouldn't have predicted twenty years earlier. China was unlike any place I'd ever known. Suddenly a squealing broke through my reverie, growing louder, a discordant note amid the street melody. A bicycle approached with a protesting pig tied on the back, feet in the air. *Going to market*, I thought, smiling. Reluctantly I turned away to get ready for the day's adventure.

Each day that first week brought new discoveries. One of my earliest impressions was of throngs of people everywhere. Throughout the day, the streets and parks were jammed. Whenever our group stopped to look at something, people gathered, encircling each of us four or five deep, pressing in and staring for minutes on end. Westerners were a curiosity then.

Those first days I observed my parents as if through a new lens. They'd been twenty-six and twenty-two when they arrived in 1930. Back again in the land of their young adult years, they took great pleasure interacting with people. They drew larger audiences than the rest of us since they could speak Chinese. I watched Mom conversing with a person who asked successive questions in English. She answered in Chinese, having so easily transitioned to thinking in that language she hadn't realized the person was speaking English. Her animated face and relaxed demeanor told me she felt the same strong ties as my father but was just more reserved with her emotions. Dad would often joke in Chinese or pull a quarter-sized one-yuan coin from behind someone's ear, to the delight of his audience.

The state television offered daily English lessons. Even homes in the poorest remote areas had televisions. One day a young woman came up to me and posed a question in English. After I answered, she asked an entirely unrelated question. This pattern continued for five or six questions. Then she bowed slightly, murmured "Thank you," and slipped away.

"That was fun," I said to Dad. "I think she was practicing the latest English lesson."

I wished I could converse in Chinese, but I knew only the few phrases Dad had taught me: *hao bu hao* (the colloquial "how are you"), *xie xie* ("thank you"), and *zai jian* ("goodbye").

Even the modes of transport fascinated me. I saw horse-drawn carts in smaller cities and occasionally people riding small tricycle-style tractors. Everywhere bicycles were the most common means of moving goods and people. The bikes all looked alike: unisex, black paint, no gears. "Parking lots" consisted of sidewalks cordoned off where riders left their bicycles with an attendant and paid a small fee. Imagine the parking space needed, I thought, if the bicycles had been cars. Double buses were common: two regular-sized bus sections joined by an accordion-like connection that made turning corners easier. The buses, always jammed, must have held a hundred people or more. Passengers' belongings were crammed on top, everything from boxes and crates to chickens and ducks. I couldn't get enough of these scenes of Chinese life.

During the second week, as I'd feared, I began to find Mom's constant company wearing. Tours often require flexibility and patience, never her strong suits. She often lashed out at Dad and occasionally others in the group. I was used to this in a home setting, but having her act this way in public embarrassed me. Needing space, I began to sit apart at some meals and on the bus. They'd made friends, so I wasn't leaving them isolated. I still sought them when I had questions or wanted to share my thoughts. On several occasions I asked them what was different from the China they'd known.

"The cities have changed," Dad said. "The city walls and gates are mostly gone, sad to say. And all these drab concrete buildings were built during the Soviet era."

"But life in the countryside is pretty much unchanged," Mom offered.

Another time she said, "Overall I think life is better. What do you think, Johnny? I don't see the extremes of wealth and dire poverty. No beggars on the street."

"General health has definitely improved," Dad said. "In the 1930s, open sores and obvious diseases like leprosy were common. I see none of that now."

We'd all noted the conformity in dress. Only children with their patterned shirts in bright colors provided contrast to the navy-blue and dark-gray Mao-style clothes worn by adults. We learned from their Chengdu friends that the countrywide restrictions on dress were to change soon.

For most people on the tour, arriving in Chengdu marked the middle of the trip—another look at a Daoist or Buddhist temple, a chance to visit the city's teahouses and sample the fiery-hot cuisine. For my parents and me, Chengdu was the highlight.

Following the touching reunion of my parents and their colleagues at the Chengdu airport, our tour group boarded a bus that took us to our hotel. With several free hours before dinner, I dropped my luggage in my room and met my parents in the lobby to go walking. From the bus they had recognized several old buildings not far from the hotel. By chance in this now-huge city of eighty-one million, our hotel was less than a mile from the university.

The three of us walked along Renmin Nan Lu, the wide boulevard that fronted the hotel and led toward the campus. The street had spacious bicycle lanes and wide sidewalks shaded by office buildings and flowering trees. Bicycles choked the street as usual, their bells offering a musical backdrop as we walked. Only half listening to my parents talk excitedly about staying so close to the campus, I watched the Chinese stare uninhibitedly as we passed and tried to determine which tree was the source of the sweet aroma drifting down.

After fifteen minutes of brisk walking, Dad spotted something familiar. "Look over there!" He pointed toward an older building partially blocked by newer ones. "Isn't that . . . ?" and he switched to Chinese.

"No, no, that's not it at all," Mom responded sharply, her good humor vanishing.

The derision in her voice caused the familiar uneasiness from childhood to rise in the pit of my stomach. Her ire was so easily provoked. I hung back to allow myself space to breathe.

Mom said, "But over there . . . ," and pointed to another building.

After Dad answered again in Chinese, she said, "No, dammit, that's not right!"

"Dr. Lenox! Dr. Lenox!" I heard the call from behind me.

Turning, I saw a slight elderly Chinese man across a side street looking expectantly at us. I tapped Dad on the arm to get his attention as the man hurried over, smiling from ear to ear. The three of them talked animatedly in Chinese for a minute, and then Dad introduced me.

"Jackie, this is Dr. Wang, a physicist. He studied in Rochester the year we lived there."

I shook Dr. Wang's hand, and he proceeded to orient us. Baptist Row, the narrow campus road along which we'd lived in the 1940s, had been torn up in creating Renmin Nan Lu, which now bisected the campus. The houses of the Baptist missionaries were gone. My heart sank. I had no early memories but had wondered if seeing my first home might prompt some recall. Dr. Wang led us to the campus entrance. In the 1930s the university campus had been outside the city wall and surrounded by rice paddies. With the wall long gone, the burgeoning city had engulfed the campus. Dr. Wang walked with us for a while. He'd known we were coming—the word had gone out—and he planned to attend the welcome for us the next day.

The campus was a mixture of old and new. As Dr. Wang and Mom chatted in Chinese, Dad took my elbow and pointed out the buildings from their time. The old medical library was on our left, two bright-red columns framing the entrance.

"Let's go in!" Dad said.

I followed, sharing his infectious delight at being back in this building he knew so well. We stood in a central space open to red-painted rafters high above a second-floor balcony with railings of a lattice design. Two rows of tables lined the room where a crush of students worked amid the thrum of Chinese voices. It appeared to still be a library of sorts.

"Anatomy classes were held upstairs in our day," Dad whispered, and I remembered the photo of Mom and her classmates sitting beside their cadavers. "The room would be too small for the number of medical students now." He gave a last glance around before turning to leave.

Back outside, the old administration building stood opposite, echoing the library's architecture only grander, with many red columns along a front portico. From studying my parents' photos over the years, I recognized several classroom buildings and in the distance the clock tower, a campus landmark. All around me, the photos came alive in full color: red doors, gray brick walls, gray-tiled roofs, and upturned eaves with dragons, horses, cranes, bats, and other animals.

"Dad, the campus is wonderful." A warmth filled me—I cared about these buildings.

"I think our university was the most beautiful of the mission-built schools. Here they used elements of Chinese architecture. Other schools were more western in style."

As we walked, I watched my parents chattering away, their earlier bickering forgotten, and was thankful I'd come on the trip. Their faces lit up with memories when they recognized a building, and they shared with me how each had been used in their time. Noting some shabbiness in places, I wondered what the future held for these structures, part of my parents' early life together.

After an hour with Dr. Wang, we said goodbye and returned to the hotel so my parents could put their feet up before dinner and work on their speeches. They'd been invited to give medical presentations at the next day's welcome and had been polishing their remarks for days. Mom planned to give her speech in English, but Dad had prepared his in Chinese. On the tour I'd seen him in the evening with his English–Chinese dictionary, checking and rechecking his terms. He knew his former students considered him their esteemed teacher, although he was too humble to have said that. He wanted to get the words right so he wouldn't lose face.

That evening I noticed he was a little hoarse.

"Are you coming down with a cold, Dad?"

"I feel fine, just a little tired," he said.

By the next morning his voice was gone. My heart went out to him. As the tour group left for a day of sightseeing, we three headed to the campus. Two dozen people awaited us in the old administration building, including Mom's friend Dr. Zhang, more classmates, and several women from graduating classes before and after Mom's. The rest were Dad's former faculty colleagues or his students who had later joined the faculty.

Our meeting began with tea in the reception room. The university president, a woman and Communist Party official, welcomed us in Chinese while our friends sat quietly in their chairs. Ten minutes later she was called out of the room, and our friends popped out of their seats and milled around, laughing and talking with my parents and among themselves. Suddenly they rushed back to their seats and sat quietly drinking their tea as the president entered. I chuckled to myself. Had someone been on watch? I realized they had to be careful in the still politically difficult times.

After our welcome, everyone but the president adjourned to a lecture hall for my parents' presentations. Additional faculty and students joined us, perhaps forty in all. A colleague read Dad's speech in Chinese. I was sad he couldn't give it himself—I would have enjoyed listening to him, even if I couldn't understand a word. Then it was Mom's turn. In a turquoise pantsuit, slim, her hair still blond, she looked younger than her seventy-two years. Standing up front animated and self-assured, she wielded a bamboo pointer as highlights of her talk on rheumatic fever were projected on a screen behind her. All discussion afterward was in Chinese. This was my first and only time seeing her give a speech, and I was quite proud. I thought again of the airport reunion and now this poised, confident woman. What else did I not know about her?

After a group photo on the steps of the administration building, we went with a dozen of their closest friends for a midday banquet. I sat next to Dr. Guo, who had visited us in Philippi in 1946. His twinkling eyes, kind manner, and short stature reminded me of Dad. His English was still impeccable, even after thirty years.

At one point he leaned toward me and said, "You will always have a home in Chengdu."

"Xie xie," I said and thanked him in English too. I knew in my heart he was speaking from his deep friendship and respect for both my parents, but Dad especially. "Your words mean so much to me. I am so happy to return to my birthplace."

During the next two days, while Dad and Mom remained with their friends, returning to the hotel only to sleep, I split my time and participated in several tour activities. When I was with my parents, I was mostly an observer and occasional photographer. They introduced me to everyone, but I couldn't keep the Chinese names straight. Several women came up with shy smiles and squeezed my hand. Had they known me as a baby? Seeing Mom with her friends was again a revelation—laughing, relaxed, and enjoying herself.

At one gathering I met Chunhua, the daughter of Dr. Zhang and about my age. My parents translated to help us "converse." Chunhua was also a physician and lived in the mountains northwest of Chengdu, where she had been assigned during the Cultural Revolution. She had traveled two days to meet us at a time when few Chinese made trips of any length. She even made a river crossing by cable—sitting on a seat suspended from a hollow log that slid along a cable high above waters raging from melting Tibetan snows. After our visit, Chunhua returned to her village and began studying English from the television classes. For years Mom coached her through letters, sharing them with me.

My parents were heartbroken to leave Chengdu. Three and a half days wasn't nearly enough time for them to catch up on thirty-five years. Being associated with a mission university had caused their colleagues hardship following the Communist takeover, yet that hadn't affected their friendships with my parents. They all picked up the threads quickly and with much joy. I was glad my parents could see the fruits of what they and their missionary friends had begun so long ago. The medical school and associated teaching hospital had become one of the top medical institutions in China.[2]

Xi'an, Luoyang, and Beijing still awaited us, each an ancient city with some of China's most treasured cultural sites. A sense of discovery continued to energize me. In these three cities I marveled at architectural beauty, the archaeological unearthing of pottery soldiers guarding the first emperor's mausoleum, massive city gates, and the finest of Chinese handwork and cultural objects. I gained an appreciation for China's millennia-long civilization that added contextual depth to what I was seeing. What captured me most, however, lay beyond the cities.

The Chinese landscapes outside my bus and train windows had a similar scale and at times a similar mountain beauty to Alaska, yet something was different. This was no wilderness landscape. People had lived here for thousands upon thousands of years, working the land and shaping it over time. I thought the vistas no less beautiful for that. Take rice cultivation, for example, long the backbone of China's agriculture.

This was springtime, a time of planting, and thick patches of intensely green rice seedlings awaited transplanting. Everywhere we went, I saw farmers stand calf-deep in flooded fields, take precious bundles of seedlings, and bend over to push the young plants into the mud one by one in arrow-straight rows. With flat land the fields appear geometric. With rolling hills they assume more rounded, asymmetrical shapes that follow the contours of the land. Narrow paths along the dikes between paddies add visual beauty, further emphasizing the lovely curving patterns. Steep slopes in more mountainous areas are sculpted by terrace after terrace of ancient fields marching upward.

At the Stone Forest near Kunming, I walked a path winding among natural gray limestone towers and rice paddies, some rock towers sporting a *tinza*, a small pavilion, on top. Rounding a curve in the path, I came upon a traditional Yi village and stepped back in time. Pigs and chickens roamed the narrow red dirt streets, and a woman sat sewing in a courtyard. Children played on a big wooden cart with wooden wheels three feet across. The small reddish stone homes contrasted stunningly with the green rice seedlings—the most brilliant shade of green I've ever seen.

These scenes affected me profoundly. My eagerness to absorb all that China offered was fed by the beauty I saw and the cultural resonance I felt inside. Despite my childhood resistance to China, I had grown up surrounded by Chinese items and my parents' love for this country. Being here, seeing these beautiful landscapes, with little that had changed since the 1930s and '40s, gave me glimpses into my parents' experience. I better understood the attraction. If Alaska had caused a paradigm shift that led to my passion for landscapes and environmental work, I sensed a similar ongoing process, an awakening growing stronger inside me as our tour progressed.

Now we were at the end. After twenty-five days of immersion in China, our group departed the same way we had come, aboard the Guangzhou–Hong Kong train. Although sad to leave, I finally had a few moments on the train to reflect. I realized I'd been so immersed in everything China had to offer that I'd thought little of Tom or my children aside from sending them postcards. Beyond showing them the beauty in my photos, I wasn't sure I could explain the impact of my experience.

The immersion in the culture and beauty of this country had changed me in some deep way I wasn't yet able to put in words—beyond the certainty that my childhood ambivalence had vanished. I had opened my heart to the Chinese people and to this country that at the same time felt strange and foreign yet welcoming and familiar. This dichotomy didn't sink in until the train had crossed the barren no-man's-land of the border and the view changed to 1980s Hong Kong. As buildings and cars and high-rises began to flash by, I thought, *No, no, I'm not ready for this. Let me go back to the bicycle bells and the beautiful countryside and a slower rhythm of life. . . .*

After years with little interest in China, I was now irresistibly drawn to the land of my birth. I'd always known of my parents' profound connection with China. Now a similar affinity blossomed within me.

 Chapter 9

When I returned from China, Tom and the kids welcomed me at Boston's Logan Airport. Because John and Steph were eager to talk, Tom whispered briefly in my ear after we hugged, "I agree we have problems, and I'm ready to work on them with you."

Relieved, I smiled and whispered my thanks. Then the kids claimed my attention, excited to bring me up to date on everything I'd missed. Tom didn't explain his change of heart, but his willingness to accept marriage counseling was enough for me then.

Ten days later we met with a therapist. Having never experienced counseling, I found even a superficial examination of my feelings painful and overwhelming. My time away had provided a respite from the insecurity, anger, and fear I'd felt at what seemed an increasingly uncertain future. The sense I'd had that China represented a new door opening in my life was soon overtaken, at least for the time being, by my probing of that internal churning stew of emotions. After our first meeting, Winnifred, the therapist, suggested weekly individual sessions with a joint meeting every several months. Changing the dynamic of a seventeen-year marriage clearly meant a lot of work. We told John and Steph we were in counseling to help us appreciate each other more. And at first the home atmosphere improved.

I thought doing something together as a family that summer might help. Backpacking was an idea I'd been mulling for a while. After living in Alaska, the rolling hills around Concord hadn't satisfied my craving for outdoor adventure. The White Mountains, two hours north, offered backcountry opportunities, but in four years we had only day-hiked there our first summer. In a phone conversation with my sister Marilyn, I shared my interest in backpacking, saying I'd found an outdoor course for women only. She suggested we backpack with her family instead—I could learn everything I needed to know from Tim, her husband.

That Sunday Tom and I were sitting with a second cup of coffee after breakfast. In counseling I'd resolved to share my thoughts more, so I offered my idea.

"I miss the outdoor life we had in Anchorage. What would you say to a family backpacking trip this summer?"

He hesitated for a moment. "It's a lot of work, you know."

"But you liked it, right? Your trip to the Brooks Range when we lived on Kodiak?"

"That was ten years ago." He looked at me and sighed. "We're older now. Our life is busier."

I weighed his comment. We were nearly the same age, thirty-eight, and indeed busier, but I was in better shape than I'd ever been. Since his knee surgery, though, Tom seemed to consider himself "older."

"I want to find something we can do together. The kids like outdoor adventures. John's twelve and can help carry things besides his clothes." I gazed out the window, trying to think of another persuasive point. "If I do the planning, would you think about it?"

"Depends where and when, how long a trip. Things like that. I'm not saying no."

I called Marilyn the next day and learned they had planned a July backpack into the Pasayten Wilderness in northern Washington. She was enthusiastic about our joining them, saying Jennie would love having Steph and John along too. I said I'd get back to her. After hanging up, I did a little happy-feet dance. That evening after dinner I told Tom of my conversation with Marilyn.

He scratched his neck and sighed. "You really want to do this?"

"Yes! I'll do the work of getting ready." My heart beat faster; he seemed to be relenting.

"Okay," he said, his voice lifting a bit. "But I'll need to look at my schedule."

I jumped up and gave him a quick hug, appreciating willingness if not excitement.

Two days later he had cleared his schedule, and I called Marilyn to say we would join them. That weekend we drove with the kids to L.L.Bean in Maine to buy the gear we needed. On the drive home Tom mentioned reserving plane tickets, and my stomach clenched. I'd considered a cross-country road trip a natural extension of the adventure. So, holding with my desire to be more forthright, I pitched a road trip rather than flying.

"I can't afford that much time away," he grumbled, keeping his eyes on the road.

I didn't say anything more. Over the next few days I talked with John and Steph about driving out west and camping along the way, saying we could pick their dad up in Seattle. They were agreeable.

At dinner that evening, I said, "John and Steph both want to drive out west."

Tom looked at the kids. "Are you sure? It means long days in the car."

They said practically in unison, "It'll be fun!"

"I'll take all the equipment in the car, even your pack," I said.

"Well, if that's what you want, go ahead," he said, seeming relieved.

Somehow before leaving, I worked in two long day hikes with the kids in the White Mountains to help prepare them—and me—for the strenuous hiking to come. I had to scramble to organize our clothes and all our gear for the backpacking and the cross-country drive. Marilyn had said Tim would take care of the backpacking food, so I only had to organize food for the westbound trip. As I packed, I thought of our drive east in the camper after leaving Alaska and knew I could do this. Giving myself a week to drive across the country, we said goodbye to Tom and set off.

To my delight, the road trip went well. John and Steph were old enough to enjoy the scenery. We played license plate games and "Animal, Vegetable, Mineral" and sang songs, beginning each day with a lusty rendition of Willie Nelson's "On the Road Again." We camped some nights and stayed at Holiday Inns with swimming pools. I heard no complaints of boredom.

A week later we picked Tom up at the Seattle airport and drove to Marilyn and Tim's home in Vancouver, BC. The next day we readied our packs, protecting our clothes and supplies by bundling them in plastic bags Marilyn had saved from a store called Woodward's. The next morning we drove south into Washington, crossed to the east side of the Cascades, parked our cars in the Pasayten access lot, and hiked into the wilderness for five nights of camping.

Backpacking—the immersion in wild nature—was everything I'd anticipated and more. I reveled in the mountain beauty and having darkness fall around us each evening, night sounds everywhere and stars twinkling overhead. Tom's initial grumpiness soon disappeared as we settled into a rhythm of breaking camp each morning and pitching our tents in a different spot each evening. Every day offered a new experience, a new vista, a new adventure—much like my China trip had. The kids carried day packs with their clothes and sleeping bags. John also carried extra gear, food, and a bird book. He was getting quite good at identifying birds.

One cold, cloudy day we were high on a ridge walking single file through a remnant snowfield when a snow squall blew in. We stopped to put on rain gear and gloves. With snowflakes falling as if it were December, I watched Steph and Jennie pull their arms in under their ponchos and start out again. Jennie began singing, "Frère Jacques, Frère Jacques, dormez-vous?" and Steph joined in.

I walked over to Tom, who was lifting his pack. We'd wondered how Steph would take to backpacking. "Snow in July, and our Alaska kid is happy," I said.

He smiled. "Conditioning her by the hikes in the White Mountains was a good idea."

One evening in the tent, getting ready to turn in, John pawed through his pack looking for his flashlight, pulling out plastic bag after plastic bag. Then he started giggling uncontrollably.

"Help! I'm being attacked by the Woodward's bags!" He dissolved again into giggles.

His humor was catching, and soon we all were laughing.

The next morning Marilyn asked, "What was going on in your tent last night?"

"You never said how dangerous backpacking is." I chuckled and told her the story.

Overall, the trip seemed a roaring success. For me, it confirmed the soul-lifting importance of adventure in mountainous landscapes. I had wanted my children to experience this too and was gratified they took to it as much as I. Even Tom seemed to enjoy himself. Before we left for home, Marilyn and I talked about backpacking again the following summer.

We dropped Tom off at the Seattle airport, and the kids and I began the drive back east. In South Dakota we had a different kind of adventure. After camping a night in Badlands National Park and exploring the badlands the next morning, I pulled onto the interstate after lunch. Only then did I notice the menacing cumulus clouds crowding the sky to the north, huge and dark and roiling, the turbulence spinning and circulating from bottom to top. I'd never seen clouds like this. A foreboding gripped my gut. Hating to alarm my children but needing to hear a weather forecast, I spun the radio dial and found a station just beginning an update.

"All of South Dakota is under a tornado watch," intoned the announcer, naming a town where a twister had touched down.

"John, could you find that town on the road map so we know where the tornado is?" I tried not to let my nervousness show.

"It's about sixty miles to the north," he said a minute later.

Fighting back fear, I racked my brain for advice I'd heard on what to do in case of a tornado. All I remembered was to get down in a ditch or culvert until it blew over. Looking at the ominous clouds and the flat, open landscape with few culverts, I didn't find this helpful. The wind gusted strongly all afternoon as we drove east, and I developed a tension headache. The storm must have crossed the interstate in the late afternoon, as we drove a stretch with several inches of hail the size of golf balls along the roadside. Through it all the kids were troupers. The tornado watch expired hours later when we crossed into Minnesota. I stopped at the first motel, exhausted but relieved we didn't have to test the "get in a ditch" advice. In reflecting that evening, I felt I'd been challenged and hadn't given in to fear. I slept well that night.

The rest of the trip went smoothly, especially when compared with driving under threat of a tornado. In those last days, I found myself at quiet times thinking about risk-taking and the importance of testing yourself in new situations. In fact, this trip from inception to carry-through had been a test in risks. I'd voiced my desire to backpack, pushed for a road trip, and handled most of the organizing. When I'd told my women friends I was driving across the country with my kids, each of them had said, "Alone?"—to which I'd answered I wasn't alone, I was with my kids. Thinking back on that, I felt pride. I'd challenged myself and dealt with whatever came up along the way. It was an important lesson for me: to trust my decisions and abilities. In the end, the sheer delight of the experience and what I'd learned about myself made the risk worth taking.

The tension between Tom and me had seemed to ease while backpacking. When I arrived home with the kids, though, he'd had a week to settle into his usual routines. As we resumed our family life, the tension soon returned. The familiar settings, especially those fraught in the past with personal doubts, seemed to trigger old habits in me and distance between us. Once again, to avoid the unhappiness at home, I buried myself in work, where I knew colleagues appreciated my efforts.

Despite considerable political wrangling, the Alaska lands legislation had been proceeding through Congress during the summer of 1980 and into the fall. I'd built solid relationships with three of the four members of New Hampshire's congressional delegation, supported by the continuing grassroots pressure from the people on my mailing list. Only my own representative had shown no support. To my surprise, though, when the bill finally passed in November 1980, he was in the "aye" column.

Only days later, I wrapped up my Audubon work and picked the kids up from their after-school art class. Arriving home, Steph ran to the mailbox as John and I went into the house.

Moments later she burst into the kitchen. "Mom! There's a letter from the White House!"

I tore open the telegram-format letter to read:

You are cordially invited to
join President Jimmy Carter
in the East Room of the White House
on December 2, 1980, at 9:30 a.m.
for the signing of the Alaska
National Interest Lands Act of 1980.

I gave a whoop of delight and hugged my children. There had been no doubt President Carter would sign the legislation, but never in my wildest dreams had I expected to be invited to the signing ceremony. The invitation was part of a celebration the Alaska Coalition had planned for people across the country who had helped in the campaign. I decided on the spot to attend. Celebrating with Anchorage colleagues and friends I'd made among Coalition staff and volunteers from other states would be a grand capstone to the hard work.

As before when I'd answered the Coalition's calls to come to DC, Tom was not happy.

"You're going again."

It was more a declaration than a question. He got the tight, angry look around his eyes that had become so familiar.

"Of course. This is the culmination of all the work I've done since leaving Anchorage."

I thought about my travels around New Hampshire to present programs and enlist people in the cause, the regular updates I'd sent to the several hundred people on my mailing list.

"All four members of our congressional delegation voted in favor of the Alaska bill, and they did it because I worked my butt off to get people to send letters and make phone calls." I felt the anger rising, which hardened my resolve. "I wouldn't miss this celebration for anything."

He retreated into irritable silence. That my own husband

couldn't even muster some enthusiasm or pride for my accomplishments saddened me. I didn't want to feel angry toward him—any positive expression from him, even if insincere, might have softened my heart. The kids were old enough for me to go away for two days. Steph, who was ten, considered being born in Alaska a unique part of her identity, and she and John were my two biggest fans. They both understood I cared deeply about this hard-won success. I wanted to be a part of this celebration regardless of how Tom felt.

Sitting with friends in the East Room on December 2nd, I thought back to the day in January 1975 when I opened the door to the Alaska Center for the Environment and all that had happened since. Discovering what would become a lifelong passion for environmental work, delivering the New Hampshire delegation in support of the Alaska Lands Act, the work I was now doing for New Hampshire Audubon—all stemmed from stepping into that log cabin six years earlier.

President Carter entered the room and welcomed everyone, breaking my reverie. My pride was immense when he said, "Never before have we seized the opportunity to preserve so much of America's natural and cultural heritage on so grand a scale."

The brief clips making the television news on these occasions don't begin to convey the atmosphere of such events, or at least what I felt that day. Underneath the palpable air of celebration was the more sobering ceremonial act that embodies the essence of democracy, of Congress and the president carrying out the will of the American people. That evening, jubilation was in the air as the Alaska Coalition's party commenced at a swank hotel in northwest Washington, complete with food, music, and dancing. It was a joyous evening celebrating with Anchorage friends who had helped me get started in my career.

Several months later I was at the Audubon headquarters composing a position statement for an upcoming state legislative hearing. Increasingly I was drafting and presenting most of the organization's statements, making good use of what I was learning in my graduate courses. I had my own desk in a room I shared with two other people on the second floor of the old farmhouse. When I went to the kitchen that day to get my lunch, Tudor was there also.

"Oh, Jackie," he said, "could you come to my office, please? I have something to discuss with you."

I followed him into his office and sat in the chair opposite him. He cleared his throat and began in his rather formal style of speaking.

"The executive committee has reviewed the budget and authorized me to offer you the salaried position of policy director," he said. "This position is new and of necessity will be part-time, two days a week."

My spirits soared. After all my volunteer work, I was being offered a paid job!

"Wow, Tudor," was all I could get out. The offer was so unexpected I had difficulty finding my voice.

"You can think about it." His smile peeked out from under his shaggy mustache. "We very much want you on the staff."

I chuckled, feeling warmth flush my face. "Oh, I don't have to think about it, Tudor. I appreciate the offer and happily accept. I'm delighted!"

That afternoon I shared the news with John and Steph, and they were excited too. They knew what it meant to me. At dinner I was eager to tell Tom. *Maybe being paid will make a difference*, I thought.

"Today at Audubon, Tudor offered me a paid job," I blurted when we were all seated. "Policy director, two days a week."

Tom frowned, then burst my bubble. "But you never told me you wanted a career!"

Clearly he didn't share the kids' excitement. He and I were both anger averse and had never once argued in front of the kids. The conversation was strained for the rest of dinner. When the kids left the table and disappeared into other parts of the house, I picked up where we'd left off.

"So it's okay to volunteer, but getting paid is different?" Hearing the stiffness in my voice, I stood and began clearing the table, avoiding his eyes. With the dishes stacked, I made eye contact. "When we married, I had no specific career in mind and took the lab job during med school because we needed the money. When you graduated, I knew lab work wasn't something I wanted to do anymore."

Taking the plates to the kitchen sink, I paused to collect my thoughts then came back to where he was still sitting at the table, chin high and eyes flinty.

"But that didn't mean I didn't want a career," I continued. "I just hadn't found what I wanted to do until Anchorage."

"I make enough money," he grumbled, his face reddening. "You don't have to work."

I rolled my eyes. "It's not about the money!" I walked back to the sink, aware of my clenched jaw. I relaxed, took a deep breath, and returned. "Audubon's paying me diddly-squat. It's about feeling good about myself. Pursuing my passion and contributing to society."

We'd never spoken to each other like this, so it seemed like a heated argument. Without another word he left the table and went to his study. I stood there, looking out the window over the sink, not seeing anything—it was dark—but thinking. Why couldn't he be happy for me just once? Or support me even a little? My stomach churned.

As I finished cleaning up, my anger grew. My desire to work seemed a personal affront to him. I was entitled to my ambitions too. As a young adult I'd lacked the self-awareness to know what I wanted in life and hadn't planned a specific career.

I'd grown up with a driven woman for a mother and hadn't wanted to be like her. Near the end of college, I was in love for the first time, and marriage seemed the least risky choice. I didn't have to confront my inner fears or decide what to do next, although those were not conscious thoughts. When the kids were little and Tom was in training, we'd assumed traditional gender roles right out of the 1950s.

Yet my mother's example—showing women are as capable as men at having careers—had burrowed inside me. This sudden realization startled me, but my thoughts roared ahead like a speeding train. I was a different person now than when I married. As the social upheaval of the 1960s and '70s exploded, I found the environmental causes that would be my life's work. The feminist upwelling had burst full force into my consciousness just as my heart opened, and I yearned for more. When the feminists spoke, they spoke to me and the life that was possible. Never having learned to share my feelings, I hadn't thought to talk with Tom about what these societal changes meant to me—and for him.

Later that evening my thoughts were still in overdrive. Realizing the similarity of my commitment to environmental work and Mom's determination to succeed in medicine had surprised me. She too had struggled to balance professional fulfillment with the personal responsibilities of parenting. But the parallel ended there. She'd had a supportive husband and a troubled relationship with her children, whereas I had a loving relationship with my children and an increasing disappointment in my marriage, despite the ongoing counseling.

With Tom and me drifting further apart, we now had little in common other than our children. I had feared the impact of divorce on them and mistakenly thought that since Tom and I never argued, they hadn't been affected. I had entered marriage counseling with an honest desire to find some middle ground and a willingness to adjust my behavior, although stopping work altogether was never an option for me. In leaving Anchorage I had turned my back on a promising situation for the sake of my family. I knew myself better now and resolved to not do that again. To be a good life partner, I had to be happy.

Over the next several years as my commitment to my career grew, our relationship languished. Each summer I drove out west with the kids to backpack with Marilyn and her family. But Tom did not join us again, saying he didn't like sleeping on the ground. Although disappointed at first, I was relieved to leave him behind and escape the constant strain. John and Steph accepted that this was what the three of us did together and never asked why their father didn't come too.

Tom and I were still in counseling, but we met less frequently and mostly in individual sessions. Throughout this time my emotions did battle inside: the old fear of being on my own, a stubborn determination to hang on to environmental work, hostility toward Tom for not being more supportive, and an utter sadness for my children and the crumbling of our family. A fragile inner hope withered as time passed and Tom seemed unable to understand or accommodate my desire for a career. Underneath it all, I felt a constant push-me-pull-you between my growing self-confidence in aspects such as my work and backpacking, yet felt a failure in my marriage. I took on too much responsibility for our eroding relationship rather than holding Tom accountable for his part in what was happening.

Finally, in late summer of 1984, our marriage therapist suggested we rent an apartment for three months to get some distance—probably a last-ditch effort to move us off the dime. We would take turns staying alone at the apartment for two-week intervals while the other remained at home with John, now sixteen, and Steph, fourteen. We found a one-bedroom apartment in a renovated mill on the opposite side of Concord and brought furniture and household items from home. I offered to stay in the apartment first, knowing Tom wasn't eager about the idea.

Sitting in the silence on my first evening, I was euphoric. *For the next two weeks, I won't have to tend to anyone's needs or desires,* I thought, *except my own. I can work at Audubon into the evenings, fix vegetarian meals as often as I want, do what interests me.* The emotional weariness of the last years lifted some. But during Tom's first stay in the apartment, he became lonely and missed the kids terribly. When he mentioned this after his first two weeks, I offered to stay at the apartment with no switching so he could stay at home.

The toughest part for me was living away from the kids. I phoned them often and went to their sporting events. John was now driving, and he and Steph came for dinner when their schedules permitted. My heartache at not being part of their daily lives couldn't disrupt my exhilaration at escaping the stress of my marriage and being responsible only for myself. Finally, I knew I could survive on my own. It was time to pay attention to my happiness.

As Christmas neared, Tom asked me to come back. He wanted to try living together again. With some reluctance, I agreed. Although there was less tension initially, I soon realized nothing had changed. When we married, he had put me in a pigeonhole marked "wife and mother," and he couldn't see beyond to the person I'd become.

At some earlier point I would have stayed if he'd been able to meet me halfway. But with his inability to see who I was and my unwillingness to give up my career, our marriage was over. We chose divorce by mediation and pledged not to drag our children into the middle of our unhappiness and hurt. Unable or unwilling to bridge our personal differences, we worked together where John and Steph were concerned.

Although neither of us had specifically prepared them for the prospect of divorce, we had not hidden the fact of our ongoing counseling, and the apartment interlude had been a clue things were not going well. Both John and Steph are perceptive, and they sensed the tension.

The process of splitting our family was excruciatingly sad—for all four of us. Nevertheless, I knew it was the right thing for me.

PART II:

Finding

My Parents

 Chapter 10

Sipping the Chinese tea I'd made from my parents' stash, I eyed the four boxes in Dad's small study, which we'd brought from basement storage that morning. Then he and Mom walked to work at the medical center, leaving me with the boxes.

My parents were back in Pittsburgh permanently in 1991 after moving four times in eight years. They lived once again near Children's Hospital and the university medical center. During their various moves they'd stored some belongings and now had everything in one place for the first time in ages. When I arrived for a short visit, they mentioned the daunting task of going through the many boxes. Some hadn't been opened for decades, including ones Dad had brought when he moved from West Virginia nearly twenty years before. I offered to help with the sorting.

I looked around at Dad's desk piled with papers, a two-shelf bookcase jammed with books on China, a comfy chair and leather ottoman, and many Chinese mementos. I set my tea mug next to a large blue Chinese vase on the bookcase. The vase had been a 1930s gift to Dad from a Chinese official for treating his ailing daughter. I moved the cartons to make room and sat down cross-legged in their midst with a sigh. Sorting through these boxes would be a thankless task—my parents saved everything.

From the first box I removed a small wooden replica of an Alaskan totem pole and a set of bamboo coasters from China that had nestled among wrapped items. Unfolding the newsprint from a flat round object, I found a small ceramic plate from Greece. The deeper I went, the more I wondered if my parents had dumped a drawer of souvenirs and trinkets from their world travels into this box. If it were up to me, I'd find a church rummage sale and donate most of this stuff, but I knew these items represented memories for my parents. I divided the contents into three piles for their consideration: keep, recycle, and toss.

One box down, three to go. I took a sip of tea and grimaced; it was cold. I was ready for a break, and my watch said almost noon, so I stood and carried my mug to the kitchen. Reheating it in the microwave, I made a sandwich and returned to my task. The second carton was marked "South Carolina." As I slogged through bank records, letters, journal articles, and other papers, my mind wandered to my parents' aborted try at retirement and southern living.

They'd moved south in 1988 after living five years in a seniors' community outside Pittsburgh. Those five years had been happy for the most part, but Mom had become increasingly outspoken about the smoking allowed in the common areas. She eventually petitioned the management to declare the dining room nonsmoking. When the petition was denied, they moved to a retirement village with a nonsmoking policy in Greenville, South Carolina, where Mom's older sister lived. Both my parents had officially retired before moving, but Mom had been unable to cut all ties with Children's Hospital and arranged to return twice a year for research purposes. They'd bought a studio apartment near the hospital for these visits.

I'd flown to Greenville to visit in April 1990 and found Dad very upset. As he and I walked a trail on the grounds of the retirement village, I learned why.

"She wants to move again. Back to Pittsburgh. I can't believe it!"

"What's this all about, Dad?" I asked, linking my arm through his.

"Everyone down here insists on calling her Mrs. Lenox, even though they address me as Doctor." He pushed his glasses higher on his nose. "And they know she's a physician too."

"Oh, boy. No quicker way to get her temper up. But it is disrespectful—she earned that title too. And probably had to fight for it more." I switched topics. "I've noticed she and Aunt Wilma fight like cats and dogs. Why did she think this would work out?"

"Short visits are different from seeing each other daily," he said. "They just clash. They're both set in their ways."

I'd given him a sympathetic smile. "That's not going to change at their ages, Dad."

"I only moved here to keep peace," he had said, his face reddening. "I'm tired of moving around. I refuse to do it again!"

Sitting on the floor of Dad's study amid the boxes, I squirmed a bit, remembering his discomfort at the time. That declaration had been a strong outburst for him. I stood and stretched to get a kink out of my back, then sat down again and continued sorting.

In the end Dad had agreed to leave, supporting Mom as always. South Carolina hadn't been a good fit for him either. I had phoned soon after my visit to see if their plans had gelled.

"We're going to de-retire," Dad announced. "We're going back to work when we get to Pittsburgh."

"Ha! De-retire," I teased. "Is that a word, Dad? Have you set a moving date?"

"The end of June," Mom said. "When our things are on the moving van, we'll start driving to Pittsburgh."

"You two are driving yourselves?"

"Of course!" she snapped. "How else do you think we'd get our car back?"

Hearing the challenge in her voice, I had pictured what the trip would be like. Two days, six hundred miles, just the two of them in the car. Mom was the main driver now since Dad had early macular degeneration. He would insist on driving some, and she would carp endlessly about that and everything else—his hearing, the shirt he'd be wearing, his less-than-erect posture, and so on. At eighty-one she was capable of driving the distance, but the stress would make her short-tempered. Dad would be the sole focus of her tirades in the close confines of their small car.

"I'll come down and help you drive."

They had both talked at once, Mom's "You don't have to . . ." on top of Dad's "Do you really want to?"

"I enjoy road trips, and it'll be like when I was a kid. Let's drive the Blue Ridge Parkway again."

The phone's sharp ringing jarred me back to the present. I stood and walked to the desk. It was Dad, letting me know he was finished at student health. Mom wasn't ready to leave, but he would walk back and be home in a half hour. I sat back down and finished with the second box, which as I'd expected had been boring. Adding the papers to the piles from the first carton, I looked at my watch and started on the third box, also from their years in Greenville. Soon I was back on autopilot, my brain once more preoccupied with the South Carolina interlude.

We had left for Pittsburgh in June, retracing part of the route from my childhood. The Blue Ridge Parkway had remained as I remembered, a narrow two-lane road with grassy shoulders, split rail fences, and a forty-five-miles-per-hour speed limit. I felt as if I'd stepped back in time, only now I was in the driver's seat, making sure to not cut the curves like Dad had always done on winding mountain roads. Mom seemed to relax and was on good behavior for the two days of our drive. I relinquished the steering wheel to her often enough for her to feel she was contributing, but not so much she became overly tense. She and Dad took turns in the passenger seat. I shared the latest news of my children—John beginning his first job after college and Steph returning from several months of study abroad. My anxiety about being in close quarters with them for two days receded as the miles went by.

On the outskirts of Pittsburgh, Mom's mood had changed. I'd driven in the city enough to know the way to their studio apartment and had been thinking ahead and concentrating on the traffic when she spoke from the passenger seat.

"No, no! What're you doing?"

She said it so sharply I jumped.

"What do you mean? What's wrong?" My shoulders tensed as I gripped the steering wheel tighter.

"You have to be in the right lane to get to the apartment."

"Mom, I know that. We still have several blocks before I need to move over." I took a deep breath, thinking of what to say to calm her rather than incite her further. I never knew how far she'd take an argument.

Then Dad spoke calmly from the back seat. "Clinky, let her drive."

Mom fell silent, but I sensed her wrath escalating beside me.

We arrived in the underground garage of their condominium seven or eight minutes later. I parked the car and they both got out on the passenger side. Gathering my purse and sweater, I looked up in time to see my mother give my father a shove, knocking him off balance. He stumbled but caught the rear door handle to steady himself.

"Mom! Stop it!" I jumped out, ran around to their side of the car, and put a hand on Dad's arm. "You okay?"

He nodded. Her shove was the closest I'd seen her come to physical abuse. She had more strength than he, given their four-year age difference. Did she do this when they were alone?

"Why did you do that?" I heard the sharpness in my voice as I looked her square in the face for an explanation.

Her eyes glittered and she pressed her lips into a hard line. Saying nothing, she turned and stormed off, going up the elevator without waiting for us.

I looked at Dad. "You sure you're okay?"

"Yes," he replied, but he was shaking a bit, still gripping the door handle.

In my mind I wanted to ask if this was new behavior for her, but what came out was, "What was that about?"

He shook his head, smiling wanly. "You know Mom. I've been trying to get her to agree to marriage counseling because of things like this, but she refuses. Could you talk to her?"

Fifteen months had passed since this incident. Yet sitting in Dad's study I could feel the apprehension grip my stomach as if he had just asked the question, as if I were back in that basement garage.

At the time I'd given him a hug—he was still trying to make peace after sixty years of marriage. How could I say no to my elderly father's request? But I'd never confronted Mom in my life, and just the thought struck terror in me. I mumbled I would try and we headed upstairs.

The rest of the day I thought about Dad's request, waiting for the right time. Mom's anger had dissipated, however, and she was back to her small talk as if nothing had happened. Not knowing how to begin, feeling like a child again and not wanting her rage focused on me, I had put off the conversation. The next day, carrying my luggage out to the taxi waiting to take me to the airport, I had carried guilt too at not being there for my father when he'd asked.

After that episode they had resumed their work and lived in the studio for about a year until this larger condo came on the market. They had moved and retrieved their boxes from the several storage locations.

Just then the front door opened, and I heard Dad call out a greeting.

"I'm in the study," I answered and stood up as he walked into the room. I gave him a hug. "I've made progress. I'm almost through the third box." I explained the three piles of things. His little clucking sound and his impish smile told me he was pleased.

"Thank you for doing this, Jackie," he said, kissing my cheek. "Mom should be home in another hour. I think I'll sit down and go through the mail."

"Can I make you a cup of tea, Dad?" I grabbed my empty mug and followed him to the dining area, where he'd dropped the mail onto the table.

"Just hot water would be wonderful, thanks." His face crinkled with pleasure as he sat down and pulled the mail toward him.

"Coming up." I smiled. Drinking hot water was a Chinese practice.

I went to the kitchen, made myself more tea, and heated a mug of water for Dad. Delivering the mug to him, I returned to the study and made quick work of the third box. When I opened the last carton, a slightly musty smell wafted into the room. Ah, an older one and hopefully more interesting than bank statements.

On top was a metal box about three by four inches. When I opened it, black-and-white photos spilled into my lap, causing my breath to hitch. The landscape and Dad's abundant hair and youthful appearance told me the photos were from 1928. After graduating from medical school, he'd spent the summer working in a small mission hospital on the Labrador coast. I'd heard his stories but had never seen pictures. I shuffled through the photos and put them aside to examine more carefully later. Next was a manila envelope with Christmas cards and letters from the 1950s and then tax returns from that period. Below these lay an old manila folder. Lifting it, I could see an inch or more of yellowed paper with crumbling corners. My curiosity spiked.

Placing the folder in my lap, I intuitively wiped my hands on my jeans before opening it. Countless sheets of tissue-thin onionskin paper fanned out before me. Carbon typing filled the fragile pages from edge to edge. Some pages had typing on both sides. My heart quickened and my mouth went dry. I took a quick gulp of tea, remembering Mom telling me years ago that Dad's mother had saved all their letters written from China. The letters had been in storage, but she hadn't known where.

Time seemed to slow down as I reached for the top page. Would it tell me about Dad's teaching or Mom's medical classes? Or maybe even something about me? Gently lifting one delicate sheet I read quickly, my senses heightened, then skimmed another page, confirming these were indeed the long-lost letters from China. At some point I vaguely registered hearing Mom talking in the next room. But this treasure trove of family history commanded my attention, and I continued to scan the pages, handling them with the utmost care.

The sheets appeared to be in random order. Dad had told me they usually typed one general letter for both families, making carbon copies to add personal notes. Postage had been so expensive at times they had often mailed one letter to Dad's mother in Pennsylvania, and she had sent it on to Hapink, my South Carolina grandmother. The letters often made a broader circuit of my parents' brothers and sisters too.

Then I realized these pages were flat. They'd never been folded or mailed and were not the letters my grandmother had kept. They were carbon copies my parents had saved, even though Mom had said they hadn't kept copies for themselves. Funny how the brain can forget something so important.

This stack of tissue-thin pages represented hours and hours of my parents' time over their fourteen years in China. I envisioned Dad putting carbon between each onionskin layer, then rolling these paper-carbon sandwiches into a manual typewriter. Each stroke of a key transferred a letter onto the onionskin page, thanks to the carbon paper, with each successive page of the sandwich fuzzier. Every now and then Dad would reverse a carbon sheet, and the typing would be transferred onto the back of a page. I found several of these while looking through the letters and had to hold the page up to a mirror to decipher the words.

Then on one sheet the words jumped off the page, bringing an immediate rush of adventure.

"We stopped for the night just below Zheduo Pass at about 11,000 feet. Our tents are pitched near a Tibetan house. Mountains to west, south, and east—some 22,000 feet high, perpetual snow. At one time today we counted six snow peaks. What a sight! Met two yak caravans carrying rice done up in yak skins. Yak are fierce-looking animals like wild cows or bison with long sharp horns and black hair reaching almost to the ground."

This was their 1932 trek into Tibet, my favorite of their stories. They'd been twenty-eight and twenty-four, still essentially newlyweds. Questions pummeled my brain. What could these letters tell me about the two people who raised me? Would I find the woman I witnessed in the reunion with her classmates? Could they tell me about my earliest childhood or my parents at the beginning of their marriage, what their life was like and what China was like then?

I put the page about Tibet back on top of the other letters and carried the entire folder of aged paper into the living room, where my parents sat talking and sorting their mail.

"Listen to what I've found!" I read the passage about Zheduo Pass and the yak caravans.

Dad pumped the air delightedly with his fists, his face beaming. Mom's grin reached from ear to ear. Warmth spread through me at seeing the joy on their faces, especially Mom's.

"The China letters!" Dad exclaimed.

"These are fascinating." An idea popped into my head. "I'd love to take the letters home and transcribe them—type them into my computer. They're so fragile. It would be the best way to protect them."

They looked at one another, pleased, and without hesitation agreed.

When I left two days later to return home, I carried the letters in a manila envelope laid carefully between layers of flat clothing in my suitcase. In the short time since I'd lifted them from the musty box, I had read more, and they had become precious to me, despite story interruptions from being out of sequence. I'd been encouraging Dad for years to write a memoir to preserve their experiences in China. More recently I'd begun recording him telling his stories. But Mom had often called corrections from the next room, and verbal sparring would follow. Once the letters surfaced with their vividness and unassailable truth, I abandoned the taping. While the tapes contained the bones of the stories, the letters infused the telling with crisp detail and vivid images—much like comparing a luminous digital color image with a 1950s black-and-white photo from a Brownie camera.

Over the next several years, I used my spare time to transcribe the letters. I first put the pages into chronological order. Piecing the letters together by matching the stories was like detective work. Once I began transcribing, I would lose myself in my parents' remarkable story, engaged by the vibrancy of their life and the significance of the work they had joined in Chengdu.

The letters were much more, however, than a chronicle of adventure, scholarship, and danger in 1930s and '40s China. They enabled me to see my parents grow as individuals and as a couple and to understand how living in China had shaped them. Few people have an opportunity to glimpse their parents as young adults, before the experience of parenting and the burdens of life inevitably transform them. The letters were a gift, providing a truer sense of my parents' relationship and deepening my fascination with my birth country.

 Chapter 11

My fiftieth birthday found me lost in thought, driving one of Vermont's rural dirt roads to meet a colleague at her house. The question preoccupying me had come from Steph, home on spring break from college the previous week. "Mom, when I was growing up, how come we never talked about our feelings?"

I was already in a contemplative mood, prompted by having just read Gloria Steinem's latest book, *Revolution from Within.*[1] The book explores stories of low self-esteem, hers included. I was surprised to learn the woman who had seemed to personify confidence had experienced doubts about herself. The more I read, the more it seemed she was speaking directly to me. When Steinem wrote early in the book of "inner feelings of incompleteness, emptiness, self-doubt," I knew exactly what she meant. A sense of kinship filled me in reading about another woman who "learned to ask a new and revolutionary question: What do *I* want?"

In the car, mulling my conversation with Steph, I knew her question went to the heart of why my marriage had failed. Our family conversations had been lively, mostly about news events or what we'd done or learned that day, but rarely how we felt about what happened, such as "I felt so good" or "I'm worried."

I hadn't asked Tom if he was happy living in Anchorage or whether the difficulties in his medical practice discouraged him. Nor had he asked me such questions. Neither of us had shared our thoughts about the direction our life was taking, not even early on when it might have strengthened our relationship. I'd hugged and cuddled my children, shown my love in myriad ways. But I had not cultivated a language of emotion.

My thoughts turned to my own childhood, and I recognized a similar pattern—dinner conversations had involved sharing facts and observations, with little probing into our sentiments about what we'd discussed. I learned not to share any worry or self-doubt that Mom might hurl at me in fury. Dad at times used mannerisms to show how he felt, like pumping the air with his fists in delight or excitement, but he too avoided voicing his feelings.

As I drove on, my mind churned in and out of these troubling revelations much like the alternating sunlight and shadows I experienced as I neared the top of the forested ridge. In a flash my brain connected Steph's question and Steinem's book. I realized I too suffered from low self-esteem. Another phrase from the book came to me then: "I've lived a seemingly aware life for more than forty years without figuring it out." Gloria and I had this in common too, but I was a decade slower on the uptake.

I had moved to Vermont in 1988 to be with a man I'd met through work, a romance with seemingly unlimited potential for openness and intimacy. We shared a love of nature and the outdoors and a similar outlook on life. I considered him a soulmate. Although our friends viewed us as a successful example of personal and professional partnership, I'd recently discovered betrayal in our relationship. This had left me angry and deeply disappointed, but I hadn't yet given up on him.

Turmoil engulfed me as my car crested the ridge. Tears welling in my eyes, I pulled to the side of the road and rifled through my purse for a tissue. Overcome by deep, gut-wrenching sobs, I pushed the seat back and let the tears flow, not knowing if I wept for myself or because it seemed I had failed my son and daughter. Probably both. I had never experienced such profound visceral pain, not even when my marriage fell apart. The floodgates of my heart opened, and long-hidden shame and humiliation surfaced, leaving me raw and vulnerable.

To have hit rock bottom on the day I turned fifty amazed me. I hadn't feared this milestone, nor had I attached any particular importance to it. But driving to Jean's, some inner voice had said, *Okay, kiddo, time to wake up. No more hiding. You must acknowledge your feelings.*

Sitting in the car, my thoughts roiling, I knew my trauma was deep-seated. My struggle involved honesty and open-ness with myself and with others. I seemed unable to trust even those I loved most with my heart and the tender core of my being.

Needing to get to my friend's house, I blew my nose and drove the remaining miles. I was still despondent when she answered my knock.

"Jean, I know we planned to work, but I need to talk," I said, my voice quavering.

"Oh my gosh! Jackie—" She pulled me in, hugging me. "What's wrong? Are you okay?"

I followed her to the kitchen, where she handed me a cup of coffee. We sat at the table, and for the next twenty minutes I shared the story of my emotionally fraught drive.

"I can't believe this all came pouring out today. I know there's a ton of shit buried from childhood, and it has to be this whole idea of self-esteem I've been reading about."

"Well, better now than on your sixtieth or seventieth birth-day—or never." She laughed. "But we shouldn't be working on such a momentous day."

I gave a rueful smile. "You're right. I can't focus, though talking with you has helped me get some perspective." I sighed.

"I think I need counseling. It helped with my divorce. But I don't know anyone here."

"I do." She tore a sheet from the notebook at her elbow and scribbled three names. "These women are all excellent." She pointed to the first name. "Peggy could probably see you the soonest. She just left county mental health services to set up her own practice."

"Thanks for the list, Jean. I would have spent a lot of time finding a good therapist. I should go now." I stood and gave her a hug. "Thanks for your friendship."

She walked me to the door and patted my shoulder. "Anytime you want to talk, just call."

That afternoon I made an appointment with Peggy for the following week. Then I phoned Steph.

"You remember asking why we never talked about feelings? It was so on target." I shared what had happened, including my appointment to begin counseling. "Your question was the best birthday present you could have given me."

"Oh, Mom, I'm glad."

"I can't change the past, but I hope to make it up to you and John in the future."

Periodically in the days before meeting with Peggy, I thought more about my insights from reading Steinem's book. Closing off my emotions had made it difficult to develop a deeper understanding of who I was and what was important to me. I lacked some of the hallmarks of self-esteem—confidence, self-reliance, empowerment—although I'd made progress in discovering my passions and skills.

I was astonished my problems had been invisible to people around me. How had I reached this point without anyone noticing I was struggling—not my parents or other family members, not my teachers or my husband or friends and work colleagues. No one. Weren't the signs there? But even I had been unaware except for a growing unhappiness and ongoing difficulty making decisions.

Only with my children had I been able to freely express unconditional love, tenderness, concern, compassion, joy, and pride. In all other parts of my life I had guarded my emotions at best but mostly buried them—and the years of marriage counseling hadn't opened that vault more than a crack. Despite seeing my parents often during my adult years, we had no familial intimacy. Our conversations remained superficial, and we resisted digging down for deeper meaning or personal connection. I had numerous friends, including work colleagues, but only a few close friendships. In truth, the only aspects of my life giving me satisfaction and a sense of self-worth were parenting and my environmental work. After divorcing I'd had public recognition for my professional work, but it had taken several years to find a niche in Vermont's environmental community, which undercut the self-confidence I'd gained from my work in New Hampshire. Now I faced the growing cracks in my personal relationship. All the agitation bursting forth threatened my capacity to sustain even the work I loved. My focus in the coming weeks and months had to be on healing myself.

Entering Peggy's book-lined office, I was ready to get started. She motioned me to sit on the couch as she pulled up a comfy-looking rocking chair. She appeared to be in her mid-thirties and had a warm, empathetic manner. I liked her immensely from our very first session. I began to tell my story, and together we peeled back the layers of my life. Over the next months no matter what topic I brought, no matter my distress, she talked me through it and lifted my spirits. Radiating a deep, alert energy, she focused solely on me and what I was conveying. Occasionally she would make notes and always had a helpful example for dealing with whatever pesky issue was distressing me. Those early months were intense, all-consuming. We first tackled my home life, but I soon realized the bigger underlying issue was my relationship with my parents. Our weekly sessions galvanized me. Knowing we were addressing long-standing issues critical to my happiness made me feel more hopeful and alive than in years. After a month I felt strong enough to call my parents.

"Hey," I said, when they both were on the phone. "Sorry to be so out of touch. Life's been crazy."

"We've been thinking about you and hoped you were okay," Dad said. "How was your birthday?"

I deflected. "Hard to believe I'm fifty, huh? I appreciated your card." Taking a deep breath, I ignored the anxious flutters inside. "I wanted you to know I've begun counseling."

I had jotted a few notes ahead of the call to make sure I covered everything I wanted to say. I told them a bit about Peggy and her credentials, knowing it would matter to them, and confided that suppressing my emotions had contributed to my breakup with Tom and was now affecting my current relationship.

Dad spoke up immediately. "You know we support you in whatever you do, Jackie."

"Thanks." I plunged ahead. "Also, I have low self-esteem, so we're working on that too."

Mom, quiet till then, asked, "What do you mean by low self-esteem?"

"Well, it's related to being out of touch with my feelings and not having a sense of self-purpose. I don't value myself very much. Everyone seems to see me as this competent, successful person, but inside I feel the opposite. Unworthy and incompetent."

"Maybe that's what's wrong with me," she mused, almost to herself.

Oh my god, I thought. But before I could process her remark further, Dad spoke.

"You *are* smart and competent, Jackie, and we want you to see yourself as such. I'm glad you're seeking help."

His comment warmed me, helping to soothe my jitters.

Checking my notes, I continued. "I also want to feel closer to you two, maybe visit more often." I paused, taking a deep breath. "Perhaps you can tell me what I was like as a little girl. I don't remember many details from childhood."

"You're welcome to come anytime," Dad said. "We'd love to have you."

"Thanks. I'll let you know when I have more definite plans. I love you both."

After hanging up, I thought about Mom's comment but pushed it to the back of my mind. I needed to stay focused on myself.

At Peggy's suggestion I began keeping a journal to explore my suppressed childhood. Several weeks later while journaling one evening, I had a sudden, crystal clear vision of a landscape, sere and brown, like a parched moonscape with no living thing in sight. Intuitively I knew this represented my childhood, bereft of love.

Feeling the same sharp, gut-wrenching pain as I'd had on my birthday, I leaned over, sobbing. I wrapped my arms around my middle, taking in the knowledge I'd grown up believing my parents didn't love me. After a few moments I went to my partner in the next room and asked him to hold me. With his arms around me, supporting me in that moment, I was able to weather the remembering.

For years an endless loop of negative commentary had played in my head: . . .*you dumb idiot . . . you can't do anything right . . . how stupid . . . you are worthless . . .* and on and on. They were my mother's words, hurled at me during her rages, augmented by my childhood shame and guilt at seeming to never get anything right. The moonscape vision was so powerful that over the next several days it subdued the critic in my head. I wrote in my journal: "Stop the negativity, Jackie. Start loving yourself. You need to fill the deficit inside."

At my next session with Peggy, I described the vision, reaching for a tissue from the box beside me as it flashed again before my eyes. Peggy scribbled some quick notes on the legal pad in her lap and leaned forward, her blue eyes radiating kindness.

"You are much stronger than you realize, Jackie. Here's what I want you to do. In your journal, make a list of your strengths. Keep that list nearby and read it periodically throughout the day. Add to it; think about how these strengths manifest in your everyday life." She smiled. "You may be surprised."

That night I did as she suggested, and the revelation heartened me: honesty, loyalty, a strong sense of values, global awareness, a belief in equality and fairness, a sense of adventure, a desire to contribute to society. Years of the endless commentary in my head had blocked my awareness of these attributes. The compilation, though, was a pedantic exercise. Recognizing these qualities was important to building confidence and esteem, but it would take longer to own them, to understand I embodied them. However, my fierce intent to make changes and Peggy's advice to stop listening to that inner critic had crushed the negative self-talk.

Over time I came to understand Mom's abusive outbursts had repressed my child's spirit—the natural spontaneity, imagination, and joy children usually have. Dad's sunny nature had made up for her words in part, but he too had struggled with her temper. He too had guarded his feelings. Neither of them had modeled a healthy way of expressing emotion. Equally important, neither had nurtured in me the ability to trust myself or to be self-reliant.

Well into midlife now, I remained trapped in my childhood fears, unsure of my ability to love anyone other than my children. As part of my environmental work, I had testified in state and congressional hearings on such topics as endangered species and acid rain. I could speak passionately to political power but couldn't find my voice with my own mother. Her put-downs, of anyone, took me back to a time when I had no sense of control.

To connect with who I was and my core strengths, I had to open emotionally and allow myself to be vulnerable. And I needed to be more proactive with my parents to bridge the gulf between us. Later, on my first visit to see them since my birthday, Dad met me at the door with twinkling eyes and a broad smile. He wrapped his arms around me in a warm, loving embrace. During my several days there, we took long walks while Mom was at work, she having longer hours than he at that point. I shared what I was learning, and Dad opened up as well, offering more of himself. His eagerness told me he'd been waiting a long time for such personal sharing. I was astonished at the more intimate side he revealed. A deeper bond developed between us, sustaining me through the tough times that followed. Mom remained uptight and closed on that trip, but subsequent visits yielded revelations.

My next time in Pittsburgh, Dad was in the kitchen one evening cleaning up after dinner while Mom and I sat chatting in the living room.

"What was I like as a child, Mom?"

She turned and called out, "Johnny, Jackie wants to know what she was like as a child."

He came into the living room, drying his hands with a towel, and sat down in his easy chair. To my shock she looked to him to speak. What was this about? She didn't usually defer to him.

"Where to start?" He passed his hand over his bald head and smiled at me. "You were a bubbly child but a bit fastidious. You didn't like to play in the mud or catch frogs or rescue dragonflies from spiderwebs like Marilyn. But you had a mind of your own and spoke up for yourself."

Before I could contemplate this latter comment, he went into storytelling mode.

"The year we lived in Rochester, you were three. You had a new blue winter coat that you loved dearly. Remember, Clinky?"

She nodded as he continued.

"We didn't realize you were so attached to this coat. Mom tried to put your old coat on you one day. You became upset— had a doozy of a tantrum—then ran to the closet and pulled on the sleeve of the new coat. Once you had it on, you patted the sleeve and made purring noises."

I didn't remember the blue coat, and Dad was on to another story. As he talked, a photo from China of me at age two came to mind. He had fixed a seat on the handlebars of his bicycle, just as he had done for Marilyn, and we were going for a ride. Then a memory surfaced of me, no more than five, standing on a stool in the bathroom watching him shave. Talking funny and joking as usual, he had dabbed a bit of shaving lather on the tip of my nose. As I took in the loving memories, Dad continued with his tales. I realized he had played a much larger role in our upbringing than I'd known, far more than most fathers then and perhaps a lot more than Mom, given her limited patience.

On another visit Mom and I were having afternoon coffee at the dining room table, with photos from our family travels to South Carolina spread out before us. Looking at pictures often made it easier to engage Mom in personal conversation. I picked up a photo of Granddaddy looking his usual sour self. He often teased us kids in his cruel, creepy way.

"Could Granddaddy ever be kind? That's not how I remember him."

"Yes, he could be kind, but he was also strict. I remember when he spanked me with a board that had a nail in it."

It was hard not to flinch, and I could almost feel a stinging pain. Her face was blank as she said this, her voice expressionless. Then she put her hand to her head and refused to say another word, appearing fragile and haggard.

I was dumbfounded. I'd had no inkling she had suffered physical abuse, but I believed her. My heart went out to my mother. Her revelation was so unexpected, though, I couldn't think what to say or do in that moment, not even to give her a hug. I've always regretted my lack of response. The impenetrable wall hiding her emotions cracked a bit that day, but I was unable to engage her ever again on the subject. But now I understood Mom to be a victim.

As my sessions with Peggy continued, I sought to reclaim memories to help reframe the story of my childhood. Could a specific experience in my early years have caused me to shut down? Had I blocked out episodes of physical violence? In the end I remembered only verbal abuse. Even several sessions of hypnotherapy shed no new light, although I gained a visceral sense of feeling very alone in my family. I decided Mom must have kept herself in check enough to stop short of anything physical other than occasionally grabbing an arm or that shove of Dad at the end of our drive from South Carolina.

With Peggy's help, I remembered the impact my mother's tirades had on me as a child. When she spewed harsh words on me, bitterness and belittlement swirled around me, sucking the oxygen out of the room. Unable to bear the guilt and humiliation that hung in the air after these episodes, I shut down inside. I took in the presumption that I was unlovable—why else would my mother say such things? Unable to bear the pain, I detached emotionally for self-preservation. In doing so, had I blocked the normal avenues for developing a sense of self?

At the same time, I had the courage to keep a place inside where I gave silent voice to my reactions at Mom's angry tirades: this isn't right; this isn't fair. This voice of authenticity gained its strength from lessons I'd absorbed from my father, embedded in his stories and his example of treating every single person he met with compassion and kindness. The moral principles he fostered provided an inner rudder that enabled me to unconditionally love my children and stop the cycle of abuse.

Accepting the truth of my childhood was the first step in growth and healing. As a parent I'd made sure my children knew they were loved. What my parenting had lacked was the openness I now sought in relationships. I began sharing with John and Steph all that had happened since my drive to Jean's and what I was learning from counseling as I put into practice my newfound desire for more honesty and intimacy with those I love.

 Chapter 12

Dad's phone call caught me at my desk preparing to leave the next day for a business trip.

"Mom's in the hospital," he said with a note of concern. "She fell and broke her hip."

"Oh no! How's she doing?" I'd worried about this. Mom had been living with osteoporosis for more than ten years. In women of her generation, a broken hip often led to deteriorating health.

"She's due for surgery first thing tomorrow to have her hip pinned."

A chill seeped into my shoulders as he told me the story. They'd been shopping at the neighborhood grocery store and rounded the end of an aisle just as a freestanding stack of extra-large dog-food bags began to slip. Mom couldn't get out of the way fast enough, and the bags had slammed her to the floor.

"How horrible! Should I cancel my trip and come down?"

"No, no, everything's under control. I'll call you after the operation."

I hung up and looked out at the woods bordering my back-yard, my trip forgotten for the moment. Mom was still working in 1993 although she was eighty-five. She didn't look her age. Her hair had remained a natural ash blond except for graying at the temples. Would she bounce back from a broken hip? Work was everything to her—what if she was unable to continue?

Both my parents were in reasonably good health, but that could change in an instant. Though their minds were sharp, I'd noticed their physical decline in the past several years. Both had shrunk in stature, Mom down to five foot four and Dad probably five foot five. They fixed nutritious meals. Despite weighing only a hundred pounds, Mom was irrationally concerned about her weight and ate like a bird. Her evening snack was ten shelled peanuts, counted out as if they were medicine and eaten one by one. They walked the mile to work and back, still at a comparatively brisk pace. Dad was spry, and while his eyes had begun to fail, he still diagnosed skin ailments at the student health center with the aid of a pocket magnifier.

Since Mom worked more hours than Dad, he now did much of the housework. On my more frequent visits I'd noticed dust on the bookshelves and grime in the corners of the bathroom. He didn't keep things up to Mom's standards, yet another source of friction. The kitchen had become his refuge. He often turned his hearing aid down so he couldn't hear her carping as he puttered around fixing meals, which only upset her more. I wondered how Dad would cope with Mom's recuperation. She was sure to be prickly when she came home from the hospital. Even though she was just skin and bones, he would have difficulty providing care if it required moving or lifting.

I called Mom that evening to let her know I was thinking of her. She was a little groggy from pain medication, so our visit was short. The next day I called Dad and found the surgery had gone well. He said a colleague of Mom's had found a solution to her postsurgical care. Everyone in the pediatric cardiology division was fond of Dad, so they too must have wondered how he would manage. Ellyn, the division's social worker, had contacted a home care aide whose now-adult daughter had been a regular patient as a baby in the cardiology outpatient clinic when Mom had been clinic director. The aide, Jeri, was happy to care for Dr. Cora, as she credited Mom with saving her daughter's life.

Dad continued with Jeri's story. Her daughter had been a "blue baby," born with a serious congenital heart defect called "transposition of the great arteries."[1] When the baby was a year old and apparently doing well, Mom and another doctor had disagreed over whether to order an imaging test on the baby's heart. The other doctor had argued the test seemed unnecessary. Mom had insisted, "With this genetic defect, shouldn't we find out what's going on and *why* she seems to be doing so well?" The test was done and showed the baby's malformed heart was nearing its limited capacity. She needed surgery soon or she would die. The operation, one of the earliest surgical corrections for this set of malformations, had been successful, and Jeri's daughter was then a grown woman in her twenties.

As Dad told this story, something inside me softened. I knew my mother was a gifted physician, but the difficulties of our relationship often blocked the respect and pride I felt for her deep down. The arrangement with Jeri seemed good for both Mom and Dad.

I flew to Pittsburgh several weeks later to meet Jeri and see how Mom was doing and was relieved at what I found. Mom had returned home determined to regain her strength and resume work. Jeri had a lively personality that matched her red hair and a friendly conversational manner. Her compassion and gentle encouragement were what my mother needed to recover fully. Mom was uncharacteristically even-tempered with Jeri and seemed to appreciate her help, which soon included cleaning the apartment and cooking. Jeri, who had never known her biological father, also spent time with Dad and quickly came to love him like a father.

Mom's prickliness was returning when I visited six weeks later, a sure sign she was feeling better. In a conversation with her, I began a question with "Mom, when you broke your hip—"

She interrupted, bristling. "I didn't break my hip; Foodland broke my hip!"

It was true. Foodland was at fault for improperly stacking the dog-food bags. The wife of one of Mom's hospital colleagues was an attorney and had begun drawing up a claim against the store. Mom eventually won a modest settlement enabling her to employ Jeri on a permanent basis, something they couldn't have afforded otherwise.

Thanks to Jeri's care, Mom recovered fully and returned to her part-time work schedule. Jeri, her husband Joe, and their children became part of our family. Jeri and Joe were loving, generous people and were open with their feelings—at times volatile with each other but never with my parents. They both had an intuitive knowledge of medical care gained from decades of dealing with hospitals over their daughter's health issues. When Joe's job permitted, he came to the apartment with Jeri. He and Dad would sit for hours and talk. Dad told stories of China, and they discussed religion and morality and debated the issues of the day. Dad had grown up with such bantering and loved it, but our family didn't banter. Joe helped fill this void in Dad's life.

Mom started back to work around the time I'd decided to expand my visits to four or five days rather than a weekend. A longer visit allowed me to get beyond superficial conversation and dig deeper into the subject matter I was seeking: to understand how we had functioned as a family. I wanted to redefine our relationship and shore up my sense of self when we were together. I knew spending more time would be challenging, but I made a commitment to myself to push through any emotional pain rather than giving in to a desire to escape—my default in confrontations with Mom.

Early in each visit Mom and I would have the same conversation.

"Jackie, what would you like to do while you're here? You could come with me to the hospital one day. The Carnegie Museum is an easy walk, and you could use our membership card. Let's go out to dinner too."

"You don't have to entertain me, Mom. I'm family," I would say. "I'm here to visit with you two and help out however I can."

I was sincere in this, but the idea of going to the hospital with her always put me on edge. It seemed a reminder I had disappointed her by not pursuing medicine. That she seemed incurious about my own job reinforced my impression. I often brought something to show my parents, a newsletter or a project report I had written. She didn't ask questions, and I never saw her reading what I had brought. But she always went on and on about my brother and what he was doing. I remarked about this once to Jeri, who reacted with genuine surprise.

"She's always talking about you and your work. She's very proud of you."

"Well, she has a strange way of showing it," I muttered.

Only later did I realize I probably misinterpreted Mom's intention in asking me to visit the hospital. She had difficulty connecting with family members and expressing her feelings. Inviting me to accompany her may have been an attempt to share herself. Although I was trying to be more open, I too struggled to move beyond the emotional barriers of the past.

On another visit, while Mom was at the hospital, I gained a critical piece of insight from Dad. Throughout our years in Philippi, Mom had endured gender harassment by one of the clinic surgeons. We had shared our first house with his family, they renting the upstairs and we the downstairs. I don't recall our families ever getting together socially, but I remember him as negative and sarcastic. Dad's explanation made sense.

Later, in transcribing the China letters, I realized Mom hadn't encountered gender bias in China. The contributions of women were highly valued in the mission field—they were teachers, nurses, physicians. When my parents went to China in 1930, women comprised more than half of the missionary contingent. My mother's medical-school class was made up of six women and three men, and there were several women doctors on the medical faculty of West China Union University—ratios unheard of in the United States at the time.

Because of the harassment she experienced in Philippi, Mom left the clinic and took a residency in pediatrics at the University of Pittsburgh. She returned to Philippi and established a solo practice, but the discrimination continued in the hospital setting. After a year she closed her practice and returned to Pittsburgh for a fellowship in pediatric cardiology. When she was asked to join the newly established pediatric cardiology division as the second of two doctors, she moved permanently to Pittsburgh. Dad followed several years later.

I was glad Dad had shared this with me, as I better understood the reasons behind Mom's career moves. The harassment she experienced also explained her obvious unhappiness in the photos from our family road trips.

Spending more time with my parents helped me realize their relationship was far more complex than I had thought. Now when visiting I noticed the many subtle ways Dad showed love to Mom. He cooked her favorite dishes and gave her tidbits such as the best cut from the roast. On occasions he made things for her. One Valentine's Day he used a red marker to draw a heart-shaped rendition of the Chinese character for "love." She kept the drawing and everything else he made for her. When Dad and I took walks on my visits, he often vented about Mom's latest rant. Before we returned to the apartment, though, he never failed to say, "But she's a really good woman." He saw her good qualities when I couldn't.

One unanticipated effect of opening to my emotions was I now felt Mom's frequent carping viscerally, as a churning in my gut. Even with Dad as the usual target, my body instantly recalled the physical unease from childhood. When he finally lost his temper and the back-and-forth picking began, I was no longer able to bury my reaction like I had as a child. I wanted to yell "Stop it!" but couldn't find my voice.

Then came a turning point. I wrote in my journal on one visit: "I need to say something the next time she starts being verbally abusive. I will no longer subject myself to it. It is too painful. I can't change them, but I can make the situation less traumatic for me."

The next day after lunch, I sensed Mom building up to another outburst. When it came, out of habit I gave in to the familiar impulse to take a walk, to escape. I opened the apartment door and started down the steps, then stopped. *No*, I thought, *I can't keep doing this.* I reversed course and walked back up the steps and opened the apartment door. Jeri gently cornered me in the living room. She'd been in the kitchen and heard the fracas.

She spoke quietly. "It's not my place to get involved, Jackie, but you have to speak up."

"You're right, Jeri." My hands trembled. "But it's really tough for me."

She took my hands in hers and gave them a squeeze. "I know, but you have to start somewhere, honey."

I took a deep breath and went to my parents in the dining area. My abrupt departure and quick return had silenced them. They looked up as I walked to the table where they still sat.

"Mom and Dad, I love you both. You each have many wonderful qualities. But so often you direct those qualities toward others and not to each other." My voice quavered. "It tears me apart when you go at each other. I've internalized the hurt ever since childhood. I can't do that anymore." I blinked back tears.

They were both silent. Dad watched me intently and Mom looked down at her hands, her knuckles white from clutching.

"I must start taking care of myself and speak out when I feel this way." Hearing strength in my voice, I continued. "Please treat each other with the kindness you show to others."

Dad came to me then and put his arms around me. "I'm so sorry."

Mom said nothing and sat stony-faced at the table. Apologies were not in her vocabulary. But my words and Dad's response had changed the atmosphere and defused the anger.

The very next day Mom started in on Dad again. "You always turn off your hearing aid so you can ignore me."

They were in the living room, Dad reading the newspaper and Mom knitting. I was in the kitchen putting dishes in the dishwasher. I shut the dishwasher and joined them in the living room, not at all sure what I was going to say. But I plunged in anyway.

"We need to talk." The confidence in my voice surprised me. "You two aren't alone in trying to cope with deafness and other aspects of aging."

Once I began, I realized even though I couldn't fix their problems, I had a responsibility to help them problem solve. I approached the subject matter-of-factly and didn't allow it to degenerate into finger pointing. Dad seemed happy to have something positive to grab on to.

His hands shook as he said, "I turn my hearing aid down because it just becomes too much sometimes." He looked at Mom. "Can't we be kinder to each other?"

My heart went out to him. He'd been fighting these battles

for so long. But Mom, still silent, stood and walked back to their bedroom. *Huh,* I thought. *Now she's the one escaping.* I turned to Dad and gave him a hug.

"Thanks for trying," he said, his shoulders slumping.

That night, lying on the hide-a-bed in the living room, I reflected on the day's events. I'd learned a valuable lesson: You don't always have to know the exact words. Stay open, tune in to your feelings, and the words will come. Several years earlier, after our drive up from South Carolina, Dad had asked me to encourage Mom to begin marriage counseling with him. I hadn't been able to help then. Finding my voice now was empowering.

Lying there in the dark, I realized that growing up I had learned to evade Mom's temper by being good and avoiding the spotlight. I'd tried always to be pleasant and smile a lot, to be agreeable, and to avoid ever speaking my mind. I had disavowed my feelings to the extent I'd become invisible to myself and didn't know who I was or what I wanted. This was the basis of my low self-esteem. But now, I didn't want to be that person. I wanted to own my feelings and express my thoughts. Turning the lamp on, I picked up my journal and wrote for a while.

On a visit several months later, Mom directed her rage at me. My parents had been discussing a particularly vexing issue with their finances. I offered several possible options, and Mom exploded.

"I'm sick and tired of how you always think you can solve every last little problem. It's not as if you're some expert."

I jumped up from the table and ran to the bathroom in tears. Sitting on the edge of the tub, I had a good cry and indulged in a few swear words. Then I took a deep breath. *Well, kiddo, you didn't vacate the scene, just escaped momentarily to the bathroom. Progress, I guess.* Steeling myself, I returned to the dining area, where Mom sat mute and sullen, examining her fingers, the muscles in her jaw knotted. Dad fiddled at the small desk just inside the kitchen.

I sat and looked directly at my mother. "I want you to know, Mom, no matter what you say or do, it's not going to drive me away. I love you both." I turned to include Dad. "I'll always be here for you and Dad."

Never had I spoken up after an outburst directed at me. I couldn't voice what I longed to say—*you have hurt me deeply.* But it was a giant step toward reclaiming myself.

Dad, ever the peacemaker, came to me. I stood and he put his arm around my waist and turned to Mom. "I think Jackie deserves a response from you."

After a moment, her face grim, she stood and came over to us. Dad put his arm around her on one side and I did the same on the other, acutely aware of her anorexic boniness. She stood silent, rigid and tense, eyes downcast, still seething. In no way a three-way embrace, it nevertheless broke the tension. After an awkward minute when she didn't respond in kind, I dropped my arm and Dad did too. The episode deepened my bond with Dad and helped me feel stronger emotionally. As for Mom, I hoped with time she might open up.

After that she and I continued to clash on my visits, though not always in a manner that sparked her temper. One day they decided to visit a longtime family friend of Dad's who lived in the Baptist Home, an eldercare facility across Pittsburgh. I hadn't ridden with Mom driving since our South Carolina trip three years before. She'd had cataract surgery in both eyes and thought her good vision meant she could drive just fine. I was dismayed at how her skills had deteriorated. She had trouble turning to look over her shoulder, seldom used her side mirrors, and often pulled out in front of other cars. She tailgated and was slow to brake. An incident with another driver sparked her temper, and she honked the horn repeatedly. Several close calls sent my heart into my throat.

I was relieved to reach the Baptist Home. Upon entering the building, a sharp antiseptic smell and the sterile institutional feel made me forget the experience in the car. We spent an hour visiting Dad's friend, who was nearing one hundred although her mind was still sharp. She shared stories of Dad's mother, the grandmother I hadn't known. I loved the image she painted in one tale when she was sixteen and sat with my grandmother in the back of the church, the two giggling together like schoolgirls during my grandfather's sermon. Maybe Dad got his playful sense of humor from his mother.

As we left the building, I thought again about the drive there. I valued my life too much to ride as a passenger with Mom. She was an accident waiting to happen.

"Can I drive back to the apartment, Mom?"

"No, thanks, I'll do it," she said.

"I insist, Mom. I can get us back. I know the way now."

She relented and handed me the keys. On the way back, thinking about her driving, I realized she shouldn't be behind the wheel at all. Later that day, as Jeri was leaving, I followed her to the stairwell.

"How often does Mom drive these days?"

"Not much. They usually walk to the hospital. When they need to go farther, Joe or I usually take them."

"She's a danger to other drivers and shouldn't be driving at all. Can we agree to an arrangement whereby you and Joe will be available so she doesn't ever have to drive?"

Jeri agreed and, as far as I know, Mom never got behind the wheel again. But she realized what had happened and connected it with my "meddling," a new focus for her grumbling. She never missed a chance to bark, "Jackie took my car keys away from me."

During these longer visits with my parents, I was increasingly comfortable with speaking up for myself and able to withstand any impulse to flee from confrontation. My inner reactions—the gnawing in my stomach, the knee-jerk expectation of shaming words—were still there, but like the fear symptoms in my presentations on Alaska, they diminished over time. In my now-less-frequent sessions with Peggy, we celebrated my growing self-confidence.

 Chapter 13

After spending most of autumn of 1994 traveling in Europe, I visited my parents the last weekend in November and found Dad's health had slipped. Nearing ninety-one, he had recently given up working after several ministrokes, or TIAs. At first glance he seemed the same old Dad, full of humor and happy to see me. But over the several days of my visit I saw disturbing changes. He was now a bit unsteady on our walks and complained of a weakness in one leg. On Saturday he steered me through the mostly empty parking lot of a Catholic church near their apartment.

"This is one of my shortcuts," he said.

"Dad, when you take this shortcut, do you look for cars before stepping out?" I hadn't noticed him looking that day.

"Oh, I always look both ways."

I wasn't convinced.

On Sunday I accompanied him to the adult discussion that preceded the main Sunday service at the Baptist church near the university. He had led this class for years and attended regularly. The group still followed the format Dad had initiated—a leader-moderated discussion on the ethical implications of two current issues. Several dozen people gathered that morning. On the first topic, prayer in public schools, the dialogue was lively and wide-ranging. Dad didn't participate, but I didn't give much thought to it. After twenty minutes the leader summarized the points made and turned to Dad.

"John, do you have anything to add before we move on to the next topic?"

"No, I haven't really made my mind up yet."

I looked at him, stunned. No opinion on prayer in schools? He'd always been a staunch believer in separation of church and state. I could do little more than note this as the group had jumped into the second topic, the "Contract with America," written by then house speaker Newt Gingrich. Another vigorous discussion ensued, but Dad said nothing. A heaviness gripped my chest. He'd never shied away from political issues. He delighted in such give-and-take.

The next day I questioned Jeri, and she confirmed he hadn't been as mentally sharp since the TIAs. Later I watched him open the mail. He took an inordinate amount of time going through the letters, reading the junk mail as carefully as the first-class letters. A sadness settled over me.

Leaving Pittsburgh, I flew on to Missoula, where Steph was living. I'd loaned her my car while I was away. Our plan was to drive east in mid-December, pick up John in Madison, then stop again in Pittsburgh before heading to New England for the Christmas holidays.

Jeri called me while I was still in Montana.

"Dad just had a stroke. How soon can you get here?"

I pulled out a kitchen chair and sat, feeling as if a rock had landed in my stomach. "Oh, Jeri, I knew something was wrong."

"I was there when it happened," she said. "I had him in the emergency room within an hour, and he's with the doctor right now."

"Thank god you were there." I pressed a palm to my head. "How is he?"

"No paralysis, but his speech is affected, and he's confused."

Calculating quickly, I said, "I think we can get there in three days, four at the most, depending on how ready John is. How's Mom holding up?"

"It's hard for her. She's with Dad right now. I'll have her call when we're back home."

After hanging up, I sat a few moments, overwhelmed by sadness. I depended so much on Jeri to hold my parents' lives together. Sometime in the past year she had begun calling my parents Mom and Dad. She had asked first, saying she felt closer to them than to her biological mother, who had been in and out of her life for long stretches. Dad was delighted, and Mom didn't object. She appreciated Jeri and didn't often get cross with her. She even encouraged Jeri to get her nursing-assistant certification.

Steph and I hurried our preparations and left early the next day. We stopped for John and continued driving east. Shortly after leaving Madison, Dad had a second stroke. Again Jeri had him in the care of a physician within an hour.

When we arrived at my parents' apartment, chaos reigned. Speech, occupational, and physical therapists came to the apartment daily. It was heartbreaking to see Dad, always so articulate, struggle for words and have them come out garbled. Mom was tense and more short-fused than usual. Jeri now bore the brunt of Mom's temper but somehow managed to maintain her calm and help Dad get through his day. My brother Don often came for the night. If Dad woke, at times he would wander around the apartment, so someone had to watch out for him. John, Steph, and I stayed only two days as Tom was expecting them in New Hampshire. Before leaving, I assured Mom and Jeri I would be back after the holidays to help out.

I'd resigned my job before traveling in Europe and had planned to begin a job search upon returning. But Dad's strokes changed everything—having no job was a blessing. The best thing, the right thing for me then, was to be there to help my parents in this stage of their lives.

In the new year I drove to Pittsburgh and stayed ten days. Dad had made some progress with his speech and understood most of what we said but continued to have trouble retrieving words. His confusion remained in other aspects too. I asked him to set the table for dinner one evening. He opened the cloth napkins and placed them diamond-shaped under the plates.

"Thanks, Dad," I said, stifling tears. "It looks very nice." I gave him a hug, my heart breaking.

Mom had difficulty coping. Her carefully ordered world, her marriage of sixty-four years had been upended. She had kept her emotions, save anger, in check for so long she was unable to react with compassion and became more rigid and controlling. She responded to Dad's confusion in the kitchen by adamantly excluding him from helping with meals.

"He's used to being in the kitchen, Mom," I said at one point. "He'd like to help. Why not let him fill the dishwasher?"

She wouldn't hear of it. "I'm afraid he'll cut himself with a knife."

I turned away with a shake of my head, swallowing a retort. I heard the concern in her words yet knew the risk was small compared to what Dad would gain by helping. I didn't push my point, though, fearing it would worsen the situation for everyone. Later, I wished that rather than stifling my words, I'd worked with her to find something he could do.

Jeri came daily, going home to her family at dinnertime. Don had hired night-duty health aides for the times he couldn't be there, but Mom slept little with a stranger in the study, which increased her crankiness. During my stay Don and I shared night duty so Mom could sleep. Dad was able to handle a good part of his personal care, but someone had to be there in case he had trouble with buttons or brushing his teeth or getting ready for bed. I found myself relating in new ways with my father, helping him with his hearing aids and dentures.

My heart ached to see him struggle in telling a story or confuse dreams with reality. Yet his quickness and sense of humor still surfaced at times. I vowed to help him keep his dignity and to treat him with love and kindness, which Mom seemed unable to give no matter what she felt inside.

On my visit a month later he seemed more settled and less confused at night. The home therapy covered by Medicare was ending, however, and we were especially concerned about losing the speech therapy. The stimulation provided by the therapists' visits also helped Dad's recovery, as he was accustomed to interacting with many different people in a normal day. Before I returned home, Mom raised the option of a limited stay at the Baptist Home for rehabilitation. Dad could get more speech and other therapy and have additional daily interaction with people. He was open to the idea.

In March I accompanied Dad, Mom, and Jeri to Dad's appointment with Dr. G., his geriatrician. Dr. G. headed geriatric education at the university medical center and was also medical director of the affiliated nursing home. As Mom presented her idea of a short rehab period at the Baptist Home, Dr. G. watched Dad, then pulled her chair up close to him so she could look directly into his eyes.

"Dr. John, do you understand what Dr. Cora is proposing? Are you absolutely certain you want to do this?" She knew Dad's mental faculties were still largely intact, albeit hindered by his speech difficulties and periodic confusion.

He struggled to find the words. "Yes, I . . . want to get better . . . get speech therapy. Maybe . . . help out . . . talk to others . . . in Baptist Home. Maybe help . . . treat skin conditions." This last idea—Dad's, not ours—spoke to his thinking of others even as he struggled to cope with his own situation.

This was my family's first direct experience with a nursing home. My parents had been predisposed to favor the Baptist Home because of its church affiliation, and they knew the facility from visits to Dad's family friend. But none of us comprehended the potential consequences of what we were proposing. Dr. G. wasn't familiar with the Baptist Home and had no consulting privileges there. But I've wondered if she had a premonition.

What happened next can only be called tragic.

Dad moved to the Baptist Home in late March for an intended period of four to six weeks. Mom and my brother, who had medical and financial power of attorney for my parents, made the arrangements, and Jeri went with them to help Dad get settled. His single room was on a first-floor wing just inside double doors that were kept closed but not locked. The nurses' station was at the far end of the hallway. After settling Dad and making his room comfortable with familiar things from home, Mom, Don, and Jeri left. Shortly afterward Dad, confused, went looking for them. He walked through the double doors and triggered an alarm. Someone brought him back to his wing where a nurse, without notifying the family, medicated him to prevent wandering. From then on, he remained medicated, although the dosage and the drug may have varied.

No one on the nursing staff had known my father previously. When he entered the Baptist Home, he was aware and alert, despite his periodic confusion and speech difficulties. From the outset the staff saw a candidate for the dementia unit two floors above. They argued for maintaining the medication, saying he wandered into the rooms of other residents on his floor or through the double doors. I thought this in part explainable. In his drug-induced or stroke-caused confusion, the rooms on his floor must have looked like countless hospital rooms he'd entered during six decades of practicing medicine. And walking was a big part of his life. But no matter what we said, no matter how much we questioned the medications in periodic meetings with the "care" team, nothing moved the staff from thinking he belonged in the dementia unit.

Dad received therapy—speech, physical, occupational, music—but his medicated state limited his improvement. Mercedes, the speech therapist, saw his personality in her interactions with him. She worked hard to help him improve. In April I arrived to visit Dad in the middle of a speech session. Mercedes motioned for me to come into the room, and I sat and watched her work. He soon fell asleep.

"This is often the situation," she said, looking at me. "He's too sedated."

I sighed. "I know. It's so frustrating. We can't seem to make headway with that."

"I want him to get better. He's such a sweet gentleman. But to continue working with him, I need to submit reports showing he's making progress." She smiled, her face empathetic. "I can give him the benefit of the doubt but only for so long, no matter how much I want to work with him."

I looked at Dad dozing then turned back to Mercedes. "Does the lack of improvement reflect another TIA? Or the sedation? Or is it a general downslide that can come at his age with lack of stimulation and suddenly becoming sedentary?"

She shrugged. "It's tough to say." Then she stood. "I'm really sorry, Jackie, but I must get to my next client. Hang in there." She gave my shoulder a sympathetic pat and left.

On my monthly visits to Pittsburgh, I drove daily to see Dad. We looked through the family picture book Mercedes had made for him with Jeri's help. Under the photos she had written names and important dates like birthdays and his and Mom's anniversary. I also read his favorite stories from the China letters, including their two summers on Mount Omei and their trip to the eastern rim of Tibet. Our conversations had become fairly simple, no longer including the intellectual discussions Dad had loved. My goal now when I visited was to provide as much stimulation as possible.

Driving to the Baptist Home on a sunny May morning, I decided to take Dad outside. He was napping in his chair when I arrived, and I touched his shoulder gently. His face lit up when he saw me. His smile never failed to warm my heart.

"Hi, Dad." I kissed his forehead. "It's pleasant and sunny outside. Want to go for a walk?"

He nodded, and I helped him get up from his chair. We walked through the double doors and out the front entrance. Benches were scattered along the walkways. I guided him to one with a view of the hills in the distance and helped him get settled.

"It's spring, Dad. See the flowering trees on the hill over there?"

He looked in the direction I'd pointed and smiled, giving me a thumbs up. I smiled back and took his hands in mine.

"You passed your love of nature along to me, Dad." He gave my hand a squeeze. "And mountains. That's another love I share with you and Mom. I wish I could see that valley with the yak and the Minya Konka and the place you and Mom camped. The photos you took are so lovely." He nodded, smiling sweetly, and gave my hand another squeeze.

I continued the chatter, but he didn't talk much. Whenever he tried, it came out garbled. I wondered whether his medication made it too tiring to search for words. At one point he started to doze off, so I walked him around a bit more and took him back to his room. I stayed briefly, but he kept falling asleep. So I kissed his forehead, told him I loved him, and said goodbye.

Driving back to the apartment, I realized this could be Dad's last spring. An acute sense of loss washed over me: loss of his companionship, his joy of life, his caring and compassion, his integrity and quick mind. That night I wrote in my journal: "The world is losing an extraordinary person, and few people beyond family and close friends will take note."

The next day I greeted him as usual with a big hug. Then I sat down, took his hands in mine, and looked into his eyes. "Dad, I love you so much. It's sad this has happened, but I treasure our relationship no matter what."

He squeezed my hands and whispered, "Love you too."

I tried an experiment that day. Wondering whether his nodding off might be boredom, I decided to see whether he could stay awake if I kept him moving around. For an hour we walked: around the grounds outside, the inside common spaces, down the hall of his floor to the nurses' station and back. I kept up a running conversation, mostly one-sided, but my purpose was to keep him awake. We sat down often as he'd lost stamina. Invariably within several minutes he would start to doze, and I would get him up and walk again. Finally I took pity and led him back to his room.

My heart was breaking. I was angry to see my father, who had always found joy in relating to people, now passive and unresponsive. Why didn't the nurses interact with him more? He was still a sweetheart even in this less responsive state, but with all the sedation his playfulness and humor couldn't surface. The drugs promoted the convenience of the nursing staff—less wandering, less trouble—at the expense of having him be present for us. It seemed the staff focused on the minutiae of routines rather than what was best for Dad.

When he'd first entered the Baptist Home, I'd hoped for enough improvement to fly with him to California to visit his brother Merrill one last time. They were so close. My uncle had physical problems and used a sit-down motorized scooter to get around, but his mind was sharp. He wrote weekly, three handwritten pages on a yellow legal pad. Determined to spark Dad's thinking, Uncle Merrill recounted childhood escapades with just enough detail to prick his memory. I didn't know the stories, but Dad did. When I read, "How about two to Glassport?" he burst into laughter. Mom said later this was the first time they had taken the train alone to a nearby town. Another time my uncle listed the names of chickens they had growing up—Biggie, Little Biggie, and No Mark—and Dad chortled. These flashes of humor showed he understood, at least in the moment.

As the weeks went by and Dad slipped more and more, I realized a trip to California was impossible. The medication sapped his energy, and the inactivity had caused his physical condition to decline. Sadly, bringing him home was also impossible. Mom was frantic about the turn of events. Unable to tolerate nighttime aides after Dad's first strokes, she would not have endured the care he now needed in his diminished state.

She seemed to have no emotional outlet for what was happening except for anger. Her need to control encompassed everything related to Dad. She felt wholly responsible for his medical care and became ever more demanding of him. He responded best to kindness and gentle encouragement, but Mom was unable to express these qualities with him. The stress and mental anguish overwhelmed the compassion she must have felt inside.

Whatever progress I'd made with Mom before Dad's strokes had now vanished. She seemed to sit on a hair trigger, and any little thing could set her off. Both Jeri and I could get Dad to respond, and she resented that. She felt the loss of Dad's company in many ways, but her grief emerged only as rancor. Everyone in the family—including Jeri, who was hurting along with the rest of us—felt the sting of her tongue. On my visits it seemed I was walking on eggshells again, just like my childhood. For decades Dad had used humor in part to ease tense situations with Mom. Could she have unconsciously relied on his humor over the years to defuse her acrimony?

In July Mom called to say Dad had had a third, more serious stroke. I was heartsick. I'd harbored some hope he might still recover if we could improve his situation. But that hope now slipped away. Time with Dad had become increasingly precious.

 Chapter 14

I caught the earliest flight to Pittsburgh after Mom's call. On the airplane my thoughts were filled with Dad. I was still upset about his four months at the Baptist Home. I couldn't shake the feeling the staff hadn't been on top of things when this third stroke occurred. I picked up a rental car and was at Mom's apartment by early afternoon. She seemed to have aged a year in the month since I'd seen her. Jeri had lunch ready, and Mom gave me a brief update as we ate.

"This stroke is more serious than the first two," she said with a sigh. "He's weaker, but there's no paralysis."

"I'm glad of that at least," I said. "How much longer will he be in the hospital?"

"Dr. G. wants him to stay to get more speech and physical therapy. I'm meeting with her later this afternoon to decide what to do next." She put her hand to her head. She was silent for a moment, rubbing her forehead, then banged her fist on the table, rattling the plates. "I'll be damned if he's going back to the Baptist Home."

Her fist bang startled me, but I agreed with her. "I'd like to see him, Mom. Are you ready to go over?"

"Just give me a minute," she said, rising unsteadily from the table and walking down the hall to her bedroom.

Mom now used a cane, except rarely in the apartment. A bout of shingles had left her with vertigo, and the constant pain reflected in her lined face, her eyes especially.

I took the dishes into the kitchen, where Jeri was cleaning up. "Thanks for the lunch." I lowered my voice. "How's she holding up?"

"Oh, you know. Keeps it all inside." She shook her head slightly and gave me a wan smile. "She's wound tighter than a drum."

"Are you coming to the hospital too?"

"It's best just you two go," she said. "Mom's been at me a lot lately. I'll drive you to the hospital. When you're ready to leave, call me. I'll stop and see Dad on my way home."

I gave her a hug. "Thanks, Jeri. I appreciate not having to deal with hospital parking."

It turned into a hellish afternoon.

When I walked into Dad's room he gave me a huge grin, which lifted my spirits some. He was not sedated for the first time in four months, so his personality shone. While I visited with him, Mom went to physical therapy for a firsthand account of his progress. I pitied the physical therapists. Mom seemed balanced on a razor's edge between grief and fury, taking on Dad's well-being, unbidden, on her shoulders. All the emotions she must have felt inside at this turn of events fed the wrath that was her only outlet.

After Mom returned, we didn't stay with Dad much longer. She didn't want to be late for the meeting with Dr. G., which was to take place in Mom's office. Since we were twenty minutes early, we sat down with Ellyn, the social worker in pediatric cardiology and Mom's friend. As we talked about the situation and options for Dad, Mom's agitation grew. She bent over in anguish, her elbows on her knees and her head propped in her hands. I knew she was hurting, so I crouched down next to her, touched her arm, and began sharing my thoughts on what we could do.

Lifting her head, she interrupted me, her hands shaking slightly and her blue eyes icy cold—*Granddaddy's eyes*, I thought with a start.

"What makes you think you know anything about this? You always have the answers, don't you? Well, I don't want to hear it. You know nothing. This is a medical decision, and you don't have the experience or the knowledge. Why don't you just go home."

A sharp pain pierced my gut like I'd been stabbed. I was used to her verbal abuse, but what cut most was the contempt in her voice and that she said this in front of Ellyn. A flush of guilt and humiliation spread up my face, and I stayed crouched for a moment to get control of my swirling emotions. How dare she speak to me like that. Did she want to alienate every family member? Did she want to be a bitter old woman, alone for the rest of her life? I didn't trust myself to speak, fearing the anger rising inside. Raging back at her, no matter how I felt, wouldn't have helped. Someone had to be the adult here.

Finally, I got up and sat back down in my chair. I glanced at Ellyn. She looked at me with sympathy in her eyes but focused on comforting Mom.

I remember little of the meeting with Dr. G. other than we agreed Dad was not returning to the Baptist Home. Dr. G. said she would admit him to Canterbury Place, the nursing home she directed. Besides that, the rest of the afternoon was a blur.

My mind kept going over and over the same thoughts: *Okay, I guess I must accept that I don't have a mother. All I have is the angry old woman who birthed me. All along I've been thinking if I deal with Mom in the "right" way—whatever that is—I can get through to her, and we can have a relationship of sorts. I want to feel love for my mother, but she makes it damned difficult. Am*

I kidding myself? Is she even capable of accepting love from me or anyone? If I'd had my car with me, I might have driven home. But that would have been escaping, and I was done with that. Besides, I wanted to spend time with Dad. I don't remember getting back to the apartment, but Jeri must have come for us.

Dinner that evening was a subdued affair. Mom acted as if nothing had happened, and I wasn't interested in conversing. Later, I sat with my journal, mulling over the day while she occupied herself in her bedroom. As always, the journaling clarified things. It seemed a veil had dropped from my eyes. I could not change my mother. I would be there for her and for Dad, but I had to put aside any hope she would respond in the way I yearned for. I had to guard my fragile, budding sense of self and cultivate my own happiness, with or without my mother's love.

That night, lying on the living room hide-a-bed after turning out the light, I resolved to let her know how much she had hurt me. I knew this was critical to my self-growth. I could not let her words slide off my back without a response. Not this time. For a while longer, I struggled with what to say, finally falling asleep with Peggy's words from our last session in my head: "Speak your truth."

The next morning I awoke determined to stand up for myself. While eating breakfast, Mom and I made the usual small talk about the day's schedule and the weather. She could act so normal when it was only small talk.

I drained my cup of coffee and sat up straight. Ignoring the clenching in my stomach, I gathered my courage. "You know, Mom, your words yesterday hurt me deeply."

She looked at me sharply, eyes narrowed, defenses up. "What do you mean?"

"What you said yesterday at the hospital while we were waiting for Dr. G. I was trying to help you think about options for Dad."

"What did I say?" She sounded puzzled.

I repeated what she had said word for word, sadness slicing through my stomach as I replayed the moment.

"I didn't say that," she bristled, her eyes hardening and her face flushing.

"Mom, you did."

A look of horror flitted across her face as she said in a tone less cutting, "I couldn't have said that."

"But you did."

She seemed to crumple, her eyes suddenly pooling. When she spoke, her tone had softened and I could hear sadness.

"But that's not what's in my heart."

Like a balloon deflating, the hurt and anger left me, replaced by the somber realization that she did not know what came out of her mouth in those out-of-control moments. Her rage, always so close to the surface, would burst forth whenever she lost control over the resentment filling her, the resentment from Granddaddy's abuse and domination and maybe even the discrimination she had faced as a woman doctor.

I went to her, my heart aching, and put my arms around her. "I love you, Mom."

She said nothing but did embrace me, sort of. I realized I'd been able to tell her how her words had hurt me, something she'd never been able to do with Granddaddy. Tenderness slipped into my heart as I gently hugged her closer. She relaxed a little, accepting my hug in a way she hadn't before.

After Dad's third stroke, I accepted he would never come home. Dr. G. assured us they would not sedate him without a medical reason to do so. If his first strokes and four months of Baptist Home sedation had affected his ability to make decisions, the third stroke extinguished all initiative. He had to be prompted to do everything short of using the bathroom. My father was now totally dependent on skilled care.

He never walked on his own again. The months of lethargy and inactivity had diminished the conditioning built over a lifetime. Now, if prompted, he went up and down the hall with a walker, a nurse or aide alongside to nudge him along and hang on to the back of his pants so he wouldn't fall. I could not watch—it hurt too much. Perhaps he felt humiliated too, or at least discouraged, as he soon was in a wheelchair all the time, joining the half circle of people also in wheelchairs who gathered daily across from the nurses' station.

Dr. G. came to see him often, and I trusted her to do what was best. As promised they never sedated him, and we had more freedom in visiting than at the Baptist Home. Still, it was a nursing home, and I had to steel myself every time I entered. I learned to accept whatever I found. Although I continued to hope Dad would improve, I acknowledged the futility of his situation, something Mom refused to accept.

At some point I called Ellyn to talk with her about Mom and the stress she was under with all that had happened to Dad.

"She feels like Dad's care is wholly her responsibility," I said. "She puts way more on her shoulders than is appropriate. The tension and stress just emanate from her when we talk."

"I know," she said kindly. "Cora has high standards, and she's the toughest on herself."

"But there's a limit to what one person can take. I'm concerned about her."

Ellyn was quiet for a moment. "Jackie, you are so like your father."

Her comparison confounded me. What came to mind immediately was Mom's comment I'd heard since childhood, that I took after Mom's family while my siblings were like Dad. I had spent so much emotional energy trying not to be like my mother. At no time had anyone said I was like my father.

I finally found my voice. "Ellyn, that's the nicest thing you could have said to me."

On my monthly visits in this new phase, Dad was fairly alert. Because of his passivity we now related mostly by just being together. Sometimes he rallied, and we had a conversation of sorts, but not often. I always brought the folder of Uncle Merrill's letters, the binders with the Tibet and China stories, or the most recent notes from my children. He listened to the stories or letters again and again and laughed or smiled as if it were the first time he'd heard them. I never knew if he just enjoyed them that much or if it was short-term memory loss. In any event, I would take my cue from whatever seemed to spark his interest and go from there.

He'd brighten and smile when he saw me, and I'd wheel him to a more private place to visit. We often ended up in the cafeteria eating ice cream, which was available anytime. Jeri on her daily visits also made sure he had ice cream. I went alone to see him when possible to spread out family visits, as they were the exception to his dull routine. But also, he shut down if Mom came along. She prodded him to be sharper, more engaged than he wanted or could be.

Although at times he was in his own world, I had many wonderful moments with him. I told him regularly how much he meant to me, how I treasured our time together and appreciated the life lessons he'd given me. He showed pleasure by closing his eyes and smiling beatifically. We communicated now with facial expressions and touching as much as words. His personality still shone through the stroke-induced fog if you looked for it. Jeri understood this. She and I talked a lot, becoming quite close. Marilyn and I now called her our adopted sister.

On a visit the following winter, Dad was among the wheelchair group when I arrived. He seemed more alert than usual and in good spirits.

"Hi, Dad," I said, putting the folders I'd brought on his lap. "Can you hold these for me while I find a place for us to talk?"

He smiled in return, his eyes almost twinkling. He promptly picked the papers up and tapped the edges on his lap as if he were straightening them.

"Here we go," I said, wheeling him down the hall. Just outside the door to his wing was a carpeted alcove with a lamp and a chair. "How about this?" Setting the brake on his wheelchair, I turned on the lamp, pulled the chair up, and sat next to him.

I started to reach for the folders in his lap, then noticed he was sitting very straight, still clutching the papers. He tapped them again to straighten them, peered out as if he were surveying an audience, and began to speak. I could not understand a word he said. He may have been speaking Chinese—this was before I began Chinese classes—or it may have been garbled speech. But I could swear he was giving a lecture. I watched in amazement, wishing to know what was going through his mind. He continued for five minutes or more before he stopped of his own accord, sinking back into his chair and becoming quiet.

"Were you giving a lecture, Dad?" He didn't seem to hear me.

I picked up the folders and began to read and talk as usual until it was time to go. He hadn't responded much, but the experience had been extraordinary. I wheeled him back to the nurses' station, told him I loved him, and gave him a hug. The now-familiar heartache spread through me as I walked to my car and drove to Mom's apartment. I so wished I could have my articulate, witty father back.

As Dad slid inexorably downhill, Mom became ever more overwrought. She had lost weight and was now gaunt at ninety-five pounds. At home she allowed no one to console her, least of all me. That brief tender moment after Dad's third stroke seemed to have never happened. I shortened my visits to three or four days—her apparent limit of civility. On more than one occasion I stayed with Jeri and Joe because Mom and I had had words. We both were in old reactive patterns, pushing each other away at a time when compassion and sincere hugs might have drawn us closer together.

My ongoing sessions with Peggy helped me hold myself together during my visits. I didn't feel closer to Mom like I did with Dad, but what I expected from her was more realistic. Her words and actions didn't throw me as much. Even on our frequent phone calls the anger would spark between us. Although no longer denying my feelings, I was frightened by the intensity I felt at times. After hanging up from one acrimonious phone call, it seemed a mirror was before me reflecting my mother, and her legacy of anger was mine also. A feeling of helplessness washed over me. I wrote in my journal: "Damn, I'm fifty-four, and I still don't have my life together."

Something unexpected happened on a visit in late summer of 1996. Usually I saw Dad in the afternoon or early evening, but this time I stopped in the morning before beginning my drive back to Vermont. I was pleasantly surprised to find him bright-eyed and delighted to see me, more alert than in months.

I kissed him on the forehead. "Would you like to go outside, Dad? It's a beautiful warm morning."

He nodded, so I wheeled him to the elevator and outside to the garden, where flowers were blooming. He spoke as soon as I had him settled.

"Tell me, did Merrill die?"

He said this with no struggle for words or pronunciation, all the while searching my face. My heart sank. I hadn't wanted to be the one to deliver this news. Uncle Merrill had passed away six months before. Mom had not told him for fear he would slip away too. We had continued to read my uncle's letters, and Dad always laughed as if he were hearing the news and stories for the first time.

"Yes, Dad, Uncle Merrill died peacefully in his sleep."

I hugged him and we both teared up.

With my arm still around him, I said, "You two were so close, doing everything together growing up."

He whispered softly, "Best friends."

"Weren't you in the same grade all the way through high school?"

Although I wished he would share memories, he only nodded. I held his hand and we sat in silence for a few moments.

"Recently I was looking at your family photos. You and Uncle Merrill were both rather short while Uncle Suds was over six feet and played football. That probably made you and Merrill like two musketeers, huh?" I squeezed his hand, and he squeezed back. "Mom told me you were valedictorian when you graduated from high school and Merrill the salutatorian. And you went to Bucknell together. The Lenox brothers must have been formidable."

I continued in this vein, talking about any aspects of family gatherings that came to mind. The only detail I left out was when Merrill had died. After talking fifteen minutes, I could tell he'd slipped back into the mists of his mind and was no longer present. I wheeled him back inside and left him at the nurses' station, murmuring my love in his ear and placing a goodbye kiss on his forehead. I hated to leave him, but I had an eleven-hour drive ahead of me.

Thinking about the episode in the car, I was struck by the clarity of Dad's speech and, for those few moments, his mind. I'd noted before that he had no difficulty in telling me he loved me— such a contrast from his usual struggle for words. What made him realize Merrill had died? That question kept my mind occupied for a while. I've never been religious, but after this episode I began wondering whether life has a spiritual dimension we don't understand. Could Dad have been visited by his brother's spirit?

A month later I was distressed to see how much he had slipped. He was groggier and less interested in things around him, almost always asleep in his wheelchair. It saddened me, but in truth his life now held little of interest. I still drove to Pittsburgh regularly, but my visits with him were shorter, which meant I spent more time with Mom. As he faded, she became ever more frantic, if that were possible.

On a Thursday a week before Christmas, Jeri called around nine in the morning, her voice breaking. "Dad's in the hospital. He was unresponsive when the Canterbury aide went to wake him. Mom had Don call an ambulance to take him to the hospital. He's in intensive care on a respirator."

My stomach lurched. "How can that be? His living will says no resuscitation."

"I know, but they did it. Mom can't let him go, and Don won't stand against her wishes."

Oh god, the end is starting. Dad's giving notice he's ready to go.

"I'll book the soonest flight I can and let you know," I said. "Keep me posted. Hang in there, Jeri. I know it's been difficult with Mom."

I put the phone down and sat in anguish, pulling my knees up and wrapping my arms around my legs. *No matter how much you've tried to prepare yourself, kiddo, it's gonna be tough. I hope I'm up to the task. I want my father to go peacefully on his own terms.*

 Chapter 15

I booked a flight for that afternoon and called my mother.

"I'm flying down, Mom. Just wanted you to know. I'll get in around six."

"Why are you coming?" The irritation in her voice was unmistakable.

"I want to see Dad." I knew she thought I was meddling. "Mom, why is he on a respirator? You know he didn't want that." Her advance directive was identical to Dad's.

"He was unresponsive." Her hostility escalated. "There's nothing you can do. You don't have to come."

I kept my tone level. "I'm coming, Mom. My flight's all set."

Her manner cold and curt, she asked, "Where are you going to stay?"

"Not with you." I sighed inwardly—so much for my level tone.

"Good. Go to Jeri's. I know you talk behind my back." She hung up on me.

I closed my eyes and shook my head. *Why does she have to be that way? I can't stand by when my father's on a damn ventilator.* Time dragged as I waited to leave, picturing him surrounded by machines and beeping monitors. I reserved a room at the

Holiday Inn close to the hospital for one night only in case Mom had a change of heart. I heard nothing more from her. Jeri called and said Dad was now alert but still on a respirator. Giving her my arrival time, I accepted her offer of a lift from the airport so I wouldn't have to rent a car.

I phoned my brother. "Don, I'm flying down this afternoon. I'm staying at the Holiday Inn near the hospital."

"You aren't staying with Mom?" He sounded surprised.

"Nope. She's mad at me for coming. We have to get Dad off the respirator, Don."

"I'll talk with the doctor," he said. "Give me a call when you get in."

Jeri and Joe were waiting when I arrived in Pittsburgh. They updated me as we drove into the city. We stopped briefly at the hotel so I could check in and leave my luggage. At the hospital Joe dropped Jeri and me off and went to park the car.

When we reached Dad's room, Jeri said, "You go in. I'll wait here for Joe."

Taking a deep breath, I steeled myself and pushed the door open. Dad was alone in the room, wide awake and surrounded by tubes and beeping monitors, as I'd pictured. My heart plummeted. He couldn't talk around the breathing apparatus, but he didn't need words. As I walked toward him, he clenched his teeth around the tube as if to bite it in two and shook his head slowly from side to side, his eyes conveying his message: GET ME OFF THIS THING!

"I'm so sorry, Dad." Needing to connect, I patted a bit of bare skin amid the tubing. "We'll get you off the respirator, I promise. I'll talk with a doctor."

I stayed with him for fifteen minutes; then Jeri and Joe visited while I went looking for the doctor in charge.

When I found Dr. D., I pointed out that Dad had a do-not-resuscitate clause. "What happened? Why was he put on a ventilator?"

"Your father was unresponsive this morning," he said kindly. "Your mother and brother directed the EMTs to revive him. He was already on oxygen when he arrived here."

"Can't you take him off?"

"We're working on that. Your brother and I talked earlier. Your father's advance directive states two doctors must declare him terminal before it can take effect. That hasn't happened yet." He said a person on a respirator must be taken off gradually—it can't be done all at once. "I've scheduled a meeting tomorrow with your family at 10:00 a.m. to review his directive. He should be off the ventilator and on a recovery floor by early afternoon."

Relieved, I thanked him and returned to Dad. After giving him the news, I kissed his forehead. "I love you, Dad. Try to get some sleep. I'll see you tomorrow."

He nodded, his eyes softening.

Declining Jeri and Joe's offer of a ride, I walked the few blocks to the Holiday Inn. My mind swirled with questions I hadn't asked. When they unhook Dad from the machine, will he be able to breathe on his own? Will he slip back into that unresponsive state? I felt heavyhearted thinking about life without my father.

I entered my hotel room exhausted but still needed to update my family. Calling across the time zones, I talked first with John in Washington, DC, then Steph in Missoula and Marilyn on the West Coast. I fell into bed at midnight realizing I hadn't talked to Mom.

The next morning, I lay awake thinking of Dad. The world was a better place because of him. He had touched the lives of so many people. I sent him my thoughts: I'll hold you within my heart always, Dad—your joy in life, your teachings, your laughter and gentle soul.

I knew the day would be sad and draining. Staying by myself close to the hospital would allow me to shore up my emotional reserves and process my grief without having to contend with Mom. My focus had to be on Dad and what I could do for him. I went down to the front desk, where the clerk said the room was mine for as long as I needed.

I arrived at the hospital and the appointed meeting room early and waited in the hall. When Mom and Don came, I hugged them hello, puzzled not to see Jeri too.

Mom asked about my room at the Holiday Inn and surprised me by asking, "Do you want to stay with me?"

"No thanks, Mom," I replied, striving for a diplomatic tone. "It's very convenient. I can easily go back and forth. So Jeri didn't come with you?"

"I told her to stay at the apartment. She doesn't need to be here. This meeting is for family."

Oh god, what a cruel thing to say. Jeri's grieving too, and she *is* family.

I was glad to see Dr. D. arrive. I hadn't known who would be meeting with us, but I sensed from last night's conversation he could handle Mom. He shook our hands and we went into the conference room and sat at the table.

"In accordance with Dr. Lenox's advance directive," he began, "I and another physician have determined he is terminal. We've begun weaning him from the respirator."

"Now hold on," Mom protested. "I'm a physician. I don't think he's terminal."

"I understand, Dr. Lenox," he said with compassion. "In this instance, though, you are family. The determination must be made by two physicians with no ties to the patient."

"No, you can't do this," Mom cried out, her face a mask of pain and fury. Don and I both tried to calm her, but she looked at each of us in turn and wailed, "You are killing your father!"

Standing abruptly and leaning heavily on her cane, she stumped out of the room. I took a deep breath and exhaled, trying to ease the tightness in my chest. Despite her words, my heart went out to her, knowing it was her grief talking. But I didn't go after her—experience told me she wouldn't welcome my comfort.

"I'm sorry about that," Dr. D. said.

"It's difficult for her to accept what's happening," Don replied.

Dr. D. nodded, then proceeded to enumerate the treatments Dad was refusing: a feeding tube, oxygen, antibiotics, hydration. He explained each one and what to expect. He questioned us about hydration.

"Withholding fluids hastens death and can be painful. Most families accept hydration."

I looked at Don. "Dad knew the implications. I think we must be true to his wishes."

Don agreed.

"Then we're all set," Dr. D. said. "He should be on this floor by early afternoon. I'm very sorry you're losing your father. I hope everything goes okay." He shook hands again and left.

Don and I looked at each other, our eyes mirroring the sadness we each felt.

"Well," he said, "I'd better go find Mom and see what she wants to do."

"I'll get an early lunch, then come back here and wait for Dad," I said.

My intent was not to ignore Mom, but I wasn't going to let her control the situation. It wasn't in her best interest nor Dad's. This time was solely his, and my goal was to ensure he left life on his terms.

Dad arrived on the floor and was put in a private room. Kissing his forehead, I pulled a chair close. His breathing was rapid and shallow. He seemed in a dream state, his eyes open and following the patterns in the ceiling tiles. I talked or read to him and touched his arm or hand often, wanting to feel connected.

This was my first end-of-life experience. Unsure how quickly death might come, I stayed watchful, trying to decipher the markers of decline. Looking at his hands in repose, I noticed for the first time how young they seemed—no swollen joints, minimal age spots, nails trimmed close: competent hands that had treated so many sick people. I wished I had a camera.

Jeri and Joe arrived in the late afternoon followed soon by Mom and Don. Dad was more alert and recognized everyone with smiles or eye contact but didn't talk. Mom appeared calmer and more accepting. She fidgeted some, patting him on the arm and checking his covers, seeming almost detached. Mostly she chitchatted with others. Sadness filled me at her inability to talk from her heart even as he lay dying.

At times Dad had spells of coughing, a residual irritation from the breathing tube. The first time it happened, Jeri, who was standing by his bed, grabbed the suction apparatus hanging on the wall above him and removed the mucus from his throat. During a later coughing attack, he pointed over his shoulder toward the suction, and again Jeri obliged. Most of the time he rested quietly with his eyes closed. Was he listening to the small talk around him, or had he turned inward? Thirty hours on the respirator had artificially slowed his state of decline. Had he resumed preparation for death? These thoughts surfaced in my mind like bubbles rising in water, heightening my desire to be present for him as he began this last journey.

Mom and Don left after an hour, but Jeri and Joe stayed into the evening. I could tell Jeri felt freer in what she could say and do without Mom there. She ministered to Dad, making him comfortable with such love and gentleness, and his eyes expressed gratitude. Their connection was so poignant. With Mom unable to show her feelings, I was glad for Jeri's love.

When I left at nine, he seemed comfortable, again in that eyes-open dreamlike state. I had arranged for a nighttime nursing assistant so Dad wouldn't be alone, and I did so on the following nights too, leaving my phone number in case any-thing happened. These competent, caring people enabled me to sleep deeply, dreamlessly. Over the next few days I settled into a routine of sorts. I went to Dad each morning refreshed, ready for whatever the day brought, and left the hospital at nine, confident Dad was in good hands. After a bite to eat at the hotel pub, I returned to my room to phone family members. Talking with them helped me process my grief.

To my surprise, I found sitting with my father in one way not unlike backpacking: with time I became more tuned-in and observant. When backpacking I see few birds or animals at first, but by the third day they're all around me. My powers of observation improve as I shed my daily rush. As I sat with my dying father, I gained an intuitive awareness and opened my heart to a deeper knowing. When Dad was brought onto the recovery floor, the word "vigil" hadn't yet surfaced in my mind. Twenty-four hours later, I knew I was sitting vigil for my father.

Dad was sleeping soundly when I arrived the next morn-ing. It was Saturday. Before long a breakfast tray mistakenly arrived, and he soon began stirring. When he awakened and saw me, his eyes twinkled—a precious, unexpected gift.

"Would you like some hot cereal, Dad?" I too had forgotten his directive.

He nodded yes. I fed him slowly, and he seemed to enjoy it at first. Suddenly he struggled to breathe, his skin gray. Fright-ened, I buzzed for a nurse. She came and inserted oxygen tubing into his nostrils, explaining the ventilator had likely interfered with his swallowing reflex. His color soon improved, and she removed the oxygen along with the breakfast tray.

That morning I read to him from *Men Against the Clouds*, the book about the mountaineering expedition my parents had traveled with into the Minya Konka on the eastern rim of Tibet.[1] Suddenly Dad began coughing, then stopped as if he just didn't have the energy. The fluids continued to rumble around as he breathed. Just then the nurse came to check on him.

"Should he be suctioned?" I asked.

"I tried that yesterday when he came over from ICU, and he bit the tube."

She tried again, though. He didn't like it but rested more easily afterward. I sat by his bed for a while holding his hand, which seemed to relax him. He was sleeping soundly when Mom and Don arrived in the early afternoon with Don's college-age son, Matt. They each kissed him on the forehead and sat down. At my suggestion Matt settled in the chair next to Dad and held his hand, periodically caressing his forehead. Mom had brought a small stuffed panda from her collection. She tucked the panda under Dad's free hand and murmured in his ear. Don turned on the television to watch the Saturday football game, and the three of them focused on the game and made small talk, Matt continuing to hold Dad's hand. The television didn't seem to interrupt Dad's sleeping, so I didn't say anything. They left soon after the game was over.

I noticed Dad's color had changed some. His hands were swollen but warm. He hadn't moved in several hours or opened his eyes. I held his hand and told him how much I had learned from him and thanked him for the love he had given to Marilyn and me, enabling us to break the generational chain of abusive anger.

Jeri and Joe came in the early evening and stayed several hours. They were leaving the next day on a long-planned Caribbean cruise. Jeri had hoped Mom would ask her to stay, but she hadn't, so this was their goodbye to Dad. Before leaving, Jeri lovingly arranged Dad's pillows and tucked his covers around him to make him as comfortable as possible.

Marilyn called that evening. She was distraught, trying to decide whether to come.

"It's snowing right now. I don't know if I can even get out."

"He may not last through the night," I said. "He hasn't awakened or responded to anyone since midafternoon. But just because he seems to be sleeping doesn't mean he's not aware. I think he knows we're here."

Then I had an idea. "I'll put the phone to his ear. You tell him whatever you would say if you were here."

She talked with him for about five minutes. A little later, Marilyn's daughter Jen called, and I let her talk to him too. He seemed more peaceful during this period.

In the silence after their calls, I thought about the time Dad had contracted typhus fever in China. Following a battle between two warlords in 1933, the hospital had been chaotic with all beds filled and more wounded soldiers lying on pallets on the ward and hallway floors. As Dad tended to the men, a louse from one must have bitten him. For a week he was in a coma with a raging fever. The other missionary doctors had been unsure they could save him. While unconscious he had several out-of-body experiences that he recorded upon recovering. In one he'd floated on the ceiling, watching doctors and nurses tending to his lifeless body.

Sitting beside him, I wondered if he had slipped into a coma. If so, could his spirit be floating on the ceiling of this room? In a coma, does the spirit experiment with leaving the body? Although lying there unmoving, he could be taking in everything in ways I couldn't comprehend.

When I awoke on Sunday with no phone call, I breathed thanks for one more day. All morning Dad lay peaceful and unmoving, his hands now cool to the touch. I made sure the little panda was tucked under his right hand, and I held his left, telling him Mom had filled the panda with the love she couldn't voice and the love of Marilyn and other family members who couldn't be there. The more I talked, the more I was convinced he was aware. I resolved to maintain a respectful atmosphere.

Anyone who wanted to discuss his condition would have to step outside his room.

Don, Mom, and Matt arrived just in time for the Sunday football game. Don kissed Dad on the forehead and headed toward the television.

"Don, please don't turn the game on."

I talked about Dad's typhus coma and my belief he knew we were there. No one disagreed, and our conversation was subdued and considerate. They left in the late afternoon, Mom and Don saying they'd be back in the morning. A friend from church and Gary, the church minister, stopped by also. Throughout the day Dad lay unmoving, unresponsive. As I sat vigil, I eased my grief by talking or reading to him and writing in my journal. That evening, running my hand over the thin blanket covering him, I felt the cold of his feet and asked the nurse for an extra blanket. The pall of sadness cloaking me all day deepened: I was losing my cherished father.

I told him, "Dad, I don't want you to go, but I know death is part of life. I'm honored to be with you as you prepare for what comes next."

Before leaving that night I realized his feet were still cold. For me, warm toes are a must for comfortable sleep. I took off my wool vest and wrapped it gently around his feet. Leaving for the Holiday Inn, I feared I would not see him alive again.

The next morning, I awoke with a start—again no phone call. My heart lifting, I rushed to the hospital. Each day I'd noticed holiday music and decorations everywhere. It was Monday, the twenty-third of December. Why hadn't I brought a tape of Christmas carols? Dad loved singing them even though he was tone deaf. He was lying quietly when I arrived, my vest still around his feet. Only his trunk was warm. I knew his body was shutting down.

When a nurse came in, I asked if the audio feed had public radio. "I'd love to find some Christmas music for my father."

"I'll find a station for you," she said, and soon carols played softly in the background.

In midmorning two aides came to give Dad a sponge bath. They asked me to step out for fifteen minutes. I went to a window at the end of the hall and looked out unseeing, tears welling and an utter sadness filling me. When I returned, the aides had just finished.

"There, now, doesn't he look better?" one said.

He did indeed. They had changed the sheets, shaved him, and dressed him in a clean johnny, rewrapping his feet in the vest and surrounding him with pillows. With the music playing and the "love panda" tucked under his hand, everything was as perfect as possible.

"Mom and Don are coming soon," I told him. "You look quite spiffy."

The aides' ministrations had loosened some mucus, and his breathing was more labored. Through his slightly open mouth I could see the space in his teeth where a bridge had been. Explaining I was using the suction to make him more comfortable, I gently inserted the tip of the tube into the space. In a flash he bit down hard. After two days of absolute stillness, his strength astonished me. Once again, he didn't need words to communicate: *Dammit, I'm dying! Leave me alone!*

"Okay, Dad, no more suction, I promise."

Over the next hour his skin took on a waxy look, and his breathing became ever shallower. Don had said he and Mom would be there late morning. But they hadn't yet arrived when Dr. G. stopped in at eleven thirty. Dad's breathing was now little more than a whisper. She stayed for a while, perhaps so I wouldn't be alone if he died. She slipped out when Mom and Don arrived just before noon.

Mom went to Dad's side and kissed his forehead. I added the fleece throw she'd brought to his foot wraps, tucking it carefully. Unable to stop being a physician, she pulled out her penlight and peered into his mouth. Don and I were standing at the foot of the bed when Dad's suddenly erratic breathing alarmed me. A pallor began to spread up his face.

"Mom, he's going!" I gasped. She didn't hear me. "Mom!"

As she pulled back to look and Don rushed to the other side of the bed, all Dad's color vanished upward, leaving a waxy mask. I felt suddenly bereft, as if a fissure had opened in my soul.

Later I learned Buddhists believe at the time of physical death the spirit leaves the body through the top of the head. I have no doubt Dad waited for Mom before he left. For two days he had lain virtually unmoving. Despite his silence, his vigor in biting on the suction tube had confirmed his presence. Just as clearly, when the color vanished from his face, he was gone.

We three remained in the room for another half hour, drained and in shock. No one wanted to leave, least of all Mom. She leaned her head against his and laid her hand on his arm. We hugged and comforted each other, all irritation gone. Some people talk of joy in death or a sense of holiness, but for me there was just a soul-deep sadness and sense of loss tempered by the relief my father no longer had to endure the indignities of a nursing home. Then Mom gently took the panda from under his hand and clutched it to her breast. We gathered our things and together we three went to Mom's apartment.

Only in the next few weeks did I realize my father had left me with one final gift, one final lesson about life: death is not something to fear.

 Chapter 16

I stayed overnight with Mom and flew home on Christmas Eve. To have left her so soon seems harsh now, but I knew Don would make sure she wasn't alone on Christmas. I needed some space. Although I loved my mother, she drained me emotionally. After losing my father, I needed to be at home to grieve and renew my energy.

Early in January, I returned to help Mom and Don plan Dad's memorial service. We agreed to hold it at the Baptist church where they had been longtime members. Dad attended regularly, but Mom had lapsed several years back after a disagreement with Gary, the minister. Although she accepted the venue, she did not want Gary officiating. Don suggested his friend Steve, an American Baptist minister then unaffiliated with a church. He arranged for Steve to come to Mom's apartment so she and I could meet him.

Steve dropped by the next day. I made tea for the three of us, and we sat in the living room to talk. He had a warm, sincere manner.

"Please tell me more about your husband's life and beliefs," he said to Mom.

Mom hesitated, interpreting his request as did I as inquiring about Dad's faith. She was uncomfortable talking about religion and looked to me to take the lead.

"Dad was American Baptist all his life," I began, leaning forward. "But he also had an insatiable curiosity about other cultures and religions." I described how my parents, studying Chinese in their first two years in Chengdu, had visited Buddhist and Daoist temples and learned five hundred Confucian proverbs. Dad was quite interested in the moral teachings of these ancient philosophical traditions. "He especially appreciated the proverbs for their pithy wisdom. Wait, I'll show you," I said, standing up. "I'll be right back."

I went to Dad's study and retrieved the pen holder from his desk, which had a Confucian proverb taped to it. Returning to the living room, I handed the pen holder to Steve so he could read the proverb.

"'Learning without thought is labor lost; thought without meaning is perilous.' I like that," Steve said.

I also talked about transcribing my parents' letters home from China and how I'd seen a change in how Dad approached his missionary work, abandoning his early desire to try proselytizing. Once he began teaching, he came to view his Chinese colleagues and students as equals, which was unusual for a missionary. "His approach became to live his beliefs, not preach them," I said. "He respected Chinese people and Chinese thought and believed he could learn from them too. For him, missionary work was not a one-way street."

Mom seemed pleased with what I said, adding, "His colleagues and students loved him. He was a born teacher."

"May I read these China letters?" Steve asked. "They might help me get a sense of Dr. Lenox as a young man."

I agreed to send him what I'd transcribed so far. I also shared my own conversations with Dad and how he had accepted that I wasn't religious. He knew my life was governed by strong ethical principles, which was most important to him.

"He saw all religions as social and cultural tools for morality," I said. "Although Dad remained in the Baptist church all his life, he wasn't constrained by its dogma."

Mom said little throughout the conversation, which I took as agreement with what I'd said. If she thought I had mischaracterized Dad's approach to life, she would have spoken. She saw herself as the guardian of his memorial-service content in much the same way she'd been fierce in wanting the best medical care for him after his strokes. Although I didn't understand at the time, these were signs of her love for him. She wanted Dad's service to reflect the full measure of the man she'd known and loved for sixty-six years.

After Steve left, Mom called Don to say we liked Steve and wanted him to officiate at the service. Meanwhile, Gary had sent a gracious condolence note saying he wanted to heal the breach with Mom. Several days later, Don picked Mom and me up, and we three met with Steve and Gary at the church office to finalize the service. We sat around a conference table, and Mom spoke up immediately, thanking Gary for his note of condolence and asking him to give the opening welcome. Her request, which I hadn't expected, set a congenial tone for the remaining discussion. I offered to talk about China as a shaping force in Dad's life. We agreed on hymns and Bible verses reflecting Dad's ecumenical beliefs and planned opportunities for the grandchildren to participate. Mom seemed pleased with these plans.

Those several days with Mom were nevertheless filled with tension. I realized how much I'd relied on spending time with Dad to help me maintain an even disposition when I visited. Living with Mom's need to control everything was difficult. My last night before returning home, I was filling the dishwasher when Mom elbowed me out of the way and began rearranging the dishes.

"They don't go in that way," she said sharply.

I stepped back and put my hands up. "Okay, Mom. Just trying to help."

How had Dad retained his positive attitude when his most intimate relationship was filled with such behavior? I let her remark slide, but not because I was cowed as in the past. What I didn't do, and still wish I had, was to hug her and express my compassion for what she was going through. She was facing the funeral of the man she had spent her entire adult life with, the man who had loved and supported her despite the challenges she presented him. Her heartbreak, which she was unable to express, must have been monumental.

Two weeks later I was back in Pittsburgh for Dad's service just days before what would have been his ninety-third birthday. All the immediate family was there: Marilyn and Jen (Tim stayed home to take care of their farm), Steph and John, and Don's family—his wife Carol, daughter Rozlyn, and Matt. The church was packed with their many medical colleagues from Pittsburgh, friends and colleagues from West Virginia, and friends from the church and their peace group. Tom had come, too; his condolences touched me.

As immediate family members began to fill the front pew, Marilyn and I brought Jeri along. Mom sat in the middle and we all held hands down the line. My role in the service helped me temporarily rein in my emotions. But when I was sitting with family again and Steve began his eulogy, the finality hit: we were saying goodbye to *my father*. Holding hands with Marilyn and Jeri helped ease my anguish as I gave in to my tears.

"Summarizing the life of Dr. John Lenox is a humbling task," Steve began. "I realized I was to speak about someone who was brilliant, disciplined, learned, cultured, accomplished. I am told this was the natural reaction of anyone first getting to know John Lenox. But he was also humble, kind, gentle, and forgiving."

Steve recounted stories he'd gathered in talking with many people who knew Dad. He called my father a citizen of the world and a friend to all, someone who cared genuinely for others, whose focus could be on the pain of one individual or expand to encompass all of humanity. I sat there with my eyes closed and let Steve's words wash over me. My emotions ran the gamut from astonishment he had grasped so well who Dad was to gratitude to Don for suggesting Steve to heartbreak at the loss of my father.

During the service Steve invited people to come to the microphone and share thoughts and stories of Dad. One woman from the church looked over at the family and said, "I know you miss him terribly, but I want you to know I do too. He came to me each Sunday and told one or two jokes, then asked, 'What do you have for me today?'" So many people spoke that the service lasted much longer than planned, but few people left. The man we were celebrating was beloved. The service ended with a Chinese friend giving a benediction in Chinese. *Perfect*, I thought.

In the weeks after Dad's service, I read Anton Grosz's *Letters to a Dying Friend* on Buddhist thinking about death. In a chapter about the first Buddha's meditations on achieving happiness, I came across this: "[The first Buddha] developed a philosophy of peace from within based on an eightfold path of right understanding, right purpose, right speech, right conduct, right vocation, right effort, right alertness, and right concentration."

Goosebumps prickled my skin as I heard my father speaking from the page. I remembered the birthday cards he made for my children every year beginning when they were ten or eleven. I went to my basement storage and found the box of mementos I'd kept for John and Steph. A little rummaging uncovered an undated handmade card. On the front is a bouquet of multicolored flowers, above which float the words "right purpose," "right speech," "right conduct," "right effort." I sat back as grief overwhelmed me, my chest aching. I wasn't surprised Dad had embraced Buddhist thought since kindness and compassion were at the core of who he was. Thinking about past conversations, I realized when he encountered a new idea or belief that he liked, he incorporated it without fanfare into his philosophy of life and passed that wisdom on to others in his everyday living.

The years following Dad's first strokes had taken a toll on Mom, and now his death left a gaping hole in her life. Although they had lived apart during the years he was in the nursing homes, she had been surrounded by items that evoked memories of him. Even in his diminished capacity, living apart from her, his physical presence had been a reminder of the gentle, humorous, loving man she had shared her life with. At restaurants I often see older couples who converse little during the meal they share. My parents had too many similar interests and Dad too much intellectual curiosity for them to be silent. Mealtimes were always filled with conversation, although sadly usually subjects of the mind, not the heart.

Now Mom was left with only memories. She still had work to occupy her time, but outside of that she seemed almost lost.

"I didn't know I would miss him so," she said to me on more than one occasion, her voice breaking.

Seeing her attempt humor was especially poignant, as her jokes usually fell flat, but then Dad was a hard act to follow. A photo from their honeymoon taken on the ocean crossing to China shows them with three other people, everyone but Dad convulsed with hilarity. He's smiling broadly, a Cheshire-cat grin on his face. I knew without a doubt he had been the instigator of this mirth. Mom had lived bathed in his humor for sixty-six years.

She felt Dad's loss in other ways as well. They had done everything together—social activities, programs, traveling, visiting relatives. Mom called her siblings often but now saw them infrequently. She had friends from church and the local peace organization but hadn't participated in either for a few years. Except for the occasional department holiday gatherings, she saw her medical colleagues seldom outside of work and socialized mainly with Don and his family and Jeri and Joe.

She still corresponded with her Chinese classmates, and their letters unfailingly brought her joy. She always told me when she heard from them. After Dad died, I helped her send word to about thirty Chinese friends—her classmates, Dad's colleagues from the 1930s and '40s, former visiting scholars at the University of Pittsburgh, and doctors they'd met on several medical trips to China in the 1980s. Assisting with this task took a burden off her shoulders and helped me feel closer to her.

Once Dad entered the Baptist Home, Mom had become increasingly fearful of living alone. She had a deep-seated dread of strangers breaking in—the reason, I realized later, she'd been unable to have a health aide stay in the apartment overnight after Dad's first strokes. She once told me about an incident when she was four or five and her family lived on a farm. Granddaddy was a part-time traveling salesman then and had been away, leaving Hapink alone with the children. She had herded them into her bedroom, moved a bureau to block the door, and shot a rifle out the window—perhaps to send a message to the hired help or thinking she'd heard someone outside.

This memory may have surfaced one morning after Dad died. The man who lived in the apartment immediately above hers had a progressive neurological disease and had awakened at 6:00 a.m. before his caregiver arrived. He took the elevator down to the ground floor and back up, getting off on Mom's floor by mistake. He pounded on her door, begging to be let in, and became increasingly frantic. Jeri told me the incident had frightened Mom terribly.

Even before Dad died, I had broached the idea of finding a place for her in an assisted living community where she would feel safe and have help if she needed it. I investigated Sherwood Oaks, the senior community where she and Dad had lived in the mid-1980s until the dispute over smoking. I called, inquiring about their current policy. Upon learning the common areas were now nonsmoking, I convinced Mom to accompany me to look at the assisted living units. Most were one room only, but a unit was available with a bedroom, sitting area, and tiny kitchen with a minifridge but no stove.

Reluctantly she agreed to take it but didn't do anything with the paperwork for several months. Leaving her apartment with its memories of Dad for a place with no history of him must have been difficult. Jeri said she would continue caring for Mom despite the greater distance, and she or Joe would take her back and forth to work. This may have made the difference with Mom and was a relief for me. She moved several months after Dad's service.

With that, I'd accomplished my goal of finding a safe place where she would have opportunities to meet people and make friends. As she came to feel more secure, I hoped with Jeri's loving care she could rebuild her life in a way that was rewarding to her. I was fully aware I had only guaranteed her safety and not her happiness. I would always be there for her, but I'd learned that for each of us, happiness is in our own hands.

I now had opportunities for environmental work and was ready to pick up the threads of my own life.

 Chapter 17

Mom called me in late 1997, her excitement echoing through the phone line. "Jackie, I've been asked to join a delegation to China. The delegation is studying women and the environment, and it's going to Chengdu and Mount Omei.[1] I want you to go in my place."

I knew Mom would have loved visiting Chengdu one last time. Mount Omei (Emeishan) was special to my parents. They had spent a second honeymoon of sorts at a cottage there the summer of 1931 and had been disappointed not to go there in 1980. If I joined the delegation, she could experience the trip vicariously.

"I'd love to see Mount Omei. Can you send the info? I'll give it serious thought."

The invitation came from the Women's International League for Peace and Freedom, a cosponsor of the trip with People to People International. For two weeks in June of 1998, the delegation would learn about China's approach to environmental issues and explore Chinese perceptions of nature through visits to cultural sites near Beijing and Chengdu.

The chance to learn about China's environmental situation was intriguing, but visiting Chengdu again and seeing Mount

Omei decided it for me. While transcribing the China letters, I had yearned to see the settings of my parents' adventures. I signed up and let Mom know.

A letter came in early March saying the delegation still had several openings. Steph was starting a master's program in environmental studies in the fall. I asked her if she wanted to join me, and after several days of consideration she said yes. Mom was delighted. Steph would be the first grandchild to visit China.

Later that month I called Mom to talk about an idea.

"I'd like to meet with your friends while we're in Chengdu," I said. "Their letters of condolence after Dad died were so heartfelt. I want them to know how much their friendship has meant to you and Dad."

"Yes, their letters were such a comfort."

I heard her voice catch and knew she still missed him deeply. Looking out the window at the sun shining on the trees, I felt sadness in my heart too.

"That would be very nice, Jackie. Thank you. I'll write to Chunhua and Jiaying and ask them to help arrange this."

She corresponded often with these two physicians. Mom had coached Chunhua, the daughter of her medical classmate Dr. Zhang, in English ever since our 1980 trip. Chunhua now lived in Chengdu. Jiaying had been a visiting scholar in Pittsburgh in the early 1990s and was married to the son of another of Mom's classmates. I'd met her at one of the teas my parents hosted for the scholars. Both agreed to help arrange a gathering.

Three weeks before I was due to leave for China, Jeri called. "Mom fell and may have rebroken her hip. She's in the hospital and not doing well. Can you come?"

My stomach churned. I arranged time off and drove to Pittsburgh a day later. I was alarmed at what I found. The problem wasn't Mom's hip—the pins inserted in 1993 were holding just fine—but her blood chemistry was off, perhaps from long-standing dehydration and anorexia. She was down to eighty-eight pounds and in and out of delirium. Even when lucid she refused to eat much and seemed to be withering away before our eyes, her skin dry and wrinkled like crepe paper. One of the doctors from her division stopped by her hospital room one day while I was there. His face told me he was shocked at her condition. Over the next few hours several more colleagues came to see her, as if they were saying goodbye.

After several days Mom's blood chemistry stabilized, but she still had bouts of delirium. Dr. G. discharged her to the skilled nursing wing of Sherwood Oaks. In her half-delirious state Mom was restless and demanding, asking to be "fluffed" (no one knew what that meant), throwing off her covers and pulling at her nightgown, and refusing to eat or drink. In her coherent moments she must have been horrified to find herself in a situation so reminiscent of what Dad had endured. The last thing she wanted was to linger in a nursing home.

Jeri and I were with her daily, and Don visited also in the evenings. With Mom's prickliness and one or more of us regularly at her bedside, the nursing staff looked in only when necessary, mostly to give medications. As her weight continued to drop, I feared a slow decline like Dad's. I called Marilyn in Vancouver.

"Mom's no better. It's hard to get her to eat and drink. She's so thin."

"Should I come?"

"I wanted to give you the choice. I know you were sad not to see Dad before he died."

Marilyn flew east for several days, and I extended my stay to overlap with hers. The next day we stopped by Mom's apartment to get the "love panda," and I explained its significance. That afternoon Mom slept quietly with the panda in her hand.

The situation eerily resembled Dad's early hours of coma, and I wondered if she'd decided to slip away.

"Mom, if you're ready to go, it's okay," I said, caressing the hand holding the stuffed toy. "The panda holds love just like it did for Dad."

Jeri and Marilyn, also at her bedside, voiced similar thoughts.

After ten minutes or so, Mom's eyes suddenly flew open. She looked around at us and then at the panda and threw it disgustedly toward the foot of the bed as if to say, *DAMN! I'M STILL HERE.* I restrained a chuckle as I silently cheered her show of spirit.

The China trip was now a week away. I was torn. I didn't want to be halfway around the world and have her die.

At a time when I knew she was fully aware, I said, "Mom, I can't go to China while you're still sick."

"Jackie, you must," she said, looking into my eyes. "I want you to see our friends."

Jeri encouraged me as well. "We'll take care of Mom; don't worry. It's what Dad would have wanted too."

I remained uneasy about traveling so far. I still carried inside the old yearnings for a more loving relationship with her. Though Don lived nearby, I knew Jeri would shoulder the daily care. It was a lot to ask of her, and I wasn't confident the nursing staff would step up and help. Another resident, whose husband had recently been in skilled nursing, heard of our plight and stopped me in the hall to tell me about Carla, a freelance caregiver she had employed to supplement the facility's nursing staff.

"If you need help, there's no one better." She gave me Carla's phone number.

"Thanks so much," I said, grateful for the reference.

Marilyn, Jeri, Don, and I talked the situation over and agreed that hiring additional help would give Mom the best chance to recover. I contacted Carla and met with her. She said she would set up twenty-four-hour care, using her network of health aides. She and Jeri would both be in the rotation.

"You go ahead and go to China, honey," Carla said, giving me a hug. "And don't worry. We'll watch out for your mom."

With Jeri and Carla anchoring the round-the-clock care, I felt able to leave. But I still fought back tears as I said goodbye to my mother.

"You keep on eating and drinking, Mom. I love you. I want you here when I get back so I can tell you about my trip."

I hugged her carefully—she was just skin and bones—and hoped fervently she would be alive when I returned.

Our delegation of eleven met in San Francisco prior to the Beijing flight for a briefing by Regina, our trip leader. Our ages ranged from Steph in her late twenties to several in their seventies. Most of the delegates were peace activists, with Regina, Steph, and me representing an environmental perspective. Once in Beijing we began a whirlwind of meetings with national environmental officials, university science professors, and the director of China's first nongovernmental environmental organization. Similar meetings were planned at the provincial level in Chengdu, the capital of Sichuan.

Every evening Steph and I compared perceptions of the day's activities. Our conversation didn't just revolve around our meetings, though. I told her of the many changes since my first visit—cars replacing bicycles, everyone with cell phones, the increased city traffic, air pollution. In 1980 I had been the novice, learning from my parents. Now I was sharing my knowledge with my daughter. As our time in Chengdu neared, I thought increasingly of our upcoming gathering and wondered how Mom was doing.

We were met at the Chengdu airport by Mr. Wong, a slight,

friendly young man who was the guide for our stay in Sichuan. He led us to a bus for the drive into Chengdu.

Before sharing some regional history, he asked, "Has anyone been to Chengdu before?"

"I was born in Chengdu," I said, pronouncing the city's name like my parents always had.

His eyes lit up with delight. "You speak the Chengdu dialect!"

This pleased me. There are regional differences in pronunciation, and few tourists pronounce "Chengdu" as the natives do.

The bus took us to the same hotel as in 1980, close to the university. Chunhua was waiting at the hotel to greet us. Steph and I visited with her for a little while. Her English was good enough for us to engage in simple conversation. She told me she had found an American woman in her eighties living in Chengdu who met with her regularly for conversation.

The next day Jiaying and her husband drove Steph and me to the campus. The gathering she and Chunhua had organized was taking place in the old administration building where the 1980 gathering had been held. The familiar red columns still lined the portico, but the paint on the columns and the decorative trim was faded and peeling, causing me to wonder about the fate of these old buildings from my parents' time.

Several dozen people awaited us in the reception room. Despite the comfortable chairs scattered around, people milled about talking to one another. I recognized many from the 1980 celebration. Then everyone had been pleased to meet me, but their focus had been on my parents. Now Steph and I were the family emissaries and the beneficiaries of the goodwill these people felt for our family. I had conversations with some of them, those comfortable speaking English. Others greeted me with smiles. I knew all of them held my parents in high esteem, and their affection warmed my heart. I thought of Mom constantly. Often on the verge of tears, I wondered how she was faring on the other side of the world.

Seeing Dad's special friend Dr. Guo, who must have been ninety or more, lifted my spirits. He was still spry and alert, his English flawless, his eyes radiating intelligence and humor. He spent time with Steph too. She said that with his gracious manner and twinkling eyes he seemed a Chinese version of her grandfather.

I'd prepared a short talk to thank everyone for their friendship, saying that Dad and Mom's fourteen years in China had shaped who they became: two people who valued cross-cultural understanding and believed in peaceful dealings among countries. My parents had never forgotten them and counted them among their closest friends. I told them their condolences after Dad's death had been of great solace to Mom. When I shared that she was ill, my eyes pooled. How I wished my parents could have been there, but I knew they were in spirit.

Steph understood this meeting was emotionally fraught for me; she felt it herself. She seemed to know what I needed— picking up my purse and papers when I left them behind, hugging me when I was down or worried, and listening as I relived poignant moments.

She said meeting her grandparents' friends was extraordinary and made their stories more tangible. "Their friends are so worldly and cultured and were immediately open with me. I hadn't expected that."

I talked with Chunhua at the end of the gathering and invited her to have dinner that evening with our delegation. I wanted to get to know her better. She did join us, to the delight of the other delegation members. Chunhua is gregarious, with dark flashing eyes and an easy laugh. When she saw some in our group struggling with chopsticks, she gave a quick lesson, demonstrating how to capture noodles. When some still found it difficult, she laughed and served us all from the communal serving bowl, being especially solicitous with the older members of our group. She was such a hit that I invited her to join us for the meals and the temple visits remaining on our Chengdu itinerary. As our time neared to visit the cultural sites outside Chengdu, I asked Regina if Chunhua could possibly travel with us. Regina liked the idea and said she would check room availability at the hotels. When she said everything was set, I approached my friend.

"Would you like to come with us to Leshan and Emeishan? Everyone would love it."

Her eyes widened, her grin reaching from ear to ear. "Yes! I talk with my husband."

When she boarded our bus a day later, her husband saw us off with smiles and a box of just-picked peaches. Everyone waved to him as the bus pulled out. For the next three days she and I were nearly inseparable even though we struggled at times with the language barrier. Her English was still somewhat limited but far better than my smattering of Chinese.

She mentioned our first meeting in 1980, when my parents had translated our first brief conversation. "I study English so you, me have friendship like our mothers."

Her comment touched me. I knew I couldn't put all the burden of communication on her shoulders. "I will study Chinese," I said. "We can write letters to each other."

She told tales of our mothers, most of them new to me, and we laughed and giggled like schoolgirls. Her mother, Dr. Zhang, had grown up in Chengdu. Mom often rode her bicycle into the city from the university campus, which was outside the city walls, and they would study in the gardens of Wenshu Yuan, a Buddhist monastery and temple near Dr. Zhang's childhood home. They also played mahjong together, which I hadn't known. It seemed so out of character for the mother I grew up with.

Mom had shared only the story of their mutual pledge to look at the full moon each month and think of the friend far away. On one of Mom's trips to China in the 1980s, Dr. Zhang had given her a painting created especially for her. Under a full moon a woman is seated at a guzheng, a traditional stringed instrument. A poem in Chinese on the painting tells their story. The painting now hangs in my home, reminding me of the friendship between our families.

The highlight of the last few days in Sichuan was our visit to Emeishan (shan means "mountain"), forty-five miles south-west of Chengdu. Emeishan received World Heritage status in 1996, bestowed for its forest diversity and the many cultural features such as its Buddhist temples. Within the protected area are two thousand animal species and three thousand plant species, including a hundred found nowhere else.

Mount Omei, as my parents called it, is more than ten thousand feet high and one of five mountains sacred to Chinese Buddhists. The first Buddhist temple in China was built on its summit in the first century AD. In the 1930s there were six-ty-five temples on the mountain. Many of these were ravaged during the Cultural Revolution, but some thirty temples still remain and welcome pilgrims today. The streams flowing off the mountain have carved steep, narrow canyons. Many paths wind around the base among huge rocks and up the mountain, connecting the temples like pearls on a string.

More than a hundred years ago, West China missionaries negotiated with a Buddhist temple to allow them to build cottages on a portion of temple land. This compound became an interdenominational summer retreat where the missionaries could escape the intense heat and humidity of the plain below. The cottages are long gone now. Dad wrote of the climb he and Mom made to the Gin Din (Golden Summit) in 1931, hiking up the stone steps of the pilgrims' path. They stayed overnight in temples, using their own cots and bedding "to avoid 'wee visitors'" in the night. Before leaving home I printed Dad's account, which included a rough hand-drawn map, to read while on the mountain.

Two cable cars had been built to carry visitors up the

mountain in two stages. A road links the two, with buses between for people who don't want, or are unable, to walk the footpath. We didn't have the time needed to walk any of the pilgrims' path, so our delegation took the cable cars. The lower one let us off near a monastery–temple complex called Wannian Si that Dad had mentioned in his account. Wannian Si commemorates the monk who brought Buddhism to China from India. Although most of the buildings in the monastery complex were of typical Chinese design, the temple was square with a rounded dome and no upturned eaves. Inside is a large golden Buddha riding a life-sized white stone elephant. Each of the elephant's feet stands in a lotus flower, the symbol of purity and enlightenment.

As we wandered the gardens, I was enchanted by the abundance of beautiful butterflies. While a large yellow one continuously flitted around my head, a story about Dad came to mind. When my parents went trekking, he carried a net to study butterflies up close. One time he brought a particularly beautiful one to show Mom—to me an expression of his love. I followed the circling yellow butterfly, thoughts of my father filling my head. "Hi, Dad," I whispered, my tears welling.

Too soon word circulated that it was time to leave. Some of our group were already waiting at the bus. I did not want to go. There was so much to learn from being in this special place. The beauty of Mount Omei and the many stories I'd heard over the years left me feeling I was walking in my parents' footsteps.

"Steph, we'll come back someday," I vowed.

When we returned to the United States after those two weeks, it seemed like I'd been gone for months. I called Jeri and learned Mom was much improved though still in skilled nursing. I drove down to see her as soon as I'd recovered from jet lag. To my delight I found my mother sitting in a chair feeding herself lunch while Carla, at her side, grinned at me. Mom had gained weight and appeared healthier than I'd seen her in years. Looking pleased with herself, bright-eyed and happy, she asked eagerly about my trip.

Unbeknownst to family members, Dr. G. had started her on antidepressant medication while she was delirious in the hospital. In the month since I'd last seen her, as Jeri and Carla and her assistants brought Mom from the brink of death, the antidepressant had been doing its work. This person with the sunny nature was not the mother I had grown up with. I was glimpsing a woman who took joy in life, the woman who had captured my father's heart.

 Chapter 18

On the last day of 1998, I was having breakfast with my mother at the small table in her sitting area. I'd driven from Vermont the previous day to spend the New Year's holiday with her, staying in a room reserved for residents' guests. She liked to start her day with a quick breakfast in her apartment but always ate her other meals in the dining room.

Regarding me with a cocked eyebrow, Mom said, "There's a New Year's Eve party tonight. Do you want to go?"

Images of what a seniors' celebration might look like flashed through my mind. "There's a party here?"

"Yes, in the activity room."

"Sure, why not?" I said, readying myself for anything.

"That's what I thought too." The corners of her mouth turned up. "Why not?"

I smiled back. "You know, I think this will be the first New Year's Eve we've celebrated together. About time, huh?"

I got up, gave her a quick hug, and carried our cereal bowls to the sink. One thing was certain, I thought as I washed the few dishes. Welcoming 1999 with my mother in a senior residential center would be the most unusual New Year's Eve of my life.

Swing music was playing that evening when we arrived in the activity room, which looked rather festive with crepe paper streamers and a lighted Christmas tree in a corner. Tables surrounded a central cleared space where a half dozen couples danced. Mom chose a place to sit while I surveyed the refreshment table and brought back two ginger ales. Over the next hour as the room became more crowded, we chatted briefly with close to a dozen people who stopped by our table—two couples and the rest women, mostly younger than Mom's ninety years.

She introduced me to everyone and gave me more information after they moved on. Two women sat down for fifteen or twenty minutes to converse, but beyond small talk I was content to let Mom chat with her friends. With the music and the room's linoleum floor and low ceiling, having a group conversation was difficult. I liked just sitting with her and watching how relaxed she was. The tension that had emanated from her in the past was gone, and she laughed easily.

Around ten thirty Mom turned to me. "Well, I think I've had enough. How about you?"

"Yes, it's fine with me to go now. I don't often stay up to welcome in the New Year."

As we walked back to her apartment, I said, "I hadn't expected a raucous evening, and it wasn't. The party was nice, and I enjoyed meeting your friends."

I stayed another half hour chatting, then returned to my room. More than anything the evening had been pleasurable because Mom had been so pleasant to everyone, me included. We spent the next day together relaxing and talking. We chatted a lot about John and Steph, and we discussed work too, hers and mine both. She seemed genuinely interested in what I was doing. As always I looked through the China photo albums, never tiring of these scenes.

"Tell me more about what you thought of Mount Omei," she asked at one point.

We'd had other conversations about my trip the previous June but hadn't talked in detail.

"It was amazing to walk around the Gin Din area and the temples, knowing you and Dad had been there sixty-six years before."

"I wish I could have been with you." Her eyes grew distant for a moment, and then her faded blue gaze returned to me. "Mount Omei was special to us."

"I know." I reached out and squeezed her hand. "From the old photo the cottage looks cozy—rustic but cute. You had a good view of the summit from there."

In the mid-1980s the son of one of their missionary friends had visited the site of the missionary compound and had written about what he'd found. Only a few buildings being used at the time for livestock had survived the Cultural Revolution.

"Our cottage was set off a bit from the others." She smiled. "Like a hideaway." For a few moments she was lost in her memories.

"Steph and I stood a while on top looking down at the lower ridges. There's a railing along that mile-high sheer drop-off now. We wondered where the cottages had been. But it was impossible both from the haze—"

"Ah, the mists of Mount Omei. . . ."

"Yes, but also there were many ridges below. It was hard to know which was yours." I gave her a smile. "I wish it had been clear enough to see the snow mountains of Tibet to the west. You know how I'd love to see the Minya Konka." I remembered reading to Dad in his final days from *Men Against the Clouds*.

"I'm so glad Steph joined the delegation too," I continued. "Sharing the experience of Mount Omei with her was special. It's a beautiful mountain—with a great aura, as Dad would say." I grinned. "The summit with its temples is so peaceful. I wish we'd had more time."

"Maybe you can go back sometime."

"I intend to." The delight in her eyes warmed me inside.

Driving home the next day, I reflected on our visit. There was an ease to our visiting now, yet speaking from the heart seemed tough for us both. *With the tension gone, why do I still feel guarded? It's simply a matter of telling her how I feel, which I can do now. She barricaded her tender feelings so long ago, she may have difficulty taking that first step. Next time I'll speak from my heart like I could with Dad,* I vowed. I felt the potential for a new relationship with her and looked forward to more visits.

Mom's hospitalization the previous May had been such a turning point. Dr. G. had recognized my mother's depression long ago, but Mom had always refused both medication and counseling. *Bless Dr. G. for adding the antidepressant to her daily pills,* I thought. That, along with the loving support of Jeri and Carla and the stable of round-the-clock caregivers, had revived in my mother a desire to live.

Mom was already a different person when I'd visited upon returning from China. The signs of stress were mostly gone from her face. With her appetite back, she was no longer gaunt as a scarecrow. She soon resumed her weekly heart lectures to medical students, nurses, interns, and others. Jeri still came daily to do things for her and take her places she needed to go.

Carla remained in Mom's life, too, after the crisis had passed. Caring and irreverent, she was quick to laugh, tossing her thick, curly black hair. She could jolly Mom out of her now-infrequent flashes of temper, teasing and making wise-cracks no one with a long history with Mom would dare make. Carla, a buxom woman, once referred to her own breasts as "jugs" compared with Mom's "fried eggs." I also heard her call Mom "Doc-a-roo." Mom took it all in good humor, which astounded me. She would never have tolerated such labels in the days before the antidepressant medication.

Carla also brought silliness into Mom's life again, some-thing missing after Dad's death. She invited Mom to her house on Halloween and dressed her as a witch—I would not have dared—and had her welcome the trick-or-treaters. Mom loved it. I was grateful to Carla for her continuing interest. She was able to show love openly to Mom when others, including me, still recovering from past emotional scars, held back.

Mom's happier outlook had allowed me to ease back into my life without constant worry. I now worked nearly full-time on projects with colleagues at the new national park in Vermont. I called Mom weekly but didn't drive to Pittsburgh as often to visit. In late autumn I called to let her know I'd split from my longtime partner. She expressed concern for me.

"Why don't you move down here so you can be closer?"

Her unexpected question touched me. "Thanks, Mom; I really appreciate the thought."

"Surely you could find environmental work down here."

"I might be able to," I said, trying to pick my words carefully to not offend her. "But my current projects are some of the most interesting I've ever had. Also, I've put roots down in Vermont, and I don't think I'd be happy in a big city."

"I don't want you to be lonely all by yourself," she said. "You're always welcome if you change your mind."

"I know, Mom, and I appreciate your thoughts. I'm doing fine, really."

As we wrapped up our call and I put the phone back in its cradle, I realized her words came closer to expressing love than ever before.

This was the changed context of our relationship when I visited her over New Year's. I had sensed in our frequent phone conversations she was more relaxed, but still the visit was an eye-opener. She had used a cane before her illness because of vertigo but never that unwanted symbol of aging, the walker. Now she used one daily. Walking with her to the dining room was a joy as she laughed and chatted with everyone she met. Jeri had given her a life-sized stuffed cat that she kept in her walker. She would grab the cat and have it meow and talk with the nurses and aides and other residents. Unlike in the months after Dad's death, her joking was engaging and unforced. She truly seemed to be enjoying life.

Mom now looked a decade younger than her ninety years. She had put twenty pounds on her once-emaciated body. The haggard look was gone from her face, and the added weight along with her good humor softened the stress lines. This is the woman Dad married, I thought, watching her laugh and talk with people. The young woman who had captured Dad's attention had finally emerged from the shadows of her tormented childhood.

Witnessing this transformation filled me with happiness for her.

In April came a 6:00 a.m. phone call from Jeri. "Mom's had a brain hemorrhage," she said, her voice tight. "It's much worse than any of Dad's strokes."

She and Joe were on their way to the university hospital to meet the ambulance from Sherwood Oaks. A nurse on her dawn rounds had found Mom unconscious on the floor beside her bed. It was the day of her weekly lecture. She always set her alarm for five o'clock on those days to be ready when Jeri and Joe picked her up to drive into Pittsburgh. The hemorrhage must have happened when she got up, as she was still in her pajamas.

As Jeri talked, my mind swirled with these images, my stomach rolling and a sour taste in my mouth.

"I'll call when I know more," Jeri said.

"What about Don?"

"Sherwood Oaks called him first, then me. He's driving to the hospital separately."

"I'll book a flight right now," I said, needing to take some action.

"Wait till I know how bad it is," she said. "We're almost there. I'll call you right back."

As I put the phone down, dread grabbed at my gut. Guilt at not having visited more often washed over me along with frustration at being a hard day's drive away. Five years earlier I was happy to live this distance from Pittsburgh, but not now. *Thank god for Jeri*, I thought for the umpteenth time since she'd entered our family circle. *She's the most steadfast of all of us*. I trusted her to be there and do what was best for Mom.

A sudden harsh *b-r-r-i-i-n-g* caused me to jump. I grabbed the phone, my heart pounding.

"It's really bad, honey. She knew me and reached out but couldn't speak."

"I'll hang up and find a flight."

"You won't make it. The bleed is massive. I just hope Don gets here in time. I have to get back. I said I'd stay with her."

My heart stopped for a second, and in that brief pause I thought of being with Dad at the end. I knew Jeri would be as loving with Mom as she was with Dad.

"Bless you, Jeri, for being there." My voice broke. I swallowed, then continued. "Tell Mom I love her."

I hung up the phone and burst into tears. How could I have let myself get so wrapped up in work that I hadn't visited since New Year's?

A little later I called Don since I hadn't heard from him. He was still at home.

"Why aren't you on your way to the hospital?"

"I'm leaving soon," he said. "I've been looking for Mom's advance directive."

"You don't need it. Get to the hospital if you want to see her before she dies."

Shortly after I phoned Don, Mom died in Jeri's arms. Jeri had called Carla, and she was there too, holding Mom's hand.

Jeri cried into the phone afterward. "She had another hemorrhage and never regained consciousness. I stayed with her to the end."

Somehow, I was able to speak despite feeling as if a sharp knife had sliced through me.

"She knew you were there, Jeri." I stopped briefly, gathering myself, knowing the tears were returning. "I'm so glad you and Carla were with her so she wasn't alone."

After a good cry, I called Marilyn and gave her the sad news.

"She didn't linger, Marilyn," I said. "She told me once she wanted to go quickly. Seeing what Dad had gone through had been her nightmare."

"I'm glad she's finally at peace," my sister said.

We held Mom's memorial service a month later at the Baptist church with Gary officiating. I wasn't as involved in the planning as with Dad's service, consulting mostly with Don by phone. I poured my feelings into preparing a photo collage of Mom's life containing all the people and places most meaningful to her. I found pictures of her with her medical-school classmates, including their 1936 graduation and the 1980 reunion. In addition to photos of Mom as a young girl with her siblings, Mom and Dad at the Minya Konka, our family, and her with Jeri and Carla, I located one with her Children's Hospital colleagues. Jeri gave me a picture taken in Mom's last months when she was happy and free from stress. I put that photo in the center of the collage—it was how I wanted to remember her.

Many of the people who came for Dad's service attended Mom's too. Again we had a microphone set up and invited people to share their memories. Ellyn told a story that gave me a glimpse of Dr. Cora, the physician.

"One thing you may not know about Cora—she wrote a personal letter to each family that lost a child to heart disease," she said. "No one asked her to do this. She did it faithfully, on her own and without fanfare."

As I sat in the family pew, tears came to my eyes while Ellyn spoke. I thought of the cards and letters that flooded my parents' mailbox every Christmas. Mom had always given me the big wicker basket of cards to look through, as some were from relatives or Chinese friends I knew. But I'd read the cards and letters from the parents of patients too. She had written to more than just those who had lost children. Many of the personal notes told of patients who were alive and thriving. In every case the writers expressed gratitude for Mom's kindness and the care they had received. Mom kept all those cards. I'm glad she did, as they spoke of the woman who was able to open her heart and show the compassion and love inside.

In the week after the service, Marilyn, Jeri, and I sorted through her things, telling stories of Dad and Mom, both funny and sad. At one point I came across Mom's 1929 college year-book and leafed quickly to her photo. In it, she's smiling rather coquettishly, her pretty face framed by dark blond curls—despite the black-and-white image, I visualized her in living color.

"Hey, listen to this," I said to Marilyn and Jeri, reading the text beside the photo: "A ripple of laughter, a gleam of bright eyes, the toss of a blond head, and who would think Cora ever had a serious thought? But underneath her love of fun there is a determination, a tenacity, and an intellect. She has cast her lot with the medical world, and 'medicine' will not be the loser."

Marilyn and I looked at each other.

"This woman wasn't the mother we grew up with," I said, "but I'm glad we got to meet her at long last."

Children have only a partial understanding of who their parents are. A child's brain is not equipped to grasp the full measure of a mother or a father, much less fathom the intricacies of adult relationships. The tributes from Mom's colleagues and the condolences of Mom's friends at Sherwood Oaks allowed me to gain a more complete picture of my mother. It was not unlike turning a crystal and seeing through a different facet, much like witnessing my mother greet her classmates in Chengdu in 1980. I welcomed this more complex, multifaceted view of her, as it allowed me to let the mother I grew up with recede in my memory.

All these experiences and insights helped me process my grief and enabled me to let go of my childhood memories and the associated guilt and shame. I may always carry inside a yearning to have had a mother who was able to show her more tender feelings. And that's okay, because now I feel only love for her and compassion for the pain she carried in her heart for so long.

Not until after the service, arriving home from a grueling eleven-hour drive, did I feel the full force of my mother's death. As I inserted the key in my front door, my first thought, from force of habit, was that I had to call Mom and report my safe arrival home. She had insisted on each of my visits that I call so she knew I'd arrived safely. Every time, this request had grated—I'd felt it was her way of treating me like a kid. With my hand still on the doorknob, I knew I'd had it all wrong. Her desire to hear of my safe arrival had come purely from her concern for me, from the love she could not show.

Never again would she be making that request. Never again would she be at the other end of the phone line. Sinking to a chair, I gave in to the fathomless grief washing over me.

 Chapter 19

On my New Year's visit Mom had asked me for a favor, to which I said yes. She wanted her papers sent to the Archives and Special Collections on Women in Medicine housed at Women's Medical College of Pennsylvania when she died.[1] In going through Mom's belongings after her memorial service, I found two long bankers boxes marked for the archive and hauled them back to Vermont. When I opened the first box several weeks later, I flashed back to the sorting I'd done when I found the China letters. She had seemingly saved every scrap of paper that crossed her desk.

Some decisions were easy—letters, journal articles she'd authored, awards, and guest lectures she'd given. When I encountered multiple copies of published journal articles, I kept one for myself. Other items I wanted a record of, such as awards, I photocopied. But when I came to her first medical diploma from West China Union University, I sat back and stared for several minutes. This first diploma, affixed to a plaque and lacquered, was stunning in its beauty and uniqueness, from the graceful hand-lettered Chinese characters to the small formal photograph. The buttons on the neck of her white dress disclosed she was wearing a Chinese silk dress under her graduation gown. My mind swirled with thoughts of what it had taken her to earn this document—including traveling halfway around the world and learning Chinese. I knew she had treasured this diploma, as it was always displayed in the most prominent spot in her office. Her second degree—the one she'd needed to get a medical license in 1948—was off to the side with other certifications.

Various emotions jostled inside as I thought about giving up this treasure, from pride at her accomplishment to admiration for her grit and doggedness to thankfulness Dad had supported her as she pursued her dream. I wasn't quite ready to part with this diploma and instead sent a good photograph to the archive. I could always donate it in the future.

When I came to her research papers, I needed help and called Dr. Z., her longtime colleague in the cardiology division of Children's Hospital.

"With most of Mom's papers, I've been able to figure out what was important to send to the archive," I said. "But with her research notes, I'm not sure what I'm looking at and what's important to keep. Would you mind looking through these?"

"I'd be happy to help. You know, Cora was one of my favorite people."

"That's very kind of you," I said. "I'm planning a trip to Pittsburgh soon and will be in touch when I know the dates."

A month later I drove the familiar route to Jeri and Joe's house, where I'd arranged to stay for several days. Dr. Z. no longer worked full-time and had invited me to come to his home outside Pittsburgh. The next afternoon I drove to his house, where he met me at the door.

"Jackie, come in." He smiled. "It's good to see you again."

"Thanks for getting together with me. I appreciate your help."

"No problem," he said, leading me into his living room.

I handed him the folder I'd brought and sat down. "These materials have me stumped."

After several minutes leafing through the folder, he looked up. "This is the documentation for her last paper. Cora's research on this congenital defect was remarkable, especially considering she was in her mideighties at the time." He told me Mom's last paper had established her as the expert on that particular heart defect and said her contributions to the literature had been considerable.

Handing the folder back, he said that in the months preceding Mom's death, the division had been planning a conference on the teaching benefits of preserved hearts in an age of computerization. For nearly two decades my mother had catalogued the malformed hearts in the Children's Hospital heart museum. These hearts, donated by parents whose children had succumbed to their congenital abnormalities, were used in teaching and research and informed treatment protocol and possible surgical corrections.

"Cora participated in planning the conference," Dr. Z. said, handing me an official brochure. "It opened just after she died. We dedicated the conference to her."

My eyes prickled with tears as I took the brochure from him. "That was nice of you to honor her in that way."

A bit later as I stood to leave, I said, "Thank you for your help and for the support you always gave my mother."

I reflected on our conversation during the long drive home several days later. Dr. Z. had known her so well. They had begun working together in the latter 1960s. She had just completed a pediatric cardiology fellowship when he offered her a position in the newly formed cardiology division at Children's Hospital. They had been the only two doctors in the beginning months. He understood her abilities as a physician and her fierce determination to deliver the best care for patients. More than any other doctor beyond Dad, he saw who my mother was and gave her the respect and recognition she deserved. He offered his friendship as well.

After taking a break in the driving to get gas, I got back on the interstate with two-thirds of the drive to Vermont ahead of me. I soon slipped back into reflection, remembering the summer before my senior year in high school when I had helped in Mom's office in the Philippi clinic. It had been fascinating to watch her with babies and toddlers, perhaps her favorite ages to treat. Children of this age often cry during a physical exam, but she had several ways to get their attention so she could proceed with the examination. One was to make a "pishing" sound similar to what birdwatchers use to bring birds closer. Hearing that noise, the baby would stop crying and squint at Mom long enough for her to hear the tiny heart and lungs through her stethoscope.

She also distracted children with big flashy rings. Some were chunky costume jewelry, but her favorites had been the Tibetan rings she bought in 1932 from Buddhist monks at a monastery in eastern Tibet. The great silver saddles were set with large rough-cut turquoise and coral stones—rings that dwarf the proximal joint of my middle finger. Mom would waggle her fingers with the big baubles and the babies would be mesmerized. I like to think she used these silver saddles to keep her memories alive of their trek into Tibet.

The tributes paid to my mother at her memorial service, and in letters and conversations after her death, helped me see a more complete picture of her. A letter from the chief of pathology at Children's Hospital said this: "Cora Lenox was a treasure. Until her final days she could be found in the pathology department at Children's Hospital, surrounded by a group of students, teaching them the intricacies of congenital heart disease she knew so well."

Tributes like this helped me trade my imperfect child's perspective of my mother for a more honest understanding of the talented, complex woman she was. I knew she was an excellent physician, giving of herself unstintingly in teaching medical students, cardiology fellows, pediatric residents, interns, and nurses. Similarly, she was uncompromising in demanding—of herself as well as others—the highest quality of patient care.

I have come to understand my mother as a pioneer woman physician. While not among the first women who fought to get into medical school, she was part of the next wave. She was among the vanguard who challenged the gender bias that made it difficult for women to obtain hospital privileges and gain further training after medical school. At an age when most people are considering retirement, Mom entered academic medicine, where women are still underrepresented today. She became a full professor of pediatrics and, for her last seventeen years, a professor emeritus.

Succeeding as a woman doctor in the 1930s and the decades that followed required tenacity, grit, and thick skin. Throughout these years my mother stayed strong in her resolve and her dedication to medicine. She spoke up to my father in China when she feared her career was being set aside during the wartime conditions of their last four years there. She was not content to be relegated to home life even then. When she faced gender discrimination in the Philippi clinic, her survivor instinct from childhood kicked in. Just as going to China provided an escape from her domineering, abusive father, pursuing further medical training enabled her to sidestep the biases of a colleague. Her native stubbornness did not allow for giving up.

After she died, I came across a photo of Mom and her siblings when she was about thirteen. She has her arm around her two younger brothers, who stand in front of her, while her sister, a year older, stands with downcast eyes behind Mom's shoulder. Mom, unsmiling, stares directly at the photographer, a "don't mess with me" expression on her face. The photo captures the fortitude and toughness that helped her succeed in medicine.

Several years ago, I read an op-ed by a woman of my generation who said her smart, college-educated mother had not pursued her desire for a career. Instead, she had stayed at home to take care of her children and ended up frustrated and unhappy. The author described a childhood resembling mine to a remarkable extent. In reflecting on my life, I've decided that given the choice between a mother who was at home, unhappy and unfulfilled, or a mother who pursued her passion, albeit troubled from other factors, I would choose my situation all over again.

I hadn't considered my mother a model to emulate as I was growing up. Yet sometime in my forties I realized she had indeed provided me with a model: that of a woman claiming her right to a career. And the traits that complicated her home life—her strong will, her demand for perfection, her "no man will treat me that way" resolve—enabled her to successfully navigate a professional world relatively closed to women at the time.

My mother's greatest passion in the last decades of her life was cardiac morphology, the study of heart structure. This was foreshadowed by a family Christmas Eve tradition beginning when I was ten or so and continuing into my teens. As a holiday treat my parents allowed us kids to stay up late while they prepared the turkey for the next day's dinner. Making giblet gravy was part of the tradition. Before dropping the turkey heart into the pan with the other giblets, Mom would cut the heart open with a paring knife and give us an anatomy lesson.

Pointing to one of the upper chambers with the tip of the knife, she explained, "This is called the right atrium, where the blood, carrying carbon dioxide, enters the heart. Then here"— she gently spread the delicate valve with the knife tip—"the blood goes into the right ventricle through this valve. When the right ventricle pumps the blood along, the valve keeps the blood from backing up into the atrium. The blood goes out here"—she pointed again with the knife tip to the opening of a blood vessel—"to the lungs, where carbon dioxide is exchanged for oxygen." She continued in this way to show how the left side of the heart sent oxygenated blood via the aorta throughout the body. I remember her deft use of the knife and the wonder I felt at understanding how the heart works. I looked forward to the ritual each Christmas. She repeated the demonstration for my children one Christmas when she and Dad spent the holiday with us.

Eight years after joining the cardiology division, Mom assumed responsibility for the Children's Hospital heart museum. The collection grew from five hundred to twenty-four hundred hearts under her watch. For every single one, she listed the diagnosis and the patient's name, age at death, and medical history. Drawing on what she had learned in overseeing the heart museum, she authored or coauthored numerous journal articles and chapters in four medical textbooks.

Several times I accompanied Mom to the heart museum while she prepared for her weekly lecture. We would first stop at her office, where she donned her white coat, then walk to the museum on the pathology floor. The sign on the door read: "The Frank E. Sherman and Cora C. Lenox Heart Museum," the former being the surgeon who had begun the collection.

I remember the wave of pride that swept over me the first time I visited the museum with her. "Nice sign, Mom," I said as she pushed the door open.

We entered a small, sterile-feeling room with floor-to-ceiling stainless steel shelves containing glass jars of hearts in a preservative solution, each numbered. She selected several jars, brought them to a steel table in the center of the room, and set out several metal probes. These hearts she would use during her lecture on cardiac morphology the next day.

On one such occasion, she decided to show me one of the hearts. "Jackie, let's look at this one," she said. "It's very interesting."

Sitting on a stool, she pulled on medical gloves to protect her hands from the preservative. When she opened the jar, a familiar smell wafted out—formalin?

"Whew! I feel like I'm back in the biology lab, Mom."

She gently lifted the heart out and proceeded to show me why it had not been viable. I understood the normal heart from college anatomy classes and those turkey-heart demonstrations from childhood. As she explained how this heart had functioned compared to normal hearts, I visualized a diagram of the blood circulating between the abnormal heart and the lungs. The session was riveting. Time passed quickly, free of the usual tension in our relationship. We both were engrossed in the examination of the heart—she the teacher, I the student. She offered her knowledge, and I accepted it appreciatively.

Although I don't remember the details, she also shared the story of the child whose heart we studied that day. She knew the medical story behind each heart, whether she had known the child personally or not. But some children had been her patients, and she knew them well. If I had listened more carefully, I might have heard compassion in her voice, but I hadn't expected this emotion from her then. I remember, though, the reverence with which she handled the heart. She gave the impression of holding something exceedingly precious. I believe when she held one of those hearts in her hands, she felt she was holding that child's spirit.

Five years after Mom's death, my brother Don sent me a short essay, written by a physician, that had appeared in a 2002 issue of an American College of Cardiology journal review.

Titled "David's Heart," the essay begins:

> I met Cora while on elective at Children's Hospital.
> She had been there for 30 years caring for children,
> teaching young doctors the evaluation and treatment
> of congenital heart disease and caretaking the thou-
> sands of tiny hearts in the pathology lab—silent and
> still in jars of Jores solution. She was thin with weath-
> ered skin and a somewhat slow, purposeful walk, but
> her eyes and fingers danced as she showcased the intri-
> cacies of the malformed hearts. . . .
>
> . . . Many of these hearts had belonged to [Cora's]
> patients, and she knew their symptoms, their physical
> findings, what interventions were attempted, [and]
> which were successful or palliative or neither. She knew
> their lives, too, and once in a while as we talked, she
> seemed to fade away to a distant encounter, her face
> only then showing the strain and sorrow of her years
> of practice. But she would quickly brighten, almost
> willing herself to return to the present.

In the essay, the author tells a story Mom had shared with
him of a resident whose brother David had died in infancy
because his aorta hadn't developed properly. The family had
donated David's body but had never heard anything more.
The resident had asked my mother after a teaching session
if one of the hearts could be David's. Mom said she would
look into it.

She brought David's heart to the next teaching session.
The essay continues:

> It fit easily in the palm of [the resident's] hand. . . .
>
> She silently caressed the little heart for several
> minutes then laid it to rest back in its jar and tight-
> ened the lid.

"Now you tell your mother that David's heart is used for teaching," Cora instructed her. The resident paused. "I think she would cry," she said faintly.

"That's good. Crying is good."...

Cora never found out whether the resident told her mother about David's heart, but generations of physicians have since held this little boy's heart in their hands.[2]

Tears came to my eyes as I read the article, and I wished I could talk again with my mother. She knew so much about the physical structure and functioning of the heart. Perhaps her greatest gift as a teacher was ensuring the hearts were not just clinical specimens in jars but represented children who should be remembered.

Mom knew intuitively that allowing emotions to surface was good for the soul. Her compassion and empathy were always there. Love was in my mother's heart, too, even if blocked at times by anger. For me, letting go of childhood resentment and feeling empathy for what Mom endured has allowed forgiveness, unconditional love, and pride for my mother to slip into my heart.

PART III:

Finding

Myself

 Chapter 20

My parents had identical wills with an opening sentence stating what they wanted done with their remains. That single sentence conveys so well who they were.

"I hereby direct that my remains be cremated and the ashes therefrom be preserved until, with the ashes of my spouse John/Cora, they be sprinkled into the waters of the Tygart Valley River in Philippi, West Virginia, eventually to mingle symbolically in infinitesimal amounts with global waters, thereby signifying my feeling of identity with peoples of all nations and races and the hope for a worldwide family of nations with justice and peace for all."

When Dad died in 1996, his ashes remained at the crematorium, waiting to be joined with Mom in death. Before I left on my 1998 trip to China, a close family friend had asked if I was taking some of my father's ashes with me. I hadn't thought of this, as I knew of the clause in their wills, but the idea stayed with me. The summer after Mom died, my siblings and I planned a trip to Philippi to honor their request. We also invited Jeri and Joe to join us. Marilyn flew east to Vermont and the two of us drove to Jeri and Joe's home on the outskirts of Pittsburgh. Jeri had invited us to stay with them the nights before and after our trip to West Virginia.

The day was clear and sunny when we four drove to Philippi, the first time I'd been back in years. We met Don and Carol at an overlook on the college campus. Dad had loved this view of the river and the railroad beside it winding through town. Our gathering had an air of celebration despite the occasion's poignancy. Don had brought our parents' ashes. We were about to launch them on a grand journey that would echo their three-month honeymoon to China in 1930.

I broached the idea I'd been considering. "I'd like to reserve some of Dad and Mom's ashes to take back to China. I don't have specific plans, but I'll be returning in the next few years."

"What will you do with their ashes?" Don asked.

"I was thinking of scattering them in places important to them, like Mount Omei and possibly their campsite opposite the Minya Konka, if I can find it. I don't think they'd be opposed, do you?"

"I think they'd love it," Marilyn said. "They probably never dreamed it could happen."

With everyone in agreement, we left the overlook and drove into town, turning onto a dirt road along the river. Dad taught me to drive on this road, I realized with a flash. The river, its banks muddy, appeared shallow and sluggish. I had remembered it as bigger and wondered how we would get their ashes into the center of the river to the better current. We drove slowly, scouting along the bank for a good spot. Up ahead Don stuck his arm out and pointed toward a small spit extending into the water. We parked and got out to investigate. The spit, just wide enough for one person, seemed our best option. After a moment for each of us to say a silent goodbye to Mom and Dad, Don carried the brown metal box with their ashes onto the spit. As I visualized the journey they were about to take, I realized we had a problem.

"Hey," I called. "Dad and Mom are never going to get to global waters. There are many dams between here and the Gulf of Mexico."

Don, halfway out the spit, turned and walked back. After a brief discussion, we decided to honor their request. Don walked to the end of the spit, took a handful of ashes, and flung them as far as he could. But there was no breeze. I watched as the ashes drifted down into the water not far from his feet and sank to the bottom in a whitish-gray blob.

"How long does it take for ashes to dissolve?" I asked, turning to Marilyn. "Will Mom and Dad just become part of the bottom muck?"

We were both horrified, but it also struck us as rather funny.

"Not even Mom and Dad thought of this," I said.

Don continued to throw ashes, and eventually some began to move downstream a bit. But a grayish mound remained conspicuously just off the spit. In the end he scattered only a third of the ashes. I became guardian of the rest for my next trip to China.

We walked back to our cars, eventually saying goodbye to Don and Carol, and the four of us drove back to Pittsburgh. That evening, in honor of Mom and Dad, we found a Chinese restaurant, pulled up two extra chairs, and requested six sets of chopsticks, as if they were there too. We ordered Mom's favorite dish, *hui guo ru* (twice-cooked pork), along with other favorites, and had a delicious, laughter-filled evening of reminiscing.

While we were still sitting around the table, I looked at Jeri and Joe and said, "These last days have been a lot of fun. Why don't you two come with us to Vermont tomorrow and stay a few days. Marilyn isn't leaving right away, so we can all visit some more. Do you have anything planned?"

Marilyn echoed the thought. "Yes, come! Getting us all together is difficult."

Jeri turned to Joe. "I can't think of anything in the next few days that requires us to be home, can you? Lisa can feed the cat."

Joe agreed, then said, "We'll drive our car. That way if Jackie doesn't treat us right, we can escape."

We all laughed. This was Joe's sense of humor—no mystery why he and Dad had become fast friends.

On our way the next morning, we stopped in Lewisburg, Pennsylvania, to visit Bucknell University, Dad's alma mater. In all my trips to Pittsburgh during my parents' last years, there never seemed to be enough time to stop. Next visit, I'd say, as I passed the I-80 Lewisburg exit.

We poked around the campus for an hour and found the quadrangle with the oldest buildings, which had been Dad's college. We sat on nearby benches and became silly, imagining Dad the jokester as a college student.

Leaving Lewisburg, as we crossed the Susquehanna River, an idea popped into my head. I pulled over after the bridge and turned the ignition off. Joe followed, and the four of us gathered by the roadside.

"We're going to give Mom and Dad another chance to reach global waters," I announced.

Chesapeake Bay—open water—was not far downstream. There might be dams between Lewisburg and the bay but far fewer than on the Ohio and Mississippi. We walked halfway across the big iron bridge and looked out high above the river. There was a good breeze blowing, and the Susquehanna flowed wide and deep, the current strong.

"This is perfect—a double-pronged strategy to get Dad and Mom to the ocean," I said, turning to Jeri. "You want to do the honors?"

"You bet!" The sparkle in her eyes spoke her love for my parents.

She launched the ashes, and as they drifted downward and away on the wind, two small yellow butterflies fluttered up from below the bridge.

Marilyn looked at me. "I think Dad and Mom just gave their blessing."

That autumn I began studying Chinese in a night class at the University of Vermont. The teacher, who was native-born, asked in our first class why we wanted to learn the language.

"Based on your answers, I will choose a Chinese name for each of you," she said. "We'll use them in class."

Names in China carry important meaning. They can be auspicious, culturally symbolic, or a thing of beauty or courage. Although a foreigner visiting China is often assigned a phonetic interpretation of their surname, our teacher wanted each of us to have a name with meaning.

When my turn came, I shared a brief version of my family story, then said, "I want to learn Chinese so I can travel on my own in China. I'd like the same surname my parents were given in 1930: Leng."

At the next class the teacher announced our Chinese names, going around the room one by one. "Your name is Leng Jie," she said to me. "Jie is a strong word, so I've given you a one-character name to go with your surname rather than the usual two characters."

I was embarrassed to learn Jie means "outstanding," never a term I had applied to myself. But perhaps the teacher had picked up on something.

Chinese is a tonal language. The same word spoken in a different tone has an entirely different meaning. From the beginning I could distinguish between the four tones because I grew up hearing my parents speak Chinese. A month later I understood the full extent of my advantage. I had struggled in class to pronounce a complex Chinese sound represented in pinyin by the letter R. (Pinyin is the linguistic system that translates Chinese characters into the Roman or Latin alphabet.) As I drove home after class, I played with the sound, not thinking much about it. Suddenly I heard myself give a decent pronunciation. I had relaxed into a configuration of mouth, tongue, and teeth that enabled me to make the sound. It felt natural to me.

My brain has a neural pathway for pronouncing Chinese that formed when, as a baby, I mimicked the sounds I heard my parents and our Chinese *amah* make. This "hear and mimic" pathway—how all babies learn their first words—is later supplanted by more complex speech and language centers that develop over succeeding years in a different part of the brain. In class I'd been using this more dominant pathway in trying to pronounce words. But in the car, without thinking, I had accessed the earlier system. From then on, I tried to relax and let the more primitive pathway lead. With grammar and vocabulary, though, I struggled like my classmates.

My proficiency in Chinese made a great leap forward in 2003 when I took a leave of absence from work and enrolled in a nine-week Beginning Chinese course at the Middlebury College summer language institute. When the course ended, I had learned more than a thousand words and could recognize and draw nearly the same number of characters. Although still a beginner, I felt more comfortable traveling on my own. I kept my eyes open for an opportunity to return to China.

A year later my friend Jeanne, who had led many tours to China before retiring from the travel business, told me she was planning a trip for friends in spring 2005 and needed a few more people. When she said the itinerary included a boat trip through the Yangzi (Yangtze) Gorges, I signed on. Dad had written in the China letters about traveling upriver through the gorges in 1930. His description had captivated me: dangerous rocks and whirlpools, wild rapids, raging currents, and men straining to pull boats upriver.

"The river wound crookedly between mountains rising abruptly two thousand feet above us, some sheer precipices overhanging the boat as if they would topple onto us at any moment. Rock strata of various colors ran in three or four directions, often twisted and whorled. Hitting a rapid, the undercurrents and force of the water set the boat rolling as if on the ocean, the bow inundated by muddy water beaten into a yellowish spray."

The following spring as I prepared for the trip, I knew my experience would be different from my parents'. The new Three Gorges Dam sat just below the gorges. For two years a reservoir had been rising behind it, already inundating the rapids and turbulent waters. But do you miss what you've never experienced? The dramatic setting would still exist: narrow gorges, steep mountains, temples perched on ridges.

My parents were on my mind as I packed. They had been my bridge to understanding China, my go-to sources when I had questions. I felt their loss immensely. *But you're coming with me,* I told them as I tucked a small red pouch of ashes into my luggage.

When our group arrived in China, I felt the same deep connection to the culture and landscapes as on my two previous visits. My anticipation grew as the time neared for the Yangzi boat trip, which began at the riverside city of Chongqing. We flew into a brand-new airport eight miles away. Industrial cranes were everywhere as our tour bus took us toward the city and the river. Block after block of concrete high-rises were under construction, the density mind-boggling. Were these office buildings? Apartments for the million people displaced by the rising reservoir?

Occasionally I saw flashes of green—remnant farmland—and once a small wooden building of traditional design. I craved these scenes from an earlier time because they connected me to a China familiar from my parents' photos and stories. With each of my visits, these glimpses of the past had become ever more difficult to find.

We saw little of the city, stopping briefly to walk through a market street before driving to the waterfront. Walking the short path to the pontoon where several Yangzi cruise boats waited, I remembered my parents' description from 1930. They had climbed hundreds of stone steps from the river to the city wall. The steps had been treacherously slippery from the water carriers constantly ascending into the city, each with a bamboo pole across his shoulders and a sloshing bucket dangling from either end of the pole. All my parents had written about was gone, torn down or covered by the reservoir. Chongqing had been known for those steps. Would Mom and Dad have recognized this place? Even before I boarded, the thought of what had been lost saddened me.

We departed at dusk as the lights of the city blinked on. Over the next several days I kept mostly to myself, staying on deck for long stretches, heedless of chill and damp and wind. This boat trip through the gorges was the main reason I'd come with Jeanne, and I wanted to wring every bit of meaning possible from the experience. I visited with others during meals. But whenever I was inside, it seemed I was in some plush western bubble, separated from the China slipping silently by outside—a China I yearned to absorb into my every pore.

At regular intervals, signs with numbers marched up from the river's edge. The highest marker—175 meters (574 feet)—was the reservoir's expected height when full. The water stood at the three-quarters mark. The slopes below 175 meters were mostly barren except for weeds and trash. Most of the old riverside towns had been torn down or blasted away, replaced by new concrete cities at higher elevations. Occasionally waters lapped at fields with ramshackle houses and tangerine trees. Here farmers continued tending the land, stubbornly waiting for the rising water to drive them away.

Not everything had been sacrificed to the reservoir. Some temples and other structures important to local people had been disassembled for reconstruction elsewhere. A few temples near the high-water mark awaited a protective retaining wall. We stopped at one such place—Shibaozhai, a red, twelve-story pavilion built against a cliff face to provide access to the temple on top. When the boat docked, I got off and walked the brief distance to the pavilion entrance and climbed the steep stairs to a round "moon" window overlooking the river and nearby farms still being worked. I looked down at the path where a few temporary food and souvenir booths still held forth for tourists, all that remained of the ancient river town.

I took photograph after photograph while in the gorges, wishing I could have experienced the river in 1930. *Oh, Dad and Mom, the river dragon has indeed been tamed.* Although the bustle at the water's edge was mostly gone, the natural beauty of the gorges remained. But, strangely for this wilderness lover, without people the riverside scenes seemed sterile. My heart ached for the farmers and the elderly who'd had to leave the Yangzi, the only life they'd known, for a China fast changing— the world of the concrete high-rises like those we'd seen on the way to Chongqing.

Dad had written about the difficult life along the river—at best a constant struggle to eke out a bare living and sometimes life-threatening, especially for the countless men who before steam power had toiled over the centuries to pull the junks upriver. I wondered, *does today's river experience inspire reverence and poetry as it did through the centuries before technology, when life in the gorges involved a unique, intimate relationship with the Yangzi?*

Throughout my time in the gorges I tried to comprehend how being born in this country defines me. No longer a tourist, I seek the China of my birth as a touchstone for understanding the China of today. The glimpses of an earlier time always resonate, always feel more authentic to me than today's concrete cities, which at first glance seem to have more in common with western cities.

I finally realized I carry that earlier China within me, much like a baby bird imprints on the first thing it sees, usually the mother, which triggers identity and bonding. In a similar sense, my earliest memories, my very first attempts at language that enable me today to speak Chinese with a Chengdu accent—and more that lies buried inside—are all part of the visceral essence of who I am.

On the last evening aboard ship, I climbed to the top deck, relieved to find myself alone. The next day we would pass through the lock at the Three Gorges Dam. The breeze, about ten knots, was a bit chilly but welcome after the stuffy lounge below. I sat watching the waning moon play hide-and-seek with the scudding clouds. I could just make out the dramatic mountain shapes floating by as the boat, engines rumbling, moved along the quiet water of the reservoir.

Taking the red pouch from my pocket, I stood and walked to the stern to catch the wind. The moon was suddenly clear of clouds as I grasped a handful of weightless ashes. With tears rolling down my cheeks, I lifted my hand and let the ashes stream back in the wind.

You're back in China, Mom and Dad, together forever. My love goes with you.

 Chapter 21

When Jeanne's tour ended after two weeks, I stayed behind in China for another three weeks. I had arranged to visit my friend Chunhua, the daughter of Mom's medical classmate, to gain a sense of her life and be immersed in Chinese culture in a way not available to a tour group. Getting to Chengdu took half a day traveling between airports. Speaking simple sentences in Chinese and aided by airport signs in English, I arrived uneventfully at the Chengdu airport, where Chunhua and her husband Yong welcomed me. We took a taxi into the city, where they lived not far from the university campus. Their two-bedroom apartment was small and simply furnished but quite comfortable.

Chunhua's friendliness put me at ease immediately. At first I wondered if Yong knew any English, but once he became comfortable with me he tried a little English now and then. My friend's English-language skills had improved since 1998. My Chinese could not support quick responses in conversation, so we spoke mostly in English, although I often asked the Chinese words for common items and wrote them in my journal.

On a typical morning I joined Chunhua and several friendly, curious women for tai chi in an outdoor courtyard of their apartment complex. After a breakfast of *xifan* (rice gruel) with pickled vegetables, she and I walked to a nearby sidewalk market where farmers displayed produce and meats. She had no refrigerator and bought vegetables and a small amount of meat daily, preparing meals using a two-burner gas stovetop and a rice cooker. The meals were delicious, mostly rice and vegetables augmented with a little tofu, pork, or chicken. The food, fragrant with spices, was at times fiery with Sichuan peppercorns. In Chengdu whenever someone asked if I liked Sichuan's spicy-hot food, I always answered, "*Wo shi Chengdu ren*," the easiest way to say I loved it like a native. The answer always drew a laugh. After washing dishes, we put them in a countertop drying apparatus, new to me, that sterilized them through heat. They had a small clothes washer, and we hung laundry in an enclosed porch to dry. On a tour one rarely sees these mundane aspects of people's lives.

Chunhua had recently retired from medicine. Retirement was mandatory at age fifty-five for professional women and age sixty for men. Yong, a civil engineer, still worked, although he accompanied us on several of our daily walks. She and I visited the old university campus one day. Seeing the buildings from my parents' time had become a pilgrimage of sorts for me. Because our house had been demolished in creating the shaded boulevard now bisecting the university, the old campus was the closest thing to my first home.

We also took the bus to Wenshu Yuan, the Buddhist temple and monastery near where Chunhua's mother had lived as a child. The original temple, built in the seventh century, had burned to the ground but had been rebuilt in the seventeenth century. Various structures dotted the thirteen acres of temple grounds—sacred halls, a pagoda, a teahouse, an underground crypt, and a three-story monastery library. As we sat in the peaceful temple gardens where our mothers had often studied, Chunhua regaled me with stories of our mothers' friendship.

Two of the university hospitals in my parents' time had been located not far from the temple, so they both had been familiar with the temple grounds. As Chunhua and I strolled the grounds, I felt connected to my parents and pictured them discovering the serenity and cultural beauty of this place.

In a different exploration, she and I browsed a shopping neighborhood near her apartment to see what was available: housewares, clothes, cameras, watches, a variety of small appliances, groceries, and more. I suspect she wanted to show me how much life in China had improved by 2005. The Chinese were proud of their society's flourishing in the decades after reopening to tourism. I reflected on my 1980 trip, when people had no such choices of consumer goods, and was glad for them. In a bookstore I bought several early reader children's books, intended for kindergarten level. When I said they were perfect for practicing my Chinese, Chunhua laughed out loud.

Those first days in Chengdu were exactly what I'd hoped for. I knew my friend had an irrepressible spirit and was fun to be with from our time together in 1998. Now I could picture her daily life. Our friendship was deepening, going beyond the connection to our mothers.

Several days into my visit, she asked, "You want to go Chongqing, meet my sister and brothers?"

"Yes, I'd like that," I said, telling her we hadn't seen much of the city on Jeanne's tour other than the restaurant where we had lunch and a quick visit to a nearby street market. I'd met Chunhua's two sons before but not her siblings, although she talked a lot about them.

"Okay, we take bus," she said.

"How long is the trip?"

"Four, five hours."

Several days later we boarded the Chongqing bus. Both brothers lived in that city, and her sister lived several hours farther east. They all came together for the few days of my visit, along with a nephew and a niece, both teenagers. We stayed with one of her brothers. They all knew the story of our mothers. I wondered if the Chinese emphasis on ancestors meant my family had become part of their family lore. The thought deepened my sense of friendship.

Historically Chongqing was known as a city of mountains, built on steep hills above the confluence of the Yangzi and Jialing rivers. Until the arrival of cars, the city's streets and alleys had been stone staircases. Several flights of old steps remained where the terrain had been too steep to modify for cars. Chunhua's family took me to see some places preserved as examples of old Chongqing. At a traditional home converted into a museum, we walked through rooms where household items and clothing from the past were displayed. Some of the clothing was especially beautiful, like the elaborately embroidered silk tunics. It would have been the home of a wealthy family in the early 1900s.

We also visited a narrow street of traditional shops now serving as a pedestrian and tourist area. The street was packed almost shoulder to shoulder with people, mostly Chinese. Crowds sometimes make me claustrophobic, but strolling this street of shops was sheer fun. Li-Li, the niece, linked her arm in mine and explained everything, practicing her already-excellent English and skills as a tour guide (her ambition) as we walked.

In one store a shopkeeper demonstrated a "singing dragon" bowl. She rubbed the rim and handles of a brass bowl eight inches across that was inscribed with dragons and half-filled with water. As she rubbed, a low moaning sound grew louder and the water began dancing from the vibrations. A few shops down, a young woman inked tiny characters that read "Meiguo–Zhonguo *youyi*" ("America–China friendship") onto a grain of rice, slipped the grain into a vial with a preservative solution, and placed the vial on a red silk thread. Chunhua's sister-in-law presented it to me as a gift. I wore it around my neck for my remaining time in China to honor our families' seventy years of friendship.

In late afternoon we made our way to the city's huge modern central square. At one point a man in straw sandals ran past, carrying a bamboo pole across his shoulders with a big plastic bag of block ice dangling from each end. I smiled to myself. He was the modern version of the 1930 water carriers. We ate at a restaurant just off the square—a sumptuous meal of nine or ten courses. My senses were sated with the array of tastes, aromas, textures, and visual delights. The variety of dishes and flavors I've experienced in China never fails to astound me. We ended the evening strolling through a park strung with lights, the people around us dancing to music from a loudspeaker. The day had been filled with laughter and the warmth and generosity of my new friends.

The next day we visited the place where Chunhua's family had lived in the 1940s and '50s, the six of them in two rooms. They had shared the dingy, damp two-story building with many other people. Some residents from that time still lived there. Chunhua took me to see one older gentleman, who pulled a chair up for me to sit as the two of them chattered away. *Dad would have enjoyed talking with this man,* I thought. They spoke too fast for me to follow, but I sensed the deep bond of people who have shared hard times.

The depth and sincerity of the friendship offered by Chunhua and her family touched me deeply and confirmed the uniqueness of my parents' missionary experience. The friendships Mom developed with her classmates were deep and lasting, founded on a sense of equality and mutual respect that continued to grow during and after their years of medical school. I suspect her cultural immersion—which by itself was unusual for a missionary—reinforced my father's natural inclination to make friends with people he met. Their first year in Chengdu he had been admonished for inviting a Chinese friend to play tennis on the missionary courts. I believe my parents became allies in these matters—they treated their Chinese friends and colleagues as equals.

On the bus returning to Chengdu, I shared with Chunhua that before leaving home I had emailed the China office of The Nature Conservancy (a US-based nonprofit group) located in Kunming, Yunnan Province, which lies just south of Sichuan. I had been a board member of the Conservancy's Vermont chapter in the 1990s before the organization had begun working in China. In my email I'd mentioned my trip, saying I wished to learn more about the work in Yunnan. I'd had no reply before leaving the United States.

"I call for you when we return. I find what happened." Chunhua was a take-charge person.

"Would you come with me if we could arrange a meeting?"

She smiled. "Yes, I come."

Chunhua telephoned Kunming immediately after getting home. As she talked, I recognized some phrases but couldn't keep up with the conversation. I hoped she had understood what I wanted to do. Hanging up, she announced we had an appointment with the China director in three days. Two days later we entered the crowded Chengdu train station for a midday departure to Kunming, a twenty-hour train ride. When our train was announced, she ran interference as we shoved our way, along with everyone else, toward the platform. The crowd flowed as one organism, like a school of fish, toward the trains. I stayed glued to my friend's back to keep the crowd from carrying me in a different direction. Unlike the airport, the train station had no signs in English.

I had splurged on sleeper accommodations for us. The sleeper car had a row of four-bunk compartments along one side of the car, open to a corridor with windows on the other side. At each window was a small table with two seats. We had brought our own food and bought tea at a snack bar several cars away. As I sat with my tea at the table opposite our bunks, it dawned on me that this was the train Dad had tried to arrange for us in 1980. He had described the landscape between the two cities as breathtaking with steep mountains and rushing rivers. It was all that and more.

I sat glued to the window much like on the train to Guangzhou in 1980. Leaving Chengdu, we passed through fields where the first planting of rice was being harvested. Newly cut stalks stood drying in bundles in shorn fields while elsewhere people flailed dried stalks on bamboo mats to release the grains. Some fields had already been burned to prepare for the next planting. The plain soon gave way to rolling hills and increasingly larger mountains. Racing alongside or crossing a rushing river, flashing in and out of the many tunnels, we made our spectacular way through mountains and narrow, steep-sided gorges. We made numerous station stops at remote villages. Dad would have loved it. Chunhua and I laughed and shared personal thoughts as if we'd been friends forever. I loved her enthusiasm for this spur-of-the-moment escapade.

Once it got dark, we moved to our compartment and pulled the narrow bunks down on one side. She insisted I take the lower, and she climbed onto the top bunk. A young European couple had the bunks on the other side. They put their packs on the lower bunk and spent most of their time together on the upper one. I wrote in my journal for a while, then pulled my blanket over me around ten o'clock and slept fitfully through the night. Sometime in the night we crossed the Yangzi River, the only disappointment of the train ride. I would have enjoyed getting a sense of the river farther upstream.

We arrived in Kunming around eight in the morning and caught a taxi to the hotel the Conservancy had booked for us. After several hours to rest and freshen up, we walked around a nearby park and found a place for lunch. Later, we took a taxi to the Conservancy office, where we met Rose, the director of the

China program. She was Chinese, of the Naxi minority, and spoke flawless English. I told her of my family's connection to China and their lifelong affinity for the country and its people, and that I too worked in conservation. Then I explained why I had come.

"My parents left me a modest inheritance when they died," I said. "I want to give the money in their name to conservation work that helps the people and environments of western China." I was considering the work of several organizations but said I liked the Conservancy's community-based approach.

"Would you like to see a project?" Rose asked.

"Oh, very much so. I hadn't expected it on such short notice," I said, glancing at Chunhua. Our discussion in English had been filled with conservation terms, and I wasn't sure how much she had grasped.

"Is it okay if we stay a few more days?" I asked her, explaining briefly what Rose was proposing.

She nodded, seemingly game for anything.

Rose left to make some phone calls. When she returned, she had everything set up—airline reservations for the next day, a room in a traditional inn, a guide, and drivers. Our base would be Lijiang, a small city three hundred miles northwest of Kunming.

The next day a Conservancy driver met us at the Lijiang airport and took us to the old town and our inn. Lijiang has two cities: the old town—a World Heritage Site with still-intact traditional streets, alleys, and canals—and the modern city next to it. On the way into the city I noticed mountains lining the horizon. The air was crisp and clear—we'd left the air pollution of Kunming and Chengdu behind. Lijiang was popular with Chinese tourists and Chunhua was excited to be there. At the inn our second-floor room opened to a balcony overlooking a central courtyard, where we ate breakfast each day. From a window in the room, I could see a snow-covered mountain, making me eager for the next day's outing.

With free time that afternoon, we followed a cobblestone path along a small canal. A centuries-old canal system brought water from natural springs to every house. The path led to a central square, where men and women in ethnic costume were dancing. The greater Lijiang region is home to two dozen tribal minorities, Naxi the most dominant. They are allotted different days to demonstrate dances and native clothing in the square. Chunhua and I sat on a low wall and watched the dancers before continuing to explore the narrow alleyways. We passed canal-side restaurants and investigated many shops until I worried we might not find the path back to our inn. But we did and had a dinner of Lijiang pancakes along the way.

After breakfast the next morning, Lifang, our guide for the day, arrived with a driver for our outing to the Laojunshan region two hours north of Lijiang. Pixie-like with apple cheeks and dark sparkling eyes, Lifang was also Naxi. Her command of English was excellent, gained from graduate courses in the UK. As we drove north, she explained her Conservancy projects. She helped people in remote villages understand the plight of the Yunnan golden monkey, which had become endangered due to deforestation. Villagers revered the monkey living in the surrounding forests but hadn't realized their firewood gathering and tree cutting were contributing to the monkey's decline. Lifang enlisted teachers and elders in her project and worked with local villagers to identify and protect key monkey habitats.

As Lifang described her work, I recognized a kindred community organizer and was impressed with her skills and the diverse solutions the Conservancy offered. Along with community education such as Lifang described, the organization provided energy-efficient means for cooking and heating to reduce the need for tree cutting, greenhouses to extend the growing season and provide extra income, and training in ecotourism, the latter our focus for the day.

After ninety minutes or so, we reached the upper Yangzi River, situated in a broad scenic valley with occasional villages nestled at the base of the high mountains on either side. We followed along the river for a while before the driver turned off the main road and ascended through undeveloped forest. As we climbed higher, the road narrowed to two tracks hugging the mountain contours. Entering a stand of conifers, I saw flashes of brilliant blue on either side. Lifang asked the driver to stop and we got out to photograph the dense carpets of lapis blue primroses on the forest floor. The air was chilly, and I saw Chunhua shiver. She'd been living in semitropical Chengdu for a while.

"You didn't expect to be doing this when you decided to come with me, did you?" I asked, smiling.

She laughed, her eyes crinkling, and shook her head.

As we continued climbing, I spotted a rhododendron in bloom and then more and more. It was spring at this elevation. I'd never seen such an array of rhododendron colors—white, yellow, all shades of pink, and one rare rhody with bloodred blooms. Soon we stopped at a new, modest building, a warming hut for people who came to hike in the mountains where the monkeys lived, Lifang explained. No one was around, but she knew how to get in. From here she had planned a half-mile hike to a ridge to view prime monkey habitat. I saw a few remnant snow patches up the slope and worried Chunhua didn't have the proper footwear or coat for the hike.

Upon exiting the vehicle, she said, "I'm cold. I wait here."

"Are you sure?" I hated to leave her behind.

"Yes. You go, I stay."

Lifang and I started up the trail, soon leaving the conifers behind as we walked among the twisted trunks of a rhododendron forest. The branches formed a canopy twenty feet over our heads, with only an occasional shrub or small tree underneath. We soon reached the rocky ridge and zigzagged around huge boulders until a valley with three lakes came into view below us.

"Ninety-Nine Dragon Pool," Lifang said, pointing to the lakes. "All the forest you see is prime golden monkey habitat."

The rhododendron forest, with conifers reappearing downslope, stretched before us, broken only by the lakes. Lifang said the lakes were revered by the local people because Laozi, the father of Daoism, is said to have concocted medicines of immortality here.

"This is beautiful," I said. "Thank you for bringing me here, Lifang."

She suggested a photo and placed her camera on a rock, setting it on shutter delay. Then she scrambled back to where I crouched. The shutter clicked, and we had the photo of us with the lakes in the background. Then we hurried back to the hut, where we picked up Chunhua and returned to Lijiang.

The next day Chunhua and I flew back to Chengdu. A few days later I left for home with much to contemplate. My intentions for these three weeks had been to gain a more authentic sense of my birth country and deepen my friendship with Chunhua. These weeks had exceeded my desire in both respects. But there was much more.

Something had shifted inside of me. I had ventured off the tourist path and beyond my parents' world to establish ties of my own. I felt a strong connection to the people I'd spent time with. Chunhua and I agreed we felt like sisters, a bond spanning cultures and two generations of our families. I also sensed a budding friendship with Lifang, a collegial attachment stemming from our conservation work. These experiences and new relationships helped me better understand the richness of my parents' life in China. Like so many other times on this trip, I wished I could have shared my thoughts with them.

And there was the land itself. The deep-seated connection I felt to the landscapes of western China was influenced by what I had found and felt in Alaska. The scale of the mountains, the raging rivers, the depth of the river gorges, the scenes both pastoral and wild—with each trip to China, they'd claimed a greater part of my soul. China hadn't replaced Alaska, but I had gently nudged Alaska over to make room for China.

As with my visit in 1998, I knew I had to return. I had to keep this connection alive, and not just because of my parents' ties. China was in my blood, and I vowed it would be part of my future as well.

 Chapter 22

The river barreled toward me from the north, several hundred yards wide, muddy and roiling, the current and power breathtaking. My eyes traced the river in astonishment as it nearly reversed course and raged off to the northeast. Here, at the Great Bend of the Yangzi River, a quarter of the way into its four-thousand-mile journey to the East China Sea, the river changes unequivocally from a southerly to an eventual easterly flow.

When I read Simon Winchester's *The River at the Center of the World* in the early 2000s, I was intrigued even in the book's first few pages by the author's description of the Great Bend and its importance to China's history. This unique feature of the Yangzi River has its origins in a tectonic collision millions of years ago when the plate bearing the land mass that is now India plowed into the continent of Eurasia. As the plate continued to move, the pressure led over time to the uplifting of the Tibetan Plateau. These inexorable forces operate even today, causing geologic instability and periodic earthquakes throughout the region.

If you look at any world atlas, you can see rivers draining east off the Tibetan Plateau to water the countries of Southeast

Asia. Three of the rivers—the Salween, the Mekong, and the Yangzi—bend south together, separated by parallel mountain ranges with peaks as high as 19,000 feet. These rivers flow in tight formation through deep, narrow canyons for several hundred miles. Then, as the Salween and the Mekong rush on southward, the Yangzi encounters a limestone massif of unremarkable size that blocks its southerly flow. The resulting hairpin turn and directional shift, which happened long, long ago, changed the future of the region that is China today.[1]

When Lifang first took me to the Laojunshan area in 2005 to see the Yunnan golden monkey habitat, we had not stopped at the Great Bend. Although I had known we were driving along the upper Yangzi River, I'd been appreciating the beauty of the landscape and hadn't realized exactly where I was. But now, in 2007, I had returned with John, Steph, and my niece Jen, Marilyn's daughter. Lifang had generously agreed to again show us her project work for The Nature Conservancy, and at my request we stopped at the roadside pull-off at the Great Bend.

After a few minutes of being mesmerized by the river's force, I looked around and noticed everyone staring at the river, lost in contemplation, even Lifang and our driver. I walked over to where my son stood, taking it all in.

"What do you think, John?"

He grinned at me, his eyes shining. "Pretty amazing, Mom."

Steph and Jen and then Lifang came over as well. Lifang talked about the world heritage site she was taking us to—the Three Parallel Rivers of Yunnan Protected Areas.[2] This designated region comprises one of the world's most biodiverse habitats, something of great interest to me and also my children and Jen.

I looked around the group. "This area we're going to is just about my favorite part of the world. And if my parents hadn't trekked to Tibet in 1932, I might never have discovered it."

My first visit to Laojunshan and the spectacular landscapes of the upper Yangzi region had me already imagining the next trip. All my previous visits to China had been with or included tours. I decided to organize this 2007 trip myself and bring John and Steph along. I proposed to visit places they knew from their grandparents' stories—Chengdu, Mount Omei, the Minya Konka—and hoped they would gain a deeper understanding of their grandparents and perhaps engage with China in a new way. When my niece Jen heard our plans, she decided to come too. I also wanted to introduce them to *my* China, the places I'd discovered and friends I'd made. I added Lijiang to the itinerary and let Lifang and Chunhua know we were coming.

The four of us jokingly said conservation was our family business. John, a university professor teaching conservation biology and ethnobotany, and Jen, a wildlife biologist, had never been to China. Steph at the time was coordinating training programs for environmental professionals from central European countries. All three knew I'd contributed to The Nature Conservancy's China program to honor their grandparents, and I wanted them to learn more.

When we arrived at the Lijiang airport, Lifang was waiting with a car and driver and accompanied us to the traditional inn in the old city where she had booked us. We had the afternoon to explore the narrow streets and shops before meeting Lifang and some of her colleagues for a traditional Lijiang dinner. The next morning Lifang picked us up after breakfast. We headed north to Laojunshan, stopping at the Yangzi's Great Bend, where we contemplated the extraordinary hairpin turn that changed the river's course.

As we continued north of the bend, Lifang pointed to a village across the river. "That's where I grew up. My father was the primary school teacher." When she began middle school (the equivalent of American high school) in a nearby village, she had lived on the campus. "My father went with me and taught there too," she said. "He encouraged me to go to university."

I felt the same connection with Lifang as I had in 2005. We were kindred spirits a generation apart, with a similar dedication and approach to our environmental work. Our driver soon left the main road and we climbed through a scenic valley toward Liming, a small village where Lifang had worked with a local teacher and students to help the community learn about the endangered golden monkey. Shortly before reaching the village, we stopped at what looked like a deserted checkpoint of some sort.

"The area where we're going will soon become a park for ecotourism and protection of monkey habitat," Lifang explained. "This will be the entrance."

The Nature Conservancy had assisted in getting the park designated. The area was within the Three Parallel Rivers World Heritage Area and would include villages—much like the British model of national parks, Lifang said.

The village of Liming has a stunning backdrop of red sandstone cliffs. We hiked a newly constructed trail—prepared for tourists—to the top of Thousand Turtle Mountain, one of the area's larger butte-like sandstone formations. Just below the top we encountered a sign in Chinese and English requesting we remove our shoes to avoid damaging the unique sandstone "turtles." Walking the last bit in socks, I saw the reason for the name—the red surface resembled so many oval turtle shells averaging five by eight inches in size. Turtle Mountain dropped off precipitously on all sides, providing a spectacular view: distant mountain vistas, the green valley we'd driven up, and many other red buttes jutting from the surrounding forest.

"Gorgeous, huh?" I said to Steph.

She nodded, preoccupied with taking a photo of John. He stood barefooted on the red turtles, photographing the distant mountains and the green valley below, and had just turned his head to look at Steph, a happy grin on his face. That moment made all the work of organizing the trip worth it. Sharing places in China that had become special to me and seeing their delight filled my heart, and we'd only just begun.

The next day Lifang took us to a village outside Lijiang to meet a family that had participated in the Conservancy's energy conservation work. While the wife fixed a lunch for us of five or six dishes, we had a tour of the greenhouse, the solar hot water setup providing hot showers for the neighborhood, and a biogas operation that transformed farm animal waste into electricity for lightbulbs and the gas for cooking our delicious meal. These were some of the earliest projects the Conservancy had undertaken in Yunnan beginning in the late 1990s. Based on their early successes, the Conservancy now worked with the central government on diverse projects. These ranged from reforestation with native trees, sustainable hydropower that balanced energy and water needs, and a land reserve model that protected critical wildlife like the panda while providing economic opportunities for farmers and local villagers.

After several days with Lifang, we left Lijiang and flew to Chengdu, where Chunhua welcomed us with a delicious restaurant meal of Chengdu specialties, mostly new to me. She accompanied us throughout our several days there. We visited the university campus first. In 2005 I'd noticed the early buildings, while in some disrepair, had metal plaques identifying them as original buildings. On this visit the old buildings were quite beautiful with freshly painted eaves and decorative trim. The main university hospital, now one of the largest in China, had a commemorative display with historic photos just outside the entrance. Steph and Jen found their grandfather in a faculty photo from the 1930s. My parents would have been pleased at the affirmation of the university's beginnings.

Another day we took a bus across the city to the Wenshu monastery and explored the temple buildings and extensive gardens. The day was beastly hot and humid, normal for Chengdu's summer. At one point we sat for a while in a slight breeze under a covered walkway and talked of our families' ties to this place.

"Do you remember the rubbings that hung in your grandparents' living room, the scrolls with the giant characters?" I asked the kids. "They were made here." I explained the monastery had once had a significant collection of ancient stone tablets or stelae—most were destroyed during the Cultural Revolution. Incised on the stelae were ethical teachings or historical commemorations. In making a rubbing, the characters on a stela are transferred to paper through an inking process.

"Mom at one point was based at one of the mission hospitals not far from this temple," I said. "She and Dad had lived in rooms at the hospital for several months. That might have been when they had the rubbings made." I looked around at the many people strolling the gardens and crowding around the nearby turtle pond. "It was no doubt a quieter scene then."

Chunhua also told stories. "Your grandmother would ride her bicycle into the city and study with my mother in these gardens. She often came for a meal, and the cook would make her favorite yellow soybean treats."

As she talked, I watched Jen sketching in her journal, capturing scenes around us: a building, a close-up of an intricate upturned eave, the turtles in the pond. Working quickly, she added delicate shading with colored pencils. I anticipated a wonderful record of our trip.

The street outside the monastery grounds was lined with traditional restaurants and shops selling Buddhist trinkets and books. We ate a late lunch at a place featuring a thirteen-bowl sampler of Chengdu specialties. The small bowls came from the kitchen alternating Sichuan-hot and "cool," the latter mostly just less hot. We sat in a courtyard open to the sky, the sunlight adding to the heat of the dishes. Those who had difficulty with the hot dishes gave their bowls to John. He ended up with twenty little empty bowls piled in front of him, sweat streaming down his smiling face. Dad would have given him two thumbs up.

Mount Omei is a half day's drive south of Chengdu—or, for my parents, several days by *hwagar*, a simple sling seat suspended between two bamboo poles and shouldered by two men, one in front and one in back. In 1931 they spent the summer at the missionary compound on Mount Omei, continuing their language study where the heat was more bearable.

When Steph and I came to Mount Omei in 1998 with the women's delegation, we'd visited several temples, taken the cable car to the top, and walked around a bit. Our time had been short then and our ability to explore limited. Looking forward to seeing more on this trip, I'd brought Dad's 1931 account of hiking to the summit and some of their ashes.

Our first afternoon the four of us explored the densely forested lower slopes, starting out on a flat dirt path with a diverse canopy of trees high over our heads. Vendors had set up shop along this stretch, selling souvenirs, tea, and medicinal herbs and roots. John bought some Mount Omei tea and perused the traditional medicines on display, indulging his interest in ethnobotany (the study of how people use plants). For a while the path traced one or another of the streams flowing off the mountain. At one point we followed a wooden boardwalk cantilevered over the stream and snaking around huge boulders. Soon we encountered stone steps and began climbing a narrow gorge beside a stream cascading over rocks of all sizes. After a half hour our trail ended at a T-intersection with a sign pointing left to "Monkey Viewing." Despite this being my first visit, the spot seemed vaguely familiar.

The trail we intersected traversed the gorge on a relatively new wooden bridge just above the confluence of two branches of the stream. A humongous boulder sat in the water right at the point of confluence. Perched on top was a *tinza*, its eaves curving gracefully upward. On either side of the boulder were matching arched stone bridges, one leading to the trail we'd just walked, the other to the trail we were intersecting. Carved stone *fu dogs* (guardian figures) and elephants with curly tails perched on the bridges' stone railings. Crossing the nearest bridge, we sat in the tinza to cool off. These bridges were old and must have been part of an earlier trail. I had a stylized map, not to scale, that labeled this place "TWINBRIDGE."

Steph smiled at me, her fingers tracing an elephant's spiral tail. "I like this place, Mom."

After ten minutes or so, we decided to go see the monkeys. As we neared the monkey reserve, the path became a boardwalk with wooden railings and posts. The first monkey I saw was sitting on a post. Soon they were everywhere, along with many other hikers. The monkeys were Tibetan macaques about two feet tall. Numerous signs asked visitors not to feed them, warning they were aggressive. Nevertheless, I saw people feeding the creatures all sorts of junk food. With monkeys the feature, not the scenery, we soon returned to our hotel.

That night I read Dad's account of their hike, encountering this passage: "At Flying Bridges the stream cuts two deep gorges through the mountain, splashing over rocks far below. A bridge spans each chasm high up in the air, hence the name." This had to be the place we'd been earlier, and my vague familiarity went back to Dad's description of Flying Bridges and an old photo I hadn't brought with me. Even after the fact, I was thrilled to have crossed my parents' path from so long ago.

The next day we followed a different path that would take us higher. We hiked first through a settled area with several homes, gardens, foraging chickens, and a small market. The day was hot and muggy, and cicadas sang all around us. After the tiny village the dirt path became stone steps leading us up into the forest. At one point we came upon ten men chanting as they carried an obviously heavy crate up the path. Bypassing them, I saw they were transporting an elephant sculpture carved from white stone—a miniature of the white elephant I remembered from 1998 in the Wannian temple, which my map indicated was not far ahead.

Soon we began a long, steep flight of steps, after which the terrain flattened. We'd arrived at the Wannian gardens with the temple just beyond. We rested there briefly in a welcome breeze, then visited the temple, where the large white elephant stands with each foot in a lotus leaf and a golden Buddha on its back. The temple was overcrowded, so I returned to the gardens to wait. A sense of tranquility settled in my heart as I sat with the gentle breeze and occasional glimpses of the valley through the trees. My thoughts turned to Chunhua. We had sat chatting in this very place in 1998. Steph had taken a photo of us deep in conversation, clearly enjoying each other's company.

This would be a good place to stay overnight, I thought, *if we were following the pilgrims' path to the Gin Din (the summit),* which I'd always wanted to do. I reached into my pack for Dad's story of their climb to the top and began reading about the sunrise from the summit.

"Arising before daybreak, we dressed, shouldering a warm blanket, and walked to the Gin Din. We watched the sunrise from the earliest reds, through yellows, greens, and blues, till the sun appeared as a large red ball in the east. Clouds reflected the colors, adding beauty to beauty. To the northeast a high range was visible through the mist. To the north were range upon range of mountains, ending in rugged peaks tipped with snow and sporting a glacier or two. To the west, the prize: nearby, mountains of all sizes and shapes, then a flat-topped mountain with waterfalls, then ranges stretching on to the snow mountains of Tibet."

We didn't have time to hike to the top so instead took a bus to the upper tram. The steep winding road led to a parking lot jammed with tour buses. A spacious gondola had replaced the 1998 cable car. Riding up, I was taking in the view and thinking about what Steph and I had found on top back then. The cable car had brought us into an open wooden shed—this was a ski lift in the winter—with varied terrain stretching to the Gin Din. We'd hiked the quarter mile to where several temples stood amid scattered conifers, each with a small plaza in front, large brass incense burners, and a metal trough filled with sand for pilgrims to place lighted prayer sticks. It had been June and practically deserted. We identified the Golden Summit Temple on the point, almost hidden by mists, and looked for another building Dad had called the nunnery. He'd said the nunnery was being rebuilt after a fire, and he and several friends helped put up one wall. Steph and I had poked around and found a dark red building off to the side and decided it could be the nunnery.

Now, nine years later, we disembarked from the gondola inside a modern stone building with food counters and gift shops. Leaving the building was like passing through a portal to an alternate universe: I recognized nothing. We followed a stone walkway a hundred yards to a wide stone-slab staircase. On every tenth step a small white elephant with golden fittings stood on either end. I climbed the steps slowly, my head spinning, trying to absorb the changes. With each step higher, a giant golden Buddha inched into view. Reaching the top, I saw an immense statue standing in the center of a flat, expansive stone plaza, its reflective presence dominating everything. The statue was a composite of four Buddha figures atop four elephants oriented to the cardinal directions.

I looked for Steph, caught her eye, and mouthed the words, "Oh my god!"

The plaza stretched between two temples, both painted entirely in metallic gold. I stood gaping, trying to make sense of what I saw. The Gin Din Temple must be the one nearest the precipice where the famous mists were now challenging the hazy sunshine, but it seemed unfamiliar.

"It's so different," Steph said beside me, her voice echoing the horror I felt.

The entire summit area had been transformed, the natural topography obliterated. The plaza was packed with people, all Chinese tourists, mostly young adults. The jammed parking lot below should have been a clue—August is peak tourist season. In 1998, the summit had seemed a place of quiet contemplation. Now it felt like a garish spectacle.

"Steph, I have to get out of here. This is too surreal. I'm going to find the nunnery and leave this madness."

"I'm coming with you."

Recollecting where we'd found the supposed nunnery, I walked away from the gleaming visages to the far edge of the plaza. We followed steps down from the elevated plaza to a small terrace and a building painted entirely in silver. Although the placement seemed familiar, the solid silver paint was disorienting, and I wasn't sure it was the building we had deemed the nunnery. Chinese temples have unusually beautiful trim around the eaves: elaborate three-dimensional wooden fretwork painted in bright blues, reds, greens, yellows, black, and gold. The solid gold or silver with no contrasting colors flattened the surfaces, making the intricate beauty and depth of the artful carving difficult to distinguish.

Perhaps the idea behind the "improvements" had been to accommodate more visitors but keep their attention focused on the golden Buddha and away from the mile-high precipice that waited beyond the nunnery. Steph and I had walked along a railing at the cliff edge in 1998, marveling at the height of the sheer rock face and wondering which of the ridges below might have once held the missionary cottages. The overlook was no longer accessible. A higher railing kept people well back from the drop-off. I understood the safety concern, though I felt a visceral disappointment and a deep sense of loss. I'd wanted my children and Jen to see a place special to their grandparents. But the Mount Omei of my parents' time had been relegated to the past.

At the silver nunnery below the main plaza, Steph and I were out of sight of the crowds and mostly out of earshot. We followed an older path away from the summit, looking for a place to sit and come to terms with this new Emeishan. (I had to use the contemporary name.) We passed men in straw sandals loaded down with big boxes, walking toward the Gin Din, probably carrying supplies to the temples. Could this path be the old pilgrims' trail? If so, I wanted to go back down this way and avoid ever having to see the golden plaza again.

A bit later and calmer, we started back and came across Jen writing and sketching in her journal. She was in a peaceful spot near the nunnery with birds singing in the trees. She and John were more accepting of the golden statue, but this was their first time here. I remembered my response to the Yangzi Gorges—you can't really mourn what you haven't experienced.

Earlier in the day I'd mentioned leaving ashes on top. Now I asked Jen, "Would you like to scatter some ashes?"

"I would," she said.

I handed her the red leather pouch, and Steph and I walked a little way off to give her some time alone. Later, she shared her journal entry with us:

"The noise of the crowd seemed to have dimmed a little, and the sounds of birdsong, insect hum, breeze, and bells were clear. Some ashes came to rest among the blackberries and elderberries, and some drifted away. Two small brown butterflies flew by, returned, then left as the mist rolled over again. It seems fitting and the tears come . . . I love you. Rest in peace."

 Chapter 23

A stunning mountain landscape hung in my childhood home, painted in oils by a missionary friend of my parents. A snow-covered summit dominates the many peaks, towering over its snow-free foothills. On a lower ridge in the foreground a lake mirrors the white pyramid. My parents' tent is pitched nearby, a wisp of smoke hinting at a hidden campfire. In 1932 they spent nine days camped at fifteen thousand feet on the ridge opposite the Minya Konka, a sacred mountain on the eastern rim of the Tibetan Plateau. Few people outside of the mountaineering world know of this mountain, but in my family the Minya Konka was the stuff of stories.

The single tent implies my parents had the lake to themselves. But they had not been alone. For two weeks they had traveled with two American mountaineers, part of an expedition to measure and climb the Minya Konka. The expedition was inspired by a map at the Explorers Club in New York City suggesting "Mt. Koonka" might be thirty thousand feet in elevation, higher than Mount Everest.[1] It was only a matter of time before someone came looking.

This was my favorite of Dad's stories. He and Mom had completed their two years of language study in the summer of 1932 and had taken six weeks off to travel into Tibet before beginning their work in Chengdu that autumn. Dad would be teaching medicine—in Chinese—and Mom would enter the university as the only non-Chinese medical student. The destination for their trek was Kangding (Tachienlu or Tatsienlu), a frontier trading crossroads on the eastern rim of the Tibetan Plateau. In the 1930s most westerners arriving in Kangding ended up at the China Inland Mission for food, lodging, or advice. My parents made the mission compound their base for exploring farther into Tibet, traveling by horseback.

They had just returned from nine days in the high-elevation grasslands when Richard Burdsall and Arthur Emmons, an advance team for the Sikong Expedition, showed up at the mission. Burdsall, a thirty-eight-year-old engineer from New York, and Emmons, a twenty-two-year-old Harvard sophomore with extensive mountaineering experience, had hired a Tibetan named Gaoma as their expedition cook. As their knowledge of Chinese was limited, the two men were seeking someone who could communicate with Gaoma and help set up and oversee a base camp while they took measurements to determine the mountain's height. My parents had been considering spending their final two weeks at a nearby hot spring, but these two men presented an intriguing alternative.

"Choosing between hot springs or riding horses to the Minya Konka, which we'd seen only from afar, was easy," Dad told me.

The next two weeks became the grandest adventure of my parents' lives.

They traveled with Burdsall and Emmons for eighteen days, fourteen of which were spent on the ridge opposite the Minya Konka. As the two men rode their horses out every day to take readings on the peak from different vantage points, my parents taught Gaoma how to cook western food, maintained the camp, and made their own shorter forays in the vicinity.[2]

Transcribing their letters and diary entries had stirred my imagination, leaving me eager to experience the Minya Konka too. As I planned our 2007 trip, though, puzzling together a route into Tibet presented a challenge. On my previous visit to China, I'd looked in bookstores for roadmaps and found none. Online searches produced nothing useful either. But having collected material on this mountain for several decades, I had a folder with two hand-drawn maps of the area, one in German showing topography and one in Chinese showing main roads and towns. In addition, the book about the expedition, *Men Against the Clouds*, had a drawing of their route from Kangding to the camp opposite the Minya Konka.

Several times I had laid these maps out—with different languages, varying scales, sparse topography, and changing place names—trying to match them with Dad's written account. Only after I studied Chinese and could sound out Dad's place names accurately did I realize some names matched phonetically with the Chinese map. Using Google Earth, I confirmed the route we needed to take to reach the Yulong Valley just west of the Minya Konka. But we would have to rely on local knowledge to find the path up the ridge to the lake where my parents had camped—the goal of our trip. I brought the maps and Dad's old photos to China to help in talking with people.

I chose a Chengdu travel company advertising tours to the lower slopes of the Minya Konka to help arrange our trip. Despite my vague description of where I wanted to go, the travel agent was accommodating, seeming intrigued with our family story. I contracted for a nine-day loop into Tibet from Chengdu, asking him to provide us with an SUV.

"I'd prefer to put you in a minivan," he said in his excellent English. "An SUV wouldn't have room for the four of you plus a guide and driver."

"I've never been to the Yulong Valley, but its proximity to the Gongga Shan makes me think we'll need an SUV." I used the Chinese name for the mountain.

The agent mulled this over. "I'll send you with Mr. Chen. He's an excellent driver. He's not fluent in English but can translate the basics."

"Sounds good. *Xie xie*."

The company would provide camping equipment and supplies for our time in the Yulong Valley, and Mr. Chen would carry *qian* (money) for three-star hotels and meals on other nights.

"One more thing," he said. "The government requires anyone going to the Gongga Shan range to have two mountaineering guides. Since you don't know exactly where your parents camped, and I want you to find it, we'll also arrange for a local guide. Does that meet your approval?"

"That sounds fine." We had become quite the entourage. Hanging up, I felt the thrill of anticipation. *After years of dreaming, this is going to happen!*

When we left Chengdu for Tibet in our shiny black Toyota 4Runner, John, Steph, and Jen took over the back seat, and I sat in front with Mr. Chen. Our conversation was tentative at first, with both of us limited in the other's language. Just outside Chengdu we came upon a horrendous traffic jam caused by an overturned truck.

"*Zaogao!*" I said and smiled. It was such a fun word to say.

Mr. Chen looked at me and laughed, surprised I knew the word for "what a mess." That broke the ice, and we managed simple conversation after that.

I had told the travel agent we wanted to take back roads rather than the four-lane highway between Chengdu and Kangding, a half-day trip of two hundred miles. We wanted to travel more slowly to get a sense of the terrain my parents had crossed. In 1932 they had been living in Ya'an, a city southwest of Chengdu. The road they traveled was part of an ancient trade route between Beijing and Lhasa. For centuries men had carried tea grown in the hills around Ya'an and in Yunnan Province to Kangding, where it was transported farther into Tibet by horses and yaks.[3] Dad had described this "tea road" as a path three to five feet wide, varying from dirt and ruts to stone steps on steeper slopes. They had encountered two tea carriers resting at the top of a mountain pass. The men were paid based on the weight they carried. In Dad's photo I counted the number of bamboo-wrapped tea bricks on one man's pack frame. His load had totaled 360 pounds—more than a yak carried, Dad had said.

I had talked with Chunhua about wanting to walk the old tea road, but she had said it couldn't be found.[4] I gave Mr. Chen the town names from a 1931 vaccination trip my father had made into the high country west of Ya'an, the same general territory traversed by the tea road. Dad had described this region as "wide fertile valleys, terraced slopes, and mountain passes as high as nine thousand feet, recently made safe from bandits."

After leaving Chengdu, we traveled through flat agricultural fields then gradually more rugged terrain. Upon reaching the raging Dadu River, a major tributary of the Yangzi, I realized with disappointment we were following the most direct two-lane route to our night's lodging in Luding rather than the higher country my parents had crossed. A short while later we came to a roadblock with two signs: "Road Closed" in Chinese, and "No Foreigners" in English.

"Build dam," Mr. Chen said.

The warning in English concerned me some, but he didn't seem bothered. He paused briefly, then turned around and took a side road that led away from the river, climbed steeply, and turned to dirt. I glanced to the back seat and we four shared grins and the same thought: perhaps an adventure after all. We topped out on an open ridge amid rice paddies, agricultural fields, and distant mountain views. The slower pace provided some sense of rural Chinese life. We passed small houses clustered in twos or threes with courtyards open to the road and large satellite dishes dwarfing the homes. Ears of corn hung drying from the rafters, while soybeans, tea leaves, and shelled kernels of corn lay on bamboo mats in the sun. We saw only Chinese.

Rounding a curve, we came upon a line of stopped cars and farm trucks. Getting out of the car for a brief look, we could see beyond the waiting cars a gigantic mudhole with several vehicles trapped to their axles. The quagmire was much worse than anything I'd seen in Vermont, where we refer to spring mud as the state's fifth season. Cars and trucks were slogging and spinning through precariously, one at a time, as bystanders stood calf-deep in the mud ready to push.

As we moved up in the line, I turned to Mr. Chen. "Can you make it?"

He shrugged, his face impassive. Then it was our turn. With aggressive confidence he gripped the steering wheel, shifted into low gear, maneuvered around a hopelessly mired truck filled with cabbages, slid a little back and forth, and made it through, our once-shiny SUV now mud splattered. This was the first of many times I appreciated being in the hands of someone who was first and foremost a driver.

Just down the road at the next village, two men approached our vehicle, blocking our way. One man came to the driver's side and spoke loudly, sounding angry to my ears, while the other leaned on the hood. Mr. Chen shook his head and answered, clearly not happy with the request. There we sat in a tense stand-off. After several more exchanges and Mr. Chen again shaking his head, he finally pulled out his wallet and forked over some cash, and they let us proceed. He never explained the situation, indicating he didn't know the English words, but I suspect he lost face in the encounter and would lose it again if he told the story.

We eventually found our way back to the main road along the river and made up some time before encountering another road barrier, this one with rocks and broken pavement ahead. As Mr. Chen mulled over the situation, a motorcycle pulled up behind us. Mr. Chen left to talk with the rider, returning to say there was dam-related blasting ahead to build a road higher upslope. Then a police car drove up. The policeman spoke briefly to our driver before going into a little office.

"Car no go today," Mr. Chen said.

A few minutes later he went to talk again with the policeman while we wondered what we would do—our itinerary had little time for delay. He soon returned and with a hint of a smile started the car. The policeman was continuing through, and Mr. Chen had paid him to let us go too. Our convoy of three, the motorcycle also, went around the barrier and onto the rough, broken pavement. The policeman set a fast pace, and we sped and bumped along behind him. I could see trucks working higher up on the slope to our right. Suddenly a poof of smoke rose from a blast area, and I watched in trepidation as small boulders began rolling down toward us. Nervous joking erupted in the back seat. Luckily, a flat area at the base of the slope slowed the rocks, and we made it back to pavement without having to dodge boulders.

We arrived in Luding in darkness having not yet eaten dinner. The girls weren't hungry, but John and I went with Mr. Chen to an outdoor food stall for a dinner of *jiaozi* (dumplings). Since he knew the local food and controlled the purse, he always ordered for us. He also ate all meals with us, the first of my trips in China when a guide had done so. Soon realizing how much we enjoyed Chinese food and that we'd try just about anything, he took pride in putting together a good meal. Between shared meals, brief conversations in Chinese, and joking in pantomime, an easy camaraderie developed among the five of us.

Continuing along the Dadu the next day, I had a flash of landscape recognition despite never having been there.

Although my parents had stayed overnight in Luding on their travels, I hadn't expected after seventy-five years to find the road in exactly the same place. But there it was in the distance, following the turns of the river like the old photo I'd brought. From Dad's account I knew we would soon come to an intersection and leave the Dadu.

Sure enough, we turned west up a narrow winding gorge with a river Dad had described as "a wild mountain stream, essentially a series of waterfalls much of the way, falling three thousand feet in thirty miles." Today a comparative trickle, the river had been tamed by a hydroelectric facility partway up the gorge. Climbing higher, we noticed the increasing presence of Tibetan prayer flags.

Emerging from the gorge, we entered Kangding, in my parents' photos a rustic town nestled in a narrow valley between steep mountain ridges. Now a modern city, Kangding has retained its frontier aura in part because the city center has remained small and compact. The river roars straight through the center of town with room on either side for only a few streets before valley slopes become too precipitous for building. Exiting the SUV, I immediately sensed the eight-thousand-foot elevation. Contrasting with Chengdu's subtropical polluted air, here the air was crisp and clear like a mountain town in Colorado. To acclimatize for the higher elevations to come, we stayed two nights at the Kangding Love Song Hotel, named after a popular 1930s tune about a Chinese man in love with a beautiful Tibetan woman. The city is a mix of Tibetans and Chinese, a trading and cultural crossroads that invites exploration. The four of us could easily have remained longer.

Departing Kangding, our party now included three Tibetans—our two mountain guides, long-haired brothers in cowboy hats, and their microvan driver. With them leading, we passed through miles of linear city along the river. As the homes petered out, I glimpsed new high-rises in a valley branching to the south. My parents had made two loops out of Kangding, both on horseback. The first had taken them over Zheduo La (*la* means "pass") to the plateau grasslands. The second led over a different, more remote pass to the Minya Konka. They had entered the Yulong Valley from the upper end, but with no auto road over that pass we would enter from the lower end. Could that branching valley have been my parents' route to the Minya Konka? Whether it was or not, we were following their first route over Zheduo La.

We ascended an old, rocky streamed with little vegetation beyond low ground cover. As the road crossed from the right side of the drainage to the left, I looked above me and with another flash of recognition took a quick photo. Later, comparing my photo to Dad's, they were almost identical. I hadn't noticed flowers even though we'd come the same time of year, but he had recorded "buttercup, dandelions, blue Tibetan poppies, edelweiss, everlastings, wild strawberry, lilies, and glorious forget-me-nots." Traveling more slowly on horseback has its perks.

Nearing the pass, a large black yak-hair tent signified an encampment of yaks and yak herders, much like my parents had seen here. Yaks resemble wild cattle with long sharp horns and horselike tails, their hair often black or mottled with white. A full-blooded yak like my parents saw has hair reaching almost to the ground. Today, most "yaks" are *dzo*s, yak-cattle hybrids with varying lengths of hair. I saw none with hair to the ground.

At the pass Mr. Chen parked near a large *mani* pile of prayer rocks, six feet square by five feet high and draped with red, yellow, green, and blue prayer flags. More flags, snapping in the stiff wind, were strung on poles toward an adjacent peak. Nearby were several *chortens* (sacred structures often containing ashes or relics). A sign gave the elevation in meters, which

John calculated to be 15,400 feet—the highest I'd ever been. I was short of breath and had a dull headache from the altitude. Steph and I walked to the west to view the other side of the pass, where the road dropped in countless switchbacks to meet the plateau. From there, I glimpsed Dad's "endless rolling plain with mountains and valleys." Amid the paved switchbacks was an earlier path. With a thrill, I visualized my parents' caravan of people, horses, and yaks.

Descending into the valley, we entered a new world geographically and culturally—the world of my parents' time. Tibetan houses soon appeared: rectangular flat-topped buildings made of gray stone with black-and-white geometric decorations, two or three stories, windows edged with white rocks or a whitewash, and often stone walls enclosing front courtyards. The homes were distinctive, a contrast to Chinese homes with their peaked roofs and upturned eaves. The upper stories of each house were living space while the ground floor provided storage and shelter for animals. The top floor, with a corner altar and large white prayer flags, was partially open and also used to dry crops.

As we traveled, I held the folder with Dad's photos and papers in my lap and tracked his account: "We followed a clear stream down a wide verdant valley and camped near a small village." The only stream in the valley was off to our right. The golden hue of the barley, their staple crop, signaled harvest time. A woman, carrying a load of barley stalks on her back, crossed a picturesque cantilevered bridge draped with prayer flags. Several houses stood on the other side of the stream. Could they be Dad's "small village"? A little farther along, a boxy two-story white building across the valley caught my eye. Dad had mentioned something like this. I felt a tug in my heart as I found the passage.

"Hey," I said to the others, "Dad wrote about that white building over there. I'm sure of it." Then I read to them: "Across the stream on the far slope stood a white stone building. Edgar said it was a lama retreat." Mr. Edgar had been their guide.

I was blown away. We really were following the path they had taken seventy-five years earlier! But before I could absorb the brief sense of connecting across time, we zipped on by. Ten miles or so down the road, we came to a Y-intersection in a small village where our guides waited. Mr. Chen went to talk with them and reported back.

"They buy food. We wait."

A bench beside a small shop offered a shady place to sit. I grabbed the old photos, Dad's account, and my maps and sat down to figure out where we were. We were covering ground so much faster than my parents. Unable to stay on top of the landmarks, I felt frustrated, wanting to know where I was in the moment, not after the fact. This was the connection with my parents. I wanted to hold on to that feeling and not let go. I was studying the photos when Mr. Chen tapped my arm. I'd been unaware that he and an elderly man had been looking over my shoulder. The man pointed to my photo of a Buddhist monastery and spoke.

"Several kilometers," Mr. Chen translated, pointing in the direction we would be heading.

Suddenly I knew where we were. Our guides had gone to buy food in the village my parents had called Yin Gwan Chai. They had stayed there for several days while taking day trips farther into the grasslands. Here the main road forked, one route heading northwest to Lhasa (the old trade route) and the other following a tributary of the Yalong River south. The monastery was up a smaller valley across the river. And near the intersection where I sat should be a chorten, "an unusually large one with a square base two stories high, a white rounded top, and a spire of gold leaf." A lama had come out and held the reins of Dad's horse while he took a photo. As I raised my head to look, John and the girls walked up, smiling.

"There's a huge chorten on the other side of the road," John said.

I turned toward where they pointed and saw the gold spire peeking above the trees. "You found it! Granddaddy wrote about it."

These waypoints of my parents' path were like beacons to my soul.

Dad and Mom had spent three nights in Yin Gwan Chai before continuing south along the river and then taking a side path back to Kangding. While still in the valley, Dad had taken a photo looking back toward the village and a distinctive flat-topped mountain above it. I'd studied that photo because of its details of the river valley.

When the guides returned, we continued toward the river. As Mr. Chen made a turn to the south, I looked north up the valley and recognized the flat-topped mountain and its neighboring peaks. Once again I was connected across time to my parents, almost as if they were hovering behind an invisible veil.

I called to John, who had the best camera, "Take a picture. Take a picture!"

"Of what?!"

Obviously, he couldn't read my mind. I'd lived and breathed my parents' story for years and looked at their photos so often that negatives had been burned into my brain. Even if I hadn't brought the photos, some of these places would have felt familiar, much like Twinbridge at Mount Omei. Mr. Chen was driving fast now, and the road had no shoulder, so stopping would be difficult. After I explained my frustration, John patted my arm.

"I'll take photos for you, Mom," he said. "Just relax, soak in the views, and tell us where we are."

Although we'd missed a photograph of the flat-topped mountain, his offer allowed me to sit back and immerse myself in the experience. My parents had traveled four days from Kangding to reach this point. It had taken us four hours. The day had already been momentous—and we weren't through yet.

 Chapter 24

Riding south along the river, the sun high in the sky, I took in every detail of the fertile landscape. The barley harvesting seemed communal in this more populated valley, with women carrying the golden stalks back to their homes, bent over from their heavy loads. The broad valley was rimmed with mountains, the grassy slopes showing the sage, gray-greens, and tans of late summer. The river, too large for lazy twisting meanders, crisscrossed the valley in long stretched-out S curves. The cantilevered bridges were festooned with colorful prayer flags.

I heard the regular click of John's camera, reinforcing his loving insistence that I sit back and absorb the experience. Listening to the excitement in the voices behind me, I felt gratified to share this adventure with the next generation.

Then I saw the most striking features so far.

"Look at those towers across the river." I pointed to a half dozen tall, crumbling stone structures set at intervals on the lower slopes: one square, the others built in a six-pointed-star shape. A few had been rebuilt. "I once read about these watchtowers in an old *National Geographic*. They were used for defensive purposes."

With each passing mile I felt a tingling building inside. After an hour or so the valley narrowed some, and trees reappeared on the slopes. With everyone hungry, we were ready when the microvan ahead of us stopped in a riverside market town for a late lunch. Afterward we four poked briefly around the nearby shops. John disappeared into one while the girls and I walked back to the car. He soon returned wearing a woven gray Tibetan cowboy hat.

"Look what I bought!" he said with a grin. Mr. Chen and the Tibetans laughed.

As we continued on our way, the valley narrowed to a gorge and entered a village where the road forked. An official road sign—edged with blue Tibetan motifs, each place name in Tibetan script, Chinese characters, and English—pointed left to Gongga Shan Town, Gongga Temple, and Gongga Shan. As Mr. Chen turned left and headed into the Yulong Valley, I could sense the thrum of our collective anticipation.

The pavement turned into a bumpy, potholed dirt road, and Mr. Chen slowed to a crawl. Ahead, the rusty microvan lurched from side to side, prayer beads swinging in a broad arc from the rearview mirror. The narrow valley had fewer houses, the slopes were thickly forested, and the stream meandered tightly. Blue sky played hide-and-seek behind dark threatening clouds. Despite it being the summer rainy season, our luck had held so far. We were one valley from the Minya Konka and influenced by its frequent cloud cover, but the mountain itself was hidden by the ridge between us—the ridge my parents had camped on. So close after years of planning and dreaming!

We passed through a compact village and the valley opened up, the trees giving way again to grassy slopes. Not far beyond the village, the microvan turned left onto a narrow track heading up the slope, stopping at the middle of three houses. Mr. Chen followed, and we all got out to stretch our legs as the guides disappeared into the courtyard. Gazing at the ridge opposite and then up the valley, I felt my excitement nearly bursting inside.

The guides soon returned, followed by a handsome, youthful-appearing Tibetan with a quick smile. He was Dawa, our local guide. Everyone crowded around as I showed him my photos and maps. He ignored the maps but was immediately interested in the pictures. With Mr. Chen translating, I told a simple version of my parents' story, pointing to the ridge opposite and then to the picture of their camp beside a small lake, saying we wanted to find that place. Dawa nodded, then smiled and pointed to the photo of an unusually long *mani* pile.

"He asks if you want to see it," Mr. Chen translated.

"*Shi de!*" (Yes!)

We climbed into our vehicles, Dawa in the microvan, and drove ten minutes up the valley. There, on the right side of the road, was a linear pile of prayer rocks about thirty feet long. Mr. Chen parked behind the van and we all got out. Dad's photo showed white-capped cairns spaced regularly along the top surface of the pile, but only a few of these remained and just one sporting a white top. The other places I'd recognized from the old black-and-white photos had been fleeting glimpses from the SUV. Now I could examine the prayer rocks closely, walk around them—always clockwise, which sends a prayer with each encircling—and appreciate the colorful riot of wildflowers around the base. Steph and I marveled at the intricate, curving Tibetan script carved on the rocks—*om mani padme hum*, the mantra said to hold the essence of Buddhist teachings. It seemed as if my parents were circling the mani pile with me.

John took a photo, aligning the ridge peaks in the background to match Dad's photo. In comparing the two, I noticed John's was missing a Tibetan house nestled at the base of the ridge. Dad had said the house belonged to Jumei, who had invited them to stay overnight. He had photographed Mom sitting in a second-floor window writing in her diary, but I hadn't brought that photo. Dawa confirmed it had indeed been Jumei's house. Then he gave me a crinkly smile. Behind me, a young man had come from a house across the road to see what was happening. Dawa introduced him as a descendant of Jumei's. Astonished at the coincidence, I reached into my envelope of papers and pulled out a copy of Jumei's picture I'd found in Dad's photos. Steph captured the moment on camera: the young man peering at the photo, a sweet smile on his face, Dawa beaming, and I gesturing while telling the story. I left Jumei's photo with the young man.

As the afternoon was slipping by, I suggested to Mr. Chen that we find a camping spot. When we returned to Dawa's house, one of the guides said Dawa had invited us to stay at his house that night. He assured us there was enough space. His wife had taken their yaks higher up the valley for summer grazing. Steph, Jen, and I could sleep in a room with three beds, and John and the other men could camp out in the main room. I accepted Dawa's offer, grateful for his hospitality and marveling at another similarity with my parents' experience.

We grabbed our sleeping bags and packs while the guides brought in food and cooking equipment. Passing through the courtyard with its horse stalls, I entered the stone house and climbed the steep wooden stairs to the second floor. Except for the room where we women would sleep and another side door, the second floor appeared to be one large room. A stove jutted out from the front wall, providing for both heat and cooking. I noted a wooden butter churn standing near the stove, its bucket about six inches across and twelve inches high, its decorative brass fittings burnished with use and age. The walls were lined with beautifully finished wooden cupboards. Platforms with thin cushions had been built into one corner and, with a low table and several chairs, made for a comfortable conversation area.

With dusk coming on, Dawa flipped a switch and we had light.

"Hydro plant." Mr. Chen translated Dawa's words. "Electricity two, three hours each night."

Dawa crossed to a front window and pointed to a small solar cell on the outside sill. He held up two fingers and said something.

"Sunshine, two hours," Mr. Chen said.

The Tibetan crossed to the back wall and opened a cupboard to reveal a television, turned it on, then pointed to the solar cell and held up two fingers again. His evening television news was powered by the sun.

"*Hao* (good)," I said, giving him two thumbs-ups.

By then our mountain guides had Tibetan butter tea ready for us. They put out cups and poured tea for us all. I tasted it, remembering Dad's account: "The Tibetans boil their tea for fifteen minutes and put it into a tall, narrow wooden bucket. Yak butter, fresh or rancid, is added and thoroughly mixed with a tight-fitting plunger. The resulting emulsion resembles dishwater in color but is quite palatable—at least I liked it."

He must have meant Mom didn't like it. But I did—when hot, but less so as it cooled. When I emptied my cup, a Tibetan immediately refilled it. Not wanting it to get cold, I drank it quickly. With my third cup, I realized Tibetan courtesy required filling an empty cup. When I'd had enough, I had to leave some.

Dawa briefly played host until other family members, including a toddler, appeared, and the four of them sat on stools around the stove eating their meal. Our mountain guides fixed a "camping" dinner for us and for themselves made *tsampa*, a Tibetan staple of roasted barley flour mixed with butter tea. They offered some to us—it had a good nutty flavor. We spent the evening talking in the conversation area. The guides spoke a little English, so at times the talk was in Chinese or Tibetan, at times English. I remember laughter and good spirits.

After breakfast the next morning, we each prepared a day pack. Dawa's horses would carry everything else. I was ready first and waited outside by a clump of intensely blue forget-me-nots, truly glorious as Dad had noted. Looking across the valley to the ridge, I felt connected again with my parents. *Their camp is up there*, I thought, anticipation singing inside me. My intuition said the trail to their ridgetop campsite began somewhere between this house and the mani pile up the valley. Dawa had nodded at the photo with my parents' tent and the lake. I had to trust he recognized the spot and would take us there.

We drove up the valley past the mani pile and kept going. The road narrowed to two tracks, and we drove on. A sinking feeling grew inside me—we were going too far. After forty-five minutes, we stopped. I didn't say anything. Having never been in this place, I couldn't second-guess a man who had probably lived his entire life in the valley.

Hoisting our day packs, we walked a short distance to the river, took off our boots, and forded the icy-cold water. Boots back on, we pushed through a band of thigh-high scrub. The scrub soon petered out as we climbed in earnest, leaving a ground cover of grass and many flowering plants of all colors. I was a little short of breath but held a steady pace. Then I realized John wasn't keeping up. I looked back and saw my botanist son detained by the wildflowers. Each time I turned to check, he was on his knees with his macro lens, in that posture so often that I took a photo of him photographing flowers.

Dawa soon passed us with the packhorses, giving a wave. When we were halfway up the slope, I could see the guides assembling tents on a flattish area several hundred feet below the ridgetop and just downslope from a lake. Tibetans consider lakes sacred, so camping directly beside it would have been disrespectful. My heart sank. There was no view to the Minya Konka. I went into a huddle with the kids.

"You know we're not in the right place, don't you?"

Three heads nodded.

"You can't see the Minya Konka from there," Steph said.

Language barriers and our lack of precise knowledge of the area had hindered our ability to convey to Dawa exactly what we wanted to find. Since our time was limited, and we wanted to be culturally respectful of our new friends, we agreed to say nothing. We would see the Minya Konka the next day, weather permitting.

"Even if we aren't in the right place, the experience will be incredible," I said.

"It already has been," Jen said, as John and Steph nodded.

We continued to our camp, where everything was set up for us. It was now midafternoon, with more clouds than sun. The guides had said the best time to see the mountain was early before clouds gathered, so they planned a hike to the ridgetop the next morning. We spent the afternoon exploring and taking photos while tamping down the desire to scamper to the pass above us. We walked to the lake and found a string of prayer flags, keeping them on our right as we made a full circle. The view up the valley was wild and beautiful, and I pictured my parents riding in from that direction. At the head of the valley, they had encountered a summer yak encampment with several black yak-hair tents. They had camped near the black tents and watched two bull yak threatening to fight. Perhaps that was where Dawa's wife had taken their yak.

As evening approached, the temperature fell. I remembered Dad's words: "As soon as the sun set, it became so bitterly cold we could not stay up even with a fire. In our bedrolls it took a long time to get warm despite hot water bottles, flannel pajamas, wool socks and sweater, six wool blanket layers, and coats piled on top of that."

In our tent we four pulled out the down and fleece layers we'd carried all this way. I thought of Mr. Chen and his small duffel, which couldn't possibly hold a cold-weather jacket. I mentioned my concern to John. He had brought an extra fleece jacket and offered his spare to Mr. Chen, who accepted it gratefully.

The next morning, with promising weather, we began climbing after breakfast. I put my hand in my jacket pocket, closing it gently around the leather pouch with my parents' ashes. *We're going to see the Minya Konka, Mom and Dad.* A warmth spread through me.

As I approached the pass, hiking steadily, snow peaks began to appear one by one. A few more steps brought the Minya Konka to view, jutting into the sky, its white pyramid dwarfing its neighbors. Stopping at the pass to allow my senses to expand fully, I let the knowledge of where I was sink into my soul. Awestruck, I felt my breath catch as the whole spectacular range spread out before me.

I've seen many mountains from a distance, but I have never before stood so intimately close to a mountain that loomed nearly two miles above me. Only a steep narrow valley separated us from the Minya Konka. Gazing at the mountain's magnificence, I felt exhilaration, wonderment, and awe combined. I thought then of Dad's words in Denali National Park three decades ago. *Yes, Dad, the Minya Konka has a sacred aura. Now I understand.*

A line of prayer flags stood just over the pass. Each person in turn moved along the ridge to a rocky ledge more directly across from the mountain where the slope was less steep. I stayed by the prayer flags, taking photos until John stood beside me.

"This is incredible," he said reverently. "Worth all the trouble, huh?"

"You bet. I can understand why they never forgot."

After a moment of silent gazing, I pulled the pouch from my pocket. "Would you like to leave some ashes up here on the ridge, John? They will be within sight of the Minya Konka."

"Yes, I'd like that."

I handed him the pouch and rejoined the others. For several hours we stayed around the rocky ledge, basking in the mountain's glory and talking quietly. At one point Dawa borrowed

Jen's binoculars to study the slopes opposite us. Everyone took photos, even the guides and the drivers. We took turns snapping various groupings of our party with the summit as the backdrop, wildflowers at our feet. The blue Tibetan poppy was achingly beautiful.

Across the way I saw the snout of a glacier and the stream of glacial melt in the gorge below. I looked for the Konka Gompa, a Buddhist monastery built near the glacier, but it was hidden. One day my parents had ridden horses to the bottom of the valley, intending to cross the stream and find the monastery. Dad always began this story by saying this was tiger country. At the bottom of the gorge, they had left their horses and crossed the torrential stream by scooting along a fallen log. They turned back after several hours without reaching the monastery. Recrossing the torrent to find their horses missing, they had begun the difficult hike back to camp. At dusk when my parents were halfway up the slope, one of the expedition porters met them with their horses. They rode the last stretch into camp, grateful they didn't have to find their way in the dark in tiger country.

The Minya Konka had been mostly surrounded by blue sky when we arrived at the pass, but clouds had been coalescing slowly ever since. We stayed until the mountain was nearly hidden and then made our way back to camp. Along the way Dawa pointed to a plant, and with Mr. Chen translating and John providing botanical knowledge, we learned the plant could help alleviate altitude sickness. When we arrived back at camp, Jen presented her binoculars to Dawa, using gestures and smiles to convey her intent. He accepted the gift with humility and grace.

As we ate a late lunch still under the mountain's spell, the Tibetans began taking down the tents. Dawa had offered his house for another night. Although the four of us yearned to stay longer, we had a schedule to follow, and I couldn't ask Mr. Chen to spend another freezing night in a tent.

Later that afternoon at Dawa's house, we all sat on the grass for a while talking. I felt a connection with Dawa, perhaps through a mutual love of the landscape. We communicated through a mixture of my limited Chinese, pantomime, and intuition. By then he realized he'd taken us to the wrong place and indicated he now knew the place I'd meant. I assured him that seeing the Minya Konka was a wonderful reward and that we all had truly enjoyed the experience. And I told him I hoped to return someday.

That evening the conversation had an even greater ease. Our guides suggested a songfest. We sang in our different languages, the Tibetans singing "Kangding Love Song," followed by Mr. Chen, with his beautiful voice. Jen has a repertoire of camp songs and led us in "Working on the Railroad" and "The Frozen Logger," about a woodsman who stirred his coffee with his thumb.

I left the next day feeling both exhilaration and a sad reluctance at having to say goodbye to the Minya Konka and the companions who had shared our experience. Our time in the Yulong Valley had been too short. As we retraced our route in the now-familiar landscape, the mood in the SUV was subdued, each of us lost in our thoughts.

Several hours into the drive, Mr. Chen asked, "You see monastery? From father's photo?"

My energy and enthusiasm spiked again. Glancing to the back seat and seeing nodding heads and sparkling eyes, I said, "Yes!"

He made an immediate left turn, following the guides' microvan onto a dirt road and over a bridge. They must have planned this earlier, bless their hearts. Three days before—had it only been three?—we hadn't had time to make this detour. A few moments later I saw the monastery buildings in the distance. Gathering my photos, I quickly reviewed Dad's account of their visit. This was where Mom had bought the saddle rings she had used to quiet crying babies.

We parked and waited in the central courtyard while the

guides checked whether we could see the place. Several monks and small boys gathered around watching. On the hill beyond the temple, I recognized the same path with switchbacks as in Dad's photo. The trees at the foot of the hill were much taller now, and there were only two instead of three. Finally, a monk with a welcoming demeanor arrived to show us around.

The front of the temple was draped in the black curtains distinctive to Tibetan Buddhist temples. My parents hadn't seen inside, as a ceremony had been in progress, but Mom couldn't have entered anyway—women were forbidden. That rule no longer applied, and the monk, gregarious and extra polite, invited us to enter.

Inside, in dim light, he opened several large shallow wall cupboards to reveal sacred *thangka* paintings depicting various Buddhist deities. The cupboards protected these ancient paintings from light. My father had had a small thangka replica on the wall in his study.

With Mr. Chen translating, I said, "My parents visited this monastery in 1932."

Mr. Chen gave the short version of our family story, and the monk seemed interested. We circled the central ceremonial area and entered a small, better-lit room in the back. A bank of deep drawers lined one wall. Our guide opened two drawers and from each lifted an ancient-looking scroll. He unrolled one partway, exposing the beautiful Tibetan script. I found myself wondering how the monks had protected the thangkas and these sacred scrolls during the Cultural Revolution.

We followed the monk into a second room filled with photographs of men who had served the monastery over the years. He stopped beside an older photo and said this man had been the head lama when my parents had visited. In response I said they hadn't met the head lama but had sent gifts in to him, and he had sent out two pounds of yak butter in return. The monk smiled broadly.

The tour of the monastery ended up being an unexpected capstone for us, from our guides' surprise suggestion of the visit and continuing with the monk's gracious hospitality and his respect for our family story. The temple's atmosphere of ritual and reflection, as embodied by the monk's reverence as he introduced the thangka paintings and the sacred scrolls, provided meaningful closure to our trip.

My initial goals for bringing my children and Jen to China had been to help them better understand their grandparents by visiting the places they had loved. The trip far exceeded my expectations, despite my sadness at the transformation of Mount Omei's summit. I had not anticipated the profound impact of finding myself in the actual settings of my father's stories, but it made the sense of connection more palpable and authentic. That I could share all this with the next generation brought me joy. Even if my children and Jen never returned, they could tell the family stories with more authenticity and a greater sense of awe.

Overall, the cultural experience had been extraordinary: sharing an adventure and a search for meaning with Mr. Chen, Dawa, and all the Chinese and Tibetans who had helped us. Our ability to form friendly connections over a brief time span reflected the common humanity of all people, no matter their circumstances or where they live. Even language need not be a barrier to friendship. The people we met serendipitously—the elderly man who told us the monastery was nearby, Jumei's descendant, and the toddler at Dawa's house who couldn't stop staring at the strange-looking people—all of them enriched our quest.

The genuine warmth of the people, the coincidences and similarities between my parents' journey and ours seventy-five years later, the tracing of place and parallel encounters across time, sharing this intergenerational journey with my son and daughter and niece—all this fills my heart to overflowing. And though I would have loved to tell Mom and Dad about this trip, they were with us in spirit. We may not have found their campsite, but we found their experience. And their grand adventure became ours as well.

The emotional ties I feel today for China and her people were awakened by my return to Chengdu in 1980 with my parents. My life has taken me on a meandering path from childhood in West Virginia, when I rejected my birth country; to Alaska, where I became a willing captive of wild mountain landscapes; to New Hampshire and Vermont—all punctuated by my further discoveries in the mountains of western China.

I find I have come full circle, embracing these two different countries: the United States, my home since 1945, and China, where I was born. I continue to learn what it means to feel connected to two quite different cultures on opposite sides of the planet, but I know the many unforgettable people I've met in China and those remarkable landscapes in Sichuan and Yunnan have changed me to my core. I now claim China as part of my identity, integral to who I am.

Looking back with the benefit of time, I have one more realization. Forgiveness, blooming inside me as I gained a more complete understanding of my mother, freed me from the childhood shackles of resentment. With an open, unencumbered heart I found an intuitive connection with my parents after their deaths—most profoundly during those weeks in 2007 as we explored the mountains of western China. With love and awe filling me, I rejoice in the marvelous congruence of my parents' and my own experiences in that valley of the yak.

They would have been pleased.

 Epilogue

One winter evening six months after returning from Tibet, Steph and I were reminiscing about our adventure. On a lark she opened Google Earth on her laptop. We wanted to find our campsite on the first ridge west of the Minya Konka. That afternoon while the guides were setting up the tents, we four had walked around taking photos and tamping down our desire to climb to the pass and see the mountain. Across the Yulong Valley we had noticed a distinctive whitish soil layer seeming to exist only in that stretch opposite us. If we could find a short whitish band on the western slope of the valley, we would surely find the lake near which we had camped.

Looking down with Google Earth on western China, we had no trouble orienting ourselves by the area's numerous snow mountains. The Minya Konka itself was recognizable and by extension the Yulong Valley. Steph zoomed in, and we easily spotted the whitish band on the western slope. Moving directly across the valley we could see the lake and the flattish area just below it where our tents had been.

I had a sudden idea. "Let's move south along the ridge," I said, knowing we'd been farther north than my parents. I smiled. "Maybe we can find your grandparents' camp."

She did something on Google Earth I hadn't known about. Rather than the familiar bird's-eye view looking down from above, she changed the perspective so we were facing east and looking at the ridgetop at eye level. Like a photograph, we could see the higher peaks of the Minya Konka range rising up in the background.

Anticipation flooded me. I ran to the bookcase for *Men Against the Clouds,* the book written about the Sikong Expedition. It contained a photo taken from Burdsall and Emmons's tent on the morning they'd awakened to see the mountain free of clouds. Dad had written in his diary: "At five thirty a.m., Burdsall called, 'Mountain clear,' and we all jumped out of bed to see. The Konka, almost on top of us, was perfectly reflected in our little lake. It was magnificent."

"Steph, all we have to do is move along the spine until the peaks align like those in the photo," I said, sitting down with the book. I was almost giddy, my heart pounding. "That should be the site!"

I found the photo and held it up beside the laptop screen. She moved slowly to the south along the ridge and we watched the peaks on the screen come into perfect alignment with the photo. Leaning forward, almost breathless as she switched to the bird's-eye perspective, I watched in suspense as she adjusted the zoom to bring the landscape detail into focus. And there it was—a nondescript little body of water, more like a pond and smaller than the lake Dawa had taken us to. Both of us now giddy and hooting, we shared an enthusiastic high five. I felt a warmth spreading inside.

Zooming back out to see more of the landscape, we saw vestiges of a track coming up to the pond. I could also see the little road going up the opposite side of the valley to Dawa's home, the middle of three houses.

That day when I stood waiting for the others outside Dawa's house beside the clump of gorgeous forget-me-nots, I had looked across the valley with a strong sense I was standing near where we needed to climb the ridge. And the path had been across from me all the time.

Although I admit to a fleeting twinge of disappointment, I cannot blame Dawa for not understanding immediately where we wanted to go. The lakes were of such different sizes. Also, Dad's photo had been taken from a higher point looking down on the lake and their tents, giving the visual sense of an aerial photo, a vantage point that may not have been familiar to Dawa. And, too, language barriers, differing expectations, and even cultural assumptions may have been at play that day. Memory is the final arbiter of our grand adventure. And the friendships, the parallels with my parents' experience, the sense of connecting with them in that extraordinary place, and the beauty and the sacred aura of the Minya Konka will be what remains with me forever.

At the same time, I have a strong motivation to return and find that lovely spot. I still have a small portion of my parents' ashes, and now I know exactly where to go.

Endnotes

Chapter 1

1. Woman's Medical College of Pennsylvania, founded in 1850, was the first medical school in the world authorized to award women medical degrees. It was the longest-lasting all-women medical school in the US. In 1970, Woman's Medical College admitted men and changed its name to Medical College of Pennsylvania, eventually being absorbed into the Drexel University College of Medicine in 2002. For more of the history, see "Woman's Medical College of Pennsylvania" by Melissa M. Mandell (Encyclopedia of Greater Philadelphia, 2016, https://philadelphiaencyclopedia.org/essays/womans-medical-college-of-pennsylvania/). For a comprehensive, scholarly study of the participation of women in medicine, see *Sympathy and Science: Women Physicians in American Medicine* by Regina Morantz-Sanchez (Chapel Hill: University of North Carolina Press, 2000; first published in 1985 by Oxford University Press).

2. All names of people in China have been changed for privacy.

Chapter 2

1. The name of this city in India and all Chinese place names are the names and spellings currently in use today. If today's names vary widely from those used in the past, the older names are included in parentheses.

Chapter 6

1. Although the name of the national park was changed in 1980, the mountain's official name remained Mount McKinley until it was changed during the National Park Service's centennial in 2016. Denali is a Native Athabaskan name and has been translated as "The Great One." I have used the name "Denali" ever since I learned it's meaning while living in Alaska, thinking it more fitting for the highest mountain in North America (21,300 feet). The debate over the official name had been ongoing for decades. For a discussion of the history of the naming controversy, including the various Athabaskan names, see "Denali or Mount McKinley?" at https://www.nps.gov/dena/learn/historyculture/denali-origins.htm.

Chapter 8

1. Hong Kong was still under British control in 1980. England had ruled the island city since 1842 when England and China signed the Treaty of Nanking ending the first Opium War. A long-term lease agreed to by the two countries in 1898 allowed the British to remain in control for an additional ninety-nine years. A 1984 declaration between Great Britain and China guaranteed return of control of Hong Kong to the People's Republic of China in 1997 ("Chronology: Timeline of 156 Years of British Rule in Hong Kong," Reuters, June 27, 2007, https://www.reuters.com/article/us-hongkong-anniversary-history/chronology-timeline-of-156-years-of-british-rule-in-hong-kong-idUSSP27479920070627).

2. West China Hospital is consistently ranked among the best hospitals in China. It is one of the largest single-site hospitals in the world with 4,300 beds and a medical staff of more than ten thousand. The hospital was the triage center following the 2008 Sichuan earthquake ("About Us," West China School of Medicine and West China Hospital of Sichuan University, 2019, https://www.wchscu.cn/About_Us.html).

Chapter 11

1. Gloria Steinem, *Revolution from Within: A Book of Self-Esteem* (Boston: Little, Brown and Company, 1992).

Chapter 12

1. In a normal heart, oxygenated blood is pumped via the aorta to cells throughout the body, where oxygen is exchanged for carbon dioxide. The blood then returns to the heart and is pumped through the pulmonary artery to the lungs, where the reverse exchange—carbon dioxide for oxygen—takes place. In transportation of the great arteries, the baby's heart forms with the aorta and the pulmonary artery switched in position, which results in two circulating systems. Often in these cases, other defects provide for minimal mixing of the two systems, enabling some oxygen to circulate through the body but never enough for a baby to survive beyond a few years without surgery. For more information, see "Facts about Dextro-Transposition of the Great Arteries," Centers for Disease Control and Prevention, last reviewed February 2, 2023, https://www.cdc.gov/ncbddd/heartdefects/d-tga.html.

Chapter 15

1. Richard L. Burdsall and Arthur B. Emmons 3rd, *Men Against the Clouds: The Conquest of Minya Konka*, rev. ed. (Seattle: The Mountaineers, 1980; New York: Harper & Brothers, 1935).

Chapter 17

1. Because I grew up with stories of Mount Omei, I prefer to use the old spelling rather than "Emeishan," the modern term. *Shan* means "mountain."

Chapter 19

1. For more about the archive and to view the index to the collection, visit https://drexel.edu/legacy-center/the-collections /women-in-medicine/.

2. Excerpt reprinted from ACC Current Journal Review 11, no. 5, Bradley D. Huhta, "David's Heart," page 100, copyright 2022, with permission from Elsevier.

Chapter 22

1. For a more scholarly description of the Great Bend of the Yangzi River, see Simon Winchester, *The River at the Center of the World: A Journey Up the Yangtze and Back in Chinese Time* (New York: Henry Holt and Company, 1996), 2–4.

2. The Three Parallel Rivers of Yunnan Protected Areas was designated a UNESCO World Heritage Site in 2003. For an overview of its geography and values, see "Three Parallel Rivers of Yunnan Protected Areas," UNESCO World Heritage Convention, accessed February 9, 2023, https://whc.unesco .org/en/list/1083/.

Chapter 23

1. Theodore Roosevelt III and his brother Kermit Roosevelt were part of the William V. Kelley–Roosevelt Asiatic Expedition, a zoological expedition to Southeast Asia in 1928–1929 sponsored by Chicago's Field Museum of Natural History. The Roosevelts were in charge of gathering large mammal specimens. They wrote about their travels through

Yunnan and Sichuan provinces in their book, *Trailing the Giant Panda*. They speculated on reports of "Mount Koonka" possibly being thirty thousand feet in elevation but did not visit the vicinity of the mountain as winter was closing in (Theodore Roosevelt III and Kermit Roosevelt, *Trailing the Giant Panda* [New York: Charles Scribner's Sons, 1929]).

2. In May of 1943, *National Geographic* carried a story of the mountaineering expedition; the scientific determination by Burdsall and Emmons that the Minya Konka was 24,900 feet in elevation; and the ascent of the Minya Konka, a feat achieved by Burdsall and fellow expedition member Terris Moore on October 28, 1932 (Richard Burdsall and Terris Moore, "Climbing Mighty Minya Konka: Americans First Scaled Mountain That Now Is Landmark of China's New Skyway," National Geographic [May 1943]: 624–650).

3. The tea road my parents traveled is part of the ancient trade route between China and Lhasa. For more than a thousand years, the Chinese used this road to trade tea for Tibetan horses. My parents traveled a smaller loop from the tea-growing region around Ya'an (Yachow) in Sichuan Province, which linked into the more extensive and better-known Tea Horse Road that extends into Yunnan Province (Jeff Fuchs, *The Ancient Tea Horse Road: Travels with the Last of the Himalayan Muleteers* [Toronto: Penguin Group, 2008]).

4. Although my friend had said the old tea road couldn't be found, writer and adventurer Mark Jenkins found the trail my parents had traveled and wrote an article for National Geographic. This article includes a map of the different routes in Yunnan, Sichuan, and Tibet that comprise the Tea Horse Road (Mark Jenkins, "The Forgotten Road," *National Geographic* [May 2010]: 94–119).

 Acknowledgments

I must thank my daughter, Stephanie Tuxill, for being my faithful first reader, providing tactful but substantive critiques, and sending me back to my laptop numerous times with the admonition to "dig a little deeper, Mom!" With her insightful understanding of our family story and her talent for word-smithing, she supported me in all ways and helped me improve my writing immensely.

I have been fortunate to have an excellent group of women writer friends in my Vermont town who have provided diplomatic critiques and supported me from the beginning, when my intention was to write about my remarkable parents. These women were with me throughout my transition from "institutional" writing to memoir writing and enabled me to find my voice. From the bottom of my heart, I thank Louella Bryant, Harriet Szanto, Sally Baldwin, Ann Kensek, Shannon Anton, Dora Coates, Tina Scharf, Sarah McGrath, and Tori Riley.

I am eternally grateful to Cami Ostman for accepting me into the "guinea pig" cohort for what she then called "Memory to Memoir" (now "The Narrative Project"), an in-depth online course that provides coaching on writing and platform-building—everything new authors need to know to get their books out there. Cami matched me with two incredibly talented writers who became my online friends and critique team, Anne Ciochetto and Barbara Clarke. Our friendship has continued to last, long after Cami's course.

As I persisted in my writing, many people encouraged me in ways that improved my manuscript for which I am most appreciative: Rebecca Mabanglo-Mayor for her developmental edit; John Elder for his encouragement of my first feeble starts at a memoir and many times along the way, including being a beta reader; Jean Arrowsmith for reading the very first of my six drafts; my brother Don Lenox for confirming my childhood memories; and beta readers Renee DeMont, Frank Lenox, Marjory Lenox, Nancy Knight, Marion Lobstein, and Peggy Sax.

Last but definitely not least are those who read the manuscript or portions of it and provided support and encouragement at various points in my writing: my dear friends Nancy Clark, Liza Myers, Janice Ryan, and Lin Johnson (who was also a beta reader); family members, including my son John Tuxill, my daughter-in-law Julie Dugger, my niece Jennifer Ballard, and my late husband Thomas Tuxill; and Peter Scholes and Peg Tileston, whom I asked to read specific portions of my manuscript to confirm that my memory of past events in Alaska resembled what actually happened. Although I gave them permission to correct me, neither did! At this point I am solely responsible for any misrepresentations in this book.

I would be remiss if I did not acknowledge the countless ways my dear sister Marilyn Ballard provided loving support from the outset for my writing. She listened countless times, always providing insights, as I read passages or chapters to her. She passed away before she could hold this book in her hands. I miss her daily.

Finally, I sincerely thank Brooke Warner, Samantha Strom, Lauren Wise, and the entire She Writes Press team for shepherding me through the publishing process this past year.

About the Author

Jacquelyn Tuxill was born in Chengdu, China, to medical missionary parents. In 1944 she and her family escaped the war that had engulfed West China by flying over "the Hump" to India, where she had her third birthday, eventually settling in rural West Virginia. Graduating cum laude from Muskingum College with a BS in biology, Jackie worked in medical research while her husband attended medical school. Living in Alaska for five years in the 1970s, she found a love of nature and outdoor adventure that led to thirty-five years of environmental work. Jackie has a son and a daughter and lives in central Vermont on the western slope of the Green Mountains. She has made five return trips to China. *Whispers from the Valley of the Yak* is her first book.

www.jacquelyntuxill.com

Author photo © Studio LaFayette

SELECTED TITLES FROM SHE WRITES PRESS

She Writes Press is an independent publishing company founded to serve women writers everywhere. Visit us at www.shewritespress.com.

48 Peaks: Hiking and Healing in the White Mountains by Cheryl Suchors. 978-1-63152-473-8. At forty-eight years old, Cheryl Suchors vows to summit the highest forty-eight peaks in New Hampshire's challenging White Mountains—and discovers, in the years that follow, that in order to feel truly successful, she will have to do much more than tick off peaks.

Naked Mountain: A Memoir by Marcia Mabee. $16.95, 978-1-63152-097-6. A compelling memoir of one woman's journey of natural world discovery, tragedy, and the enduring bonds of marriage, set against the backdrop of a stunning mountaintop in rural Virginia.

Seeing Red: A Woman's Quest for Truth, Power, and the Sacred by Lone Morch. $16.95, 978-1-938314-12-4. One woman's journey over inner and outer mountains—a quest that takes her to the holy Mt. Kailas in Tibet, through a seven-year marriage, and into the arms of the fierce goddess Kali, where she discovers her powerful, feminine self.

When the Red Gates Opened: A Memoir of China in the 1980s by Dori Jones Yang. $16.95, 978-1-63152-751-7. In the 1980s, after decades of isolation, China opened its doors—and Communism changed forever. As a foreign correspondent during this pivotal era, Dori Jones fell in love with China and with a Chinese man; this memoir recalls the euphoria of Americans discovering a new China, as well as the despair of Tiananmen.